The Socius of Architecture

THE SOCIUS OF

ARCHITECTURE

Amsterdam . Tokyo . New York

Arie Graafland

010 Publishers, Rotterdam 2000

ARCHITECTURE
Part One

Introduction

Constructivism

The Sublime

CITIES Part Two

Amsterdam

Rhizome city

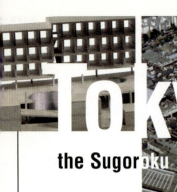

Tokyo

the Sugoroku Board

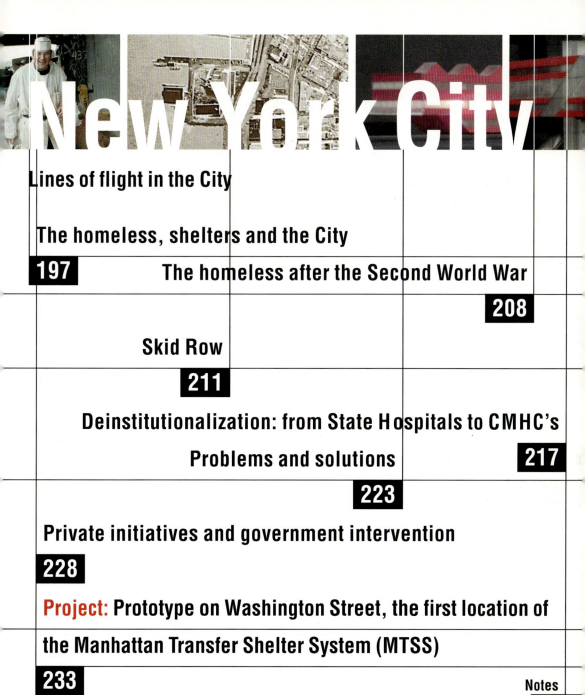

New York City

Acknowledgments

The beginning of every book is a leap into the unknown. To finish it well requires the faith of others.

This book would not have existed without the faith of both the Programming Committee Loft for New York City of the Ministry then entrusted with Public Welfare, Public Health and Culture (the former Ministry of wvc) and The Japan Foundation. For two long summers I had the opportunity to work undisturbed in the wvc Loft, once in Tribeca and once in Soho. Two years later I spent a long hot summer in Tokyo where I was a visiting scholar in the Faculty of Architecture at Tokyo University. In New York, Bernard Tschumi supported my efforts by opening the doors to the library of Avery Hall at Columbia University; while in Tokyo, Hidetoshi Ohno kindly guided me through the faculty as well as the University research facilities. Joel Blau, professor at the School of Social Welfare of the State University of New York in Stony Brook, generously took time to read through the manuscript on the homeless in Manhattan with me and I remain grateful for his expert commentary. Paul Colson, the coordinator of the Critical Time Intervention project of Columbia University, department of Psychiatry, College of Physicians and Surgeons, introduced me to the shocking world of Fort Armory. In the Netherlands, I owe a special thank-you to Ton Banning, director of the HVO Association in Amsterdam for providing me with an internship in the Amsterdam Transient Shelter. As a result, I acquired a more realistic grasp of the world of the homeless and I hope a greater empathy and understanding which subsequently informed my design decisions on the homeless shelter project. In Japan my gratitude goes out to the director of the Urban Planning Bureau of the City of Yokohama, Michio Kinoshita and to Kiyoshi Ishimaru who is in charge of the development of Minato Mirai 21 in Yokohama. I would like to thank Hidetoshi Ohno and Hajime Yatsuka for their remarks on the Tokyo and Yokohama chapter. Furthermore, I am grateful for the design work provided by Diana Ishida and Toshikazu Ishida and his team at the Kyushu Institute of Design in Fukuoka. I am deeply grateful to Deborah Hauptmann for her critical comments and collegial cooperation during the editing of this text. Finally, for financial support, I thank the Faculty of Architecture of the TU Delft for initiation funds as well as the Netherlands Architecture Fund (Stimuleringsfonds voor Architectuur) in Rotterdam for the primary funding. This publication would not have been possible without their support.

Preface

The questions about Modernism, Postmodernism, Deconstructivism, and urban planning that are raised in this book would appear to be typically Dutch. Modern architecture in the Netherlands of the beginning of this century was related to a social program. Construction in cities such as Amsterdam and Rotterdam took place in a socio-political context. The reconstruction period in the Netherlands was largely given form by modern architects such as de 8 en Opbouw. This, the Dutch equivalent of CIAM, consisted of two groups (based in Amsterdam and Rotterdam respectively) in the 1920s, and in 1932 a magazine with the same name was launched. Modernism and social democracy came into frequent contact with each other. These relationships between architecture, urban planning, society and politics have now changed greatly. Urban planning and architecture have largely developed into independent disciplines, politics has had to revise its socialist ideas, and society is no longer the society of Nieuwe Bouwen during the post-war reconstruction period. Buildings are no longer constructed for the workers, housing associations have lost their socialist aura following privatization, architects are now Postmodern; and urban planners will never again design an autonomous urban master plan in the manner of architects like Berlage, van Traa or Witteveen. New technological and informational relationships have come into play. The two disciplines are influenced by internationalization in professional practice and in education, architects are no longer interested in politics, and politicians themselves have no ideas about the design and furnishing of public spaces; and no one any longer knows exactly what 'society' means. However the profession hasn't suffered from these changes – architecture has never been as popular with the general public as it is now. The success of influential practices such as OMA in the Netherlands has only contributed to the popularity of the architectural profession.

Whether or not they seek it, architects acquire the status of celebrities; there are innumerable books about architecture and design, and politicians are glad to associate themselves with the high-profile names.

All attention seems to have shifted from the building to its architect. Once the architect has made a name for himself his buildings become 'interesting' or 'beautiful'. Criteria used to assess them are increasingly based on what the designer himself has to say about his building. Critical distance from the building is thus totally eliminated. The question is then: what role can a critic play if he wants to be more than just someone expressing an opinion (and merely attached to the architect's strings)? Of course a critical distance is still possible – and there is more than enough literature available, both inside and outside the profession to support this. I believe that it is now more important than ever that criticism should associate itself with architectural thought. This, too, is nothing new. The American architect Peter Eisenman has followed this approach from the beginning of his career. Rem Koolhaas also entered the profession after publication of *Delirious New York*. By naming these two architects I have also introduced the two most important architectural positions in the present book. By 'positions' I understand a theoretical position with respect to Eisenman, and a building (Rotterdam's Art Hall or Kunsthal) and an urban plan (the IJ-bank in Amsterdam) with regard to Koolhaas. Both architects belong to the school of Deconstructivism – a movement that in fact isn't a movement, because there is neither a common style nor a program. However the 1988 New York exhibition in the MoMA did contain all the ingredients I have just summarized above: architecture, politics and society. If what Mark Wigley says is true, i.e. that Deconstructivism has its roots in the Russian Constructivism of the 1920s and '30s, then an analysis of Koolhaas's work is only feasible when this is borne in mind. However this book is not a description of his work; his architecture does play an important role, but only when architectural lines of thought are needed for the criticism. As with Eisenman, the line of argumentation that I present here is philosophical, argued by using the body of architecture itself. The philosophical positions that are brought into play retain their autonomy relative to each other, and consequently their critical distance.

The social machines of the Russian Constructivists made a relationship between social production and architectural production; architecture was a vehicle for revolutionary change. The *dom-kommunas* were designed to vanquish the bourgeois family, and the ultimate goal was the total transformation of Man and society. Russian society at the beginning of the 1920s was a '*socius*', as the French theorists Deleuze and Guattari put it, of architectural and revolutionary inscription, a surface on which the whole process of production was inscribed. Lewis Mumford used the term *mega-machine* to designate the social machine as a collective entity. Deleuze and Guattari redefine his terminology in their *Anti-Oedipus* (1972). They are in agreement with Mumford when they characterize this mega-machine as a socius, roughly equivalent with the term society. But Deleuze and Guattari differ from Mumford when they introduce desire into the heart of this machinery. This socius, which they describe as a full body, constitutes the surface on which all production, material and immaterial, is recorded. Whereupon the entire process of the revolution appears to emanate from this recording surface. Desire, as affective and libidinal energy, has so many aspects that Deleuze and Guattari also characterize it as *desiring machines*. In opposition to this they refer to the *Body without Organs* (BwO) as the unindividuated mass, a term they borrow from Antonin Artaud. They consider this BwO to be the unproductive, the non-consumable, and it serves as a surface to record the entire process of the production of desire. In this context socius should be understood as a social machine which encloses desire. Desire, or more correctly desiring production, isn't something that comes later, after social production. Desiring production exists from the moment there is social production and reproduction. The socius serves to code and give shape to architectural and aesthetic desires and to inscribe them, and record them. This is also applicable to the counterflows, because little in the social flows in the same direction. Melnikov, who is often considered to be an individual amongst the Russian masses, is one such counterflow that also needs to be channeled, regulated, and dammed. They are these counterflows which require our attention. The unstable, restless geometry of artists such as Tatlin and Rodchenko in pre-Revolutionary Russia was undoubtedly increasingly absorbed into the functional pattern of architecture following the Revolution. Wigley argues that a critical shift in thinking took place. He states that the more the Constructivists became committed to architecture, the more the instability of their pre-Revolutionary work was removed.

Instability had been marginalized. The Russian avant-garde was corrupted, and adopted the purity of the modern movement. The desire to vanquish the 19th century tradition of decoration and to become a machine coded a flow of architectural perfection of steel and glass. In Wigley's view today's Deconstructivism draws on the instability of the early

Russian avant-garde and the stability of high modernism. Deconstructivism is the shock of the old. However, I believe that this shock is becoming increasingly ineffective. In spite of its renewing force Deconstructivism threatens to be overwhelmed by its own success. It is under the threat of becoming precisely what Eisenman has contested from the very beginning: a stabilized style. The question that first needs to be answered is how social Deconstructivism actually is. An obvious answer would seem to be that Russian Constructivism was extremely social in view of the revolutionary vanguard pretensions of the OSA architects, for example; and that this is no longer applicable to the Deconstructivism of, say, Peter Eisenman or Frank O. Gehry. However, in my opinion this answer is too simple. Society and architecture are directly mediated only by the program and the functions of the architecture. This is undeniably a socio-political choice; there is a clear difference between low-cost housing, a shelter for the homeless and a museum. Socio-political priorities are applicable to such choices. However, design in architecture follows aesthetic-ideological driving forces. This machinery is not subject to direct political mediation. What I hope to show in this book is that other concepts are required to be able to analyze this aesthetic production process. In my opinion the Russians were also unable to create convincing ties between architectural form and society. On the contrary: the ideological political debates about architecture at the time were indeterminable. And in fact this is still true for the rare discussions about the subject, even though they are in a different context from those of the Russians. To clarify this issue I begin this book with a discussion about this relationship between architecture and society.

A decade ago Jacques Derrida challenged Peter Eisenman to respond to the question of the relationship between poverty and architecture. As I will discuss later, this question contained within it a subsequent query into the social problem of today's homeless in the United States. Eisenman's answer was that neither architecture nor philosophy is able to solve this problem. I would think that that is correct; but there is more to be said. A political will is needed to tackle this problem using architecture; i.e. more and, in particular, better shelters. But the possible construction of these shelters would betray little of their significance as architecture. In other words the *Socius* of architecture is not equivalent to the *Social* in architecture. In this book this distinction is made in the following manner: the relationship between *socius* and architectural meaning is primarily developed in Part I, while the urban social is primarily discussed in Part II, which examines three *cities*: Amsterdam, Tokyo, and New York. Or, in the words of Deleuze and Guattari, society is a Socius of inscription where the essential thing is to mark and to be marked. Philosophy serves to read the results of this process. I shall engage this type of 'reading' with the aid of an old concept: the sublime. Both Edmund Burke and Immanuel Kant have described the sublime as an experience that is different from the more harmonic experience of beauty. Although the concept was considered to be inapplicable to architecture, Boullée did make use of it in his *Traité sur l'Architecture*, in what I provisionally call his architecture of shadows. For Kant this concept always involves magnitude; it seems to overwhelm our senses. The revolutionary architectures of the end of the 18th century and the beginning of the 20th both appear to be associated with the sublime. I shall also relate Koolhaas's 'bigness' to the sublime. However this sublime is divorced from its 18th century meaning by means of Elaine Scarry's interpretation of the body in pain, associated with the body without organs (BwO). In philosophical terms this constitutes the core of the book: a Man-Nature relationship in Scarry's sense replaces that of the architectural style meaning. This is how Deleuze's inscription is read.

Of course socius and social cannot be separated from each other. Philosophical themes will also be discussed in Part II, which will refer to the significance of architecture. However, they will be related more to the modern urban experience, and less to individual works of architecture. I have introduced a number of terms to describe the specific nature of these three cities in relation to modernity. Although the notion is general, elaboration on the theme is case-specific. In Chapter 4 on Amsterdam this seems possible through the proposed urban development along the banks of the IJ, which form the border of the existing medieval city structure. What is proposed here is the implanting of new tissue upon the old, a still modern issue in urban development. The metaphor of the 'Venice of the North' will be nothing new to those who are familiar with the Old City of Amsterdam. The oldest part of the city is transected by small canals and embankments, and this medieval system of waterways is enclosed by the three larger canals excavated at a later date. This part of the city is in fact best visited on foot, or by boat. I relate the specific experience of this city to the philosophical concept of the *rhizome*. Deleuze and Guattari compare the rhizome to a map with an infinite number of entrances. Here the rhizome refers both to the socius and to the social. It was initially a mental concept they used in their book *Mille Plateaux* (1980). In my opinion the term can also be used to describe the specific morphology of the Old City, and the dominating experience of the area. On the northern side the City opens up to the IJ, the river on which the city originated. As is the case in many cities, a design has been made for the development of this waterfront. Such a plan inserted in this kind of medieval structure is by definition 'modern': an implantation of new tissue into old. OMA supervised the development of a plan for this area – a plan that failed to gain political support. Nonetheless the plan is of interest, as it is illustrative of a specific idea about contemporary urban planning. It is a form of flexible urban planning that retains little of the ad hoc planning that is so characteristic of today's Amsterdam. In my analysis I shall discuss OMA's planning ideology – a concept that is closely associated with instability, uncertainty about the context of the planning, and speculative architecture.

In Chapter 5 I extend this problem of modern urban design to the cities of Tokyo and Yokohama. Tokyo used to be what Amsterdam still is – a city of water. The water has disappeared from modern Tokyo, but in the 1960s Kenzo Tange rediscovered it with his Bay project. Tange does what Koolhaas conscientiously avoided thirty years later: Tange extends his design to the smallest details. As far as the method is concerned, Tange's plan is somewhat comparable with the Pampus plan for the IJ designed by van den Broek and Bakema in the same period (1964-1965). Both base the design on Modernism, resulting in a fixed definitive plan with univocally-designed architectural components. The characteristic pattern of Tokyo is sometimes compared to a Sugoroku board, *Sugoroku* being a game for a number of players that takes you from one famous place to another. I consider the discrete nature of the city to be characteristic of the urban experience of Tokyo. The city is divided into a heterogeneous field of different wards, each with its own character and with strongly inwardly-focused elements such as parks, gardens, and brothels. I use a term of Foucault's to describe the character of the spaces, i.e. their inward-looking nature, and the way in which they accumulate history. He calls this a *heterotopia*. This is the very quality I consider to be so characteristic of the squares on the Sugoroku board. They are small enclaves in the urban tissue, entities that store and present the Japanese culture. These heterotopias are contrasted with recent large-scale urban plans for the Bay, Ariake in Tokyo Bay and Minato Mirai 21 in Yokohama. I consider both projects to be homotopias – late-modernist enclaves, or 'Cyber-Cities' (M. Christine Boyer).

The last chapter contains an analysis of the Modernists' urban plan for the waterfronts of 1930s Manhattan that was drawn up by the *Regional Plan Association* (RPA). This plan for the revitalization of the Lower East Side provided for the construction of housing for the middle class and for low-income groups. The plan was supplemented by the construction of a series of independent commercial skyscrapers on both sides of the projected Chrystie-Forsyth Parkway. This boulevard was an important component of the entire plan, which covered the area enclosed by 14th Street, the East River, Manhattan Bridge and Third Avenue. The plan was characterized by the advent of the automobile: examples of this were the Henry Hudson Parkway on the West Side of the island, and the projected Chrystie-Forsyth Parkway. Nowadays the example is the South Street Elevated Highway, which provides access to Brooklyn Bridge. Speed rules on top of the highway, but underneath the contrast could not be greater. This desolate area consists of car parks and empty spaces, and a juvenile penitentiary located immediately on the water's edge. Here the homeless of New York live, in makeshift structures made of fabric, sticks and supermarket pushcarts. This evinces the *imperfection* of perfect Modernism, the blind spot on the retina of the Modernist planner. The homeless form the central theme of the last chapter, which examines the social conditions under the roads of modernity. Terms such as 'space', 'place', 'time' and 'architecture' play a role in the worlds of both the planners and the homeless. I consider Giedion's *Space, Time and Architecture* (1967) as the reverse side of Manhattan's homeless. All the frequently used terms are to be found but with inverse meanings. This is the language of the homeless. Furthermore, researchers' endeavors to find an unequivocal explanation for the phenomenon of 'homelessness' have been fruitless. It has transpired that the term cannot be reduced to a categorization or a classification, and earlier definitions of marginality or social stratification such as low income, proletariat, or class proves insufficient to explain the phenomenon. From a philosophical point of view the term to describe this is a *line of flight*, while an unequivocal definition remains impossible. It slips out of our hands as a result of the immense complexity of the factors involved. In this manner the social in architecture touches on the socius, in which the definition of the term plays an important role.

To elaborate on this bipartite character in full detail we have conceived of and designed a project for each city. These design projects form the conclusion of each chapter in Part II. The design for Amsterdam consists of a housing project on the Westerdok bank of the IJ, that for Tokyo a hiring hall for day laborers, and for New York a shelter for the homeless. The subject for each project was chosen on the basis of the prevailing local circumstances and politics. Each design is the result of a specific analysis, and in a political context it constitutes a strategic intervention in the respective cities. The plans are not mutually interchangeable, because both the concept on which the design is based and its social context are rooted in the location. However, the architecture of the three plans is largely based on the question of the meaning of beauty in architecture as discussed in Part I. The sublime experience of architecture as reflected and transformed social imperfection plays a major role in the designs. An important reason for this combination of a theoretical treatment with design proposals is that, in my opinion, architecture and philosophy have undergone a transmutation. Until recently architectural theory consisted largely of manuals, tracts and political manifestos; but nowadays architecture intervenes directly in the field of philosophy. In my opinion Eisenman's work is the best example of this. He has opened a new field, which I term *archi-philosophy*. In order to obtain some clarity about these complex relationships between beauty, society, and the social I make an analysis of the work of the one Dutch 'Deconstructivist' architect, who in my opinion certainly is not one, and who himself finds that Deconstructivism has in fact become hopelessly decorative: Rem Koolhaas. Koolhaas, as one of the most successful Deconstructivists, would appear to have stayed closer to Modernism. In my analysis this 'closer to' is regarded as an intelligent architectural *paraphrasing* of Modernism. Using linguistic analogy we might say that we may sometimes recognize the 'words', but the syntax is fundamentally different. Consequently the meaning of the words, as well as that of the sentence, has changed. However, discussion on the work of OMA is not resolved through semiotic analysis. It requires an analysis of the desire to disrupt the rules of Modernism with the quasi-nonchalant, the quasi-ugly and the provisional, the quasi-maladjusted, and the quasi-unmanageable size in the perfect body of Modernity. This is achieved by retaining a critical proximity to the corpus of modern architecture. OMA's strategic position is that of the judoist; keeping too great a distance results in the contest being lost. This same position can also be adopted by criticism.

Finally, it is important to take a moment to introduce the reader of this book to its written structure. Within the academic world, the imperative of systematics and hierarchy is generally adhered to. Much can be said in favor of this. However, in the past few decades an increasing number of authors appear to want to match Adorno's parataxis. Some of these books are inspired by Walter Benjamin, or more recently by Gilles Deleuze and Félix Guattari. A recent example is Derek Gregory's *Geographical Imaginations* (1994). Gregory organizes his book as a set of essays that consider diverse geographical imaginations, with an emphasis on plurality. Following Deleuze and Guattari, he calls it a nomadic project, and compares the open-essay structure to a rhizome. This structure is analogous to the organization of Deleuze and Guattari's *Mille Plateaux*. Edward W. Soja pointedly criticizes Gregory's book by using an uncontrived reference to Foucault – calling it a labyrinthine Chinese Encyclopedia of geographical thinking. Both authors, though, exhibit an equally acute grasp of Foucault's work. Soja's *Thirdspace* (1996) overrides an important portion of Gregory's criticism of the former's earlier *Post-modern Geographies* (1989), at least as far as a feminist critique is concerned.

Although Gregory presents his arguments with exceptional lucidity and has written what is to me a remarkably interesting book, Soja's critique is largely accurate. The labyrinthine structure doesn't make for light reading. To an author, books may seem to enter an anonymous market, but this market is not entirely undesignated. Almost everything ends up within the educational institution of its inception. Each of these books thus acquires a local character. To a less initiated reader the nomadic expeditions are rather exhausting and sometimes inimitable. In this aspect, *Thirdspace* is more linear, making it easier to follow. Naturally, the presentation of the discourse is linked to the knowledge and assessment of the potential of postmodernism. Adorno set up his parataxis as a critical answer to Hegel's systematic, although the paratactic elements he related to the essay are not the same as those within the postmodern discourse. Adorno, Benjamin, and Deleuze remained faithful to Marx in their thinking. Postmodernity is a different thing entirely, especially within the discourse itself. Postmodernity is undoubtedly a glorification of consumption, as Celeste Olalquiaga states, but the question remains whether and how this is still related to Marxist thought. To her, an articulation of novel and often contradictory experiences seems to appear through the relinquishing of depth, linear causality, and univocality.

For example, in her book, *Megalopolis* (1992) — which is also composed as a collection of related essays — this is the case in the 'third-degree kitsch' of Amalia Mesa-Bains's work as a conscious gesture of political reaffirmation of Chicano cultural values. The same is true of Superbarrio where a masked stranger arises out of the governmental inefficiency regarding the handling of the 1985 earthquake that destroyed vast areas of Mexico City. This type of descriptive analysis used in *Megalopolis* is well suited to the essay format. Conditions of readability become different however when content revolves around more abstract texts, which is precisely what makes Gregory's book difficult to enter. His critical philosophical discourse would perhaps benefit from some level of overview, even though he emphatically dismisses the prospect of any such idea.

The structure of this book, *The Socius of Architecture*, can be found provisionally in its subdivision into two primary parts, where Part I works to develop a new and critical understanding of architecture, and Part II presents an analysis of three urban phenomena. Architectural understanding is developed on a theoretical level from Kant to Marx. Urban critique evolves within a recognizably sociological discourse. Furthermore, as I have mentioned above, there is what might be considered a critical *thirding* within the book where, concluding each urban analysis, a design proposal which addresses the critical questions raised in the respective analyses is put forward. Architecture is inevitably interpreted contextually, even when context is fully dismissed. These urban interpretations necessarily require the theoretical perspective that precedes them. Yet equally, the theoretical positions utilize these concluding proposals as frameworks of visibility. Soja never tires of reminding us that for Henri Lefebvre binary categories are never sufficient to reveal conceptual schemes, that there is always an-Other: *Il y a toujours l'Autre*. In *The Socius of Architecture* this 'other' is made present with the project designs. With them I have sought to mediate, perhaps even conciliate, the ill-perceived distance too often retained between theory and practice.

One of the questions I shall be raising is whether the general public has more than a superficial interest in today's increasingly autonomous architecture. If 'left' and 'right', and 'beautiful' and 'ugly' are not suitable for the description of a building, then what categories can we use? I propose that we should make use of terms derived from philosophy, such as the concept of the 'sublime'. However, before we can use them they will first need to be adapted to the field of architecture. Elsewhere, I have shown how 'rhizome' can be used for architecture in my chapter on Amsterdam. As the meaning of sublime becomes clarified we shall discover that other commonly-used terms become more obscure. Until now there didn't appear to be a problem with the use of terms such as formal, purist, modernistic or abstract; but now we ask ourselves what these words mean precisely. This book will make many revelations, but it will also make some frequently-applied terms less clear; it will be necessary to revise certain terms.

The reader of this book need not search for a single, underlying 'principle' (intentional or derivative) with which to frame the arguments presented here. Nor does this subsequently mean that the contents, whether theoretical, analytical, or project-based, are disjointed: it is not a dictatorship of fragments without a common theme. The reader is requested to exercise a little patience in obtaining an insight into the critical contents of this work since many of its themes will refer to each other in a horizontal as opposed to a vertical manner. By this I mean that the concepts presented here develop meaning not in terms dependent on a linear, continuous reading, but are conditioned by a lateral, contiguous reading. This structure inherently suggest that the reader will only be able to map the various courses that the book has taken once he or she has finished reading it.

PART ONE

Architecture

ARCHITECTURE Introduction

Deconstructivism and the postmodern condition

The architecture of the last two decades has been one of experiment, prompted by a critical attitude towards modernism. For many architects, proclaiming the end of modernism meant juggling with the remnants. The new architectural parameters were fragmentation, rotation, and the use of 'classical references' against the background of the tatters of modernism. This iconoclasm was reinforced by the 'loss' of philosophical totality. The question as to how this loss should be assessed formed the boundary between modernism and postmodernism. While the disintegration of totality was experienced as a loss by present high modernists such as Habermas, the postmodern architects of the 1970s regarded it as a liberating development. They found it to be a positive experience which opened the way to new experiments and to a much freer and plastic use of ornament and fragments. Modernism was exposed as regimentation; the modernists of the 1920s might have been an avant-garde, but the realization of their program ultimately led to the uniformity of the *International Style*.[1]

These postmodernist architects were assessed both favorably and unfavorably. For Habermas they were an avant-garde with the wrong fronts, whilst another German philosopher, Welsch, welcomed them as liberators freeing architecture from the delimiting nature of conformity. An important distinction between modernist vision and postmodernist view was that postmodern architects deliberately (if not critically) ignored the social and political contexts.

Postmodernism's heyday was celebrated in the us, where the French philosophy fell on fertile soil. More links were made between architecture, art and philosophy than in Europe, as was exemplified by the journals *Oppositions*, and more recently *Any* and *Assemblage*. They took root in the years that the American economy was reorganized, a period during which personal profit was paramount. Unemployment, homelessness, increasing poverty and growing contrasts were rationalized away during the Reagan period with an appeal to the traditional values of entrepreneurship and individual responsibility. There was a shift from social problems towards aesthetic questions. A new type of beauty appeared, the beauty of decay. The ruin became architecture's *leitmotiv*. It marked the definitive end of the framework of modernism.

The unprecedented cooperation between a French philosopher and an American architect was found to be possible in New York sooner than it was in France. However, this cooperation was not without its problems, because the 'languages' of architecture and philosophy differ greatly. In the Netherlands we viewed this with a degree of skepticism, and wondered whether there ever was a 'dialogue'. However, I think that this was unjustified: I believe that the willingness to cooperate, and the resulting collaboration are of greater importance. We also learn something about Derrida's views, which ultimately proposed that there was little benefit in the excessive autonomy of Eisenman's architecture. Which is remarkable, as Derrida has rarely been received as a politically-engaged philosopher.

During their collaboration on the *Choral Work* project Derrida requested that Eisenman pursue the theme of the ruin in relation to the palimpsest: the architectural experience of memory. This question referred to Walter Benjamin's essay *Erfahrung und Armut* from 1933. In this essay Benjamin calls attention to a modern poverty of experience, which for him is part of a much larger poverty caused by our technology. This poverty is not merely subjective, it refers to the development of a schism between technological development as opposed to the world of yoga, astrology, Christian Science and spiritualism. Modernism cherished few illusions about the situation in the 19th century, but did accept the technological possibilities it offered. Benjamin mentions the use of glass by Loos and Le Corbusier, and of steel by the Bauhaus. Glass is a sober material; it is secrecy's enemy, and consequently that of the civil culture around the turn of the century. This is how 'modernistic poverty' should be understood. The search is focused on an attempt to break from civil culture, rather than on new experiences. Benjamin made a magnificent analysis of this situation in his unfinished masterpiece, the *Passagen-Werk*. This 'book', which isn't actually a book but a collection of thematic essays, reflections, philosophical conceptions, descriptions of everyday life, critical views on fashion, architecture, the 'flâneur', etc., offers a fascinating glimpse of the 19th century. It is a unique attempt to understand the transition of life and its philosophy from the romanticism of the previous century as it evolved into modernism. Benjamin's particular insight coupled with his ability to link everyday life with philosophy and history is particularly striking. Rolf Tiedemann compares the *Passagen-Werk* with the building materials for a house. We know only of the drawings for its construction, and the excavated site; although the rest is present, the house is not finished.[2] Whilst the *Pariser Passagen* fragment is an important section, it is no more than a theme amongst many others. For Benjamin the street is the home of the collective, an ever-restless and continually-moving being, a being that undergoes, experiences and dreams outdoors just as much as individuals do within the privacy of their homes.[3] The cities Benjamin describes are for him the realization of the dream of the labyrinth. Here the flâneur passes his days without realizing the characteristic nature of his life. The covered passages or arcades of the last century are a central theme. Benjamin considered them to be a material duplication of the consciousness of the time. Everything that was wrong with that consciousness was to be found there (an existence turned in on itself), but also the utopian dream (fashion, prostitution, gambling).[4] Furthermore the arcades constituted the first 'international style' of modern architecture; they were part of the metropolitan experience. The arcade was the outstanding characteristic of the modern world.

Anyone reading this book will also realize how dramatically the world has changed. It seems as though the tramp in *Konvolut* M 1,3 is the only person in that world who has survived into *our* time. The flâneur could still go out for a walk with a tortoise, now everything seems to happen at an increasingly rapid pace.[5]

Benjamin's texts possess an unmistakable topicality. Some of today's critics, like Benjamin, have had enough of the present culture of Deconstructivism and postmodernism: 'Sie haben das alles gefressen, "die Kultur" und den "Menschen" und sie sind übersatt daran geworden und müde', Benjamin wrote in 1933.[6] In some respects the situation as it was then is comparable with the situation today.[7]

A return to the values of modernism is impossible. An architecture that wishes to shun both Deconstructivism and postmodernism cannot avoid an *anamnesis* of modernism itself. This anamnesis is more than just an analysis of the culture and the outline of designs of the modernists. Later in this book I will further elaborate this analysis within the proposed project designs. Not only the type of building plays a role; in New York it also involves homelessness, a term that is almost impossible to delimit and cannot be reduced to classifications and definitions in the sense of social stratification, low income, proletariat, classes or unemployment.

Derrida's challenge to Eisenman to examine the question of the relationship between architecture and poverty referred to poverty as understood by Benjamin in his *Erfahrung und Armut* of 1933; and furthermore to the other form of poverty, that of housing in general, and of inhabitable or uninhabitable housing in particular.[8] Ultimately he is referring to today's homeless people in the United States. Eisenman's answer is characteristic of the new position in which Deconstructivism has landed. It is a new enclave, typified by the distance it keeps from the social and political consequences of its designs. The designs of Deconstructivism are remarkably mute where the more specific problems of our society are involved. However, the question remains whether architecture can do nothing other than indicate its *political* powerlessness. On this account I agree with K. Michael Hays, who is of the opinion that 'despite the intransigent anti-humanism of postmodernist deconstructivist discourse, the practical result has often been the construction of a canon of individual oeuvres and authors whose domain is the gallery, the journal, and the jewelry boutique'.[9] The aim of Hays's theoretical reconstruction of the work of Hannes Meyer and Ludwig Hilberseimer is to protect, at least, the social character of their work from the present wave of 'deconstruction'. Later, I will discuss the relationship between architecture and society in more detail in connection with Russian Constructivism. However, it is, to say the least, remarkable that the architectural significance of this poverty problem remains untouched.

Benjamin's writings further raise a number of important questions, which are not restricted to social or philosophical issues. He also inquires into the meaning of architecture, both to society, and in an ideological sense. Nothing is achieved with the choice of the object: for New York a shelter for the homeless is no more 'social' than a museum. Nor is housing in Amsterdam's Westerdok inherently more social than the office buildings in the same plan. Such buildings readily invite pseudo socially-motivated opinions. This book maintains a great distance from these kinds of noncommittal social viewpoints. The real question is whether there is an *architecture of poverty*, not so much in a financial as in a conceptual sense. The duty of the architect is to create architecture, that of the critic to criticize. Which may well seem self-explanatory, but it is increasingly less so.

'Homelessness' is a term that has been adopted by the media: around Christmas time the newspapers deal with the subject in great depth. What I particularly wish to demonstrate is that the phenomenon of homelessness is the result of a historical process, which in the USA is connected with real-estate speculation, gentrification, alcohol, and drug abuse, and the increasing disintegration of normative systems. This is an important point, both for the architect and the critic. In this book I will fulfill both roles – it will be seen that they are actually very similar.

Homelessness consists of a whole gamut of experiences, and this should be the material the architect works with. Neither the modernist concept of the pure form nor the Deconstructivism of the tormented form can be of assistance here. Their ideas of time and space, the parameters of the architecture of spatial configuration, are fundamentally different from the way in which these theoretical ideas are actually experienced by the homeless. Benjamin's writing is exemplary in this respect. To a certain extent this book is also montage. Benjamin himself described the *Passagen-Werk* as a *literary* montage. 'I have nothing to say', says Benjamin about the method he adopted, 'I only show. I shall purloin nothing of value, nor lay claim to any profound phrasing'. For him it was just a question of the rags, the garbage of history. He wanted them to be given the place they deserve.[10] I believe that there is much inspiration still to be drawn from the ideas posed, as well as the quality of investigation illustrated, in the *Passagen-Werk*.

The street also remains an important subject throughout this book – but now it is the streets of Manhattan, Amsterdam and Tokyo at the end of the 20th century which are brought into focus. *The Socius* also contains many critical comments about architecture and society, in particular attention is given to the street culture and the way in which this is reflected in the buildings. The flâneur has become extinct; today the only permanent residents of the street are the homeless and numerous sections are devoted to the 'lived space' of their lives. It should be realized that the homeless are a sign of the imperfection of our world. I will make clear the significance of this for architecture in discussions on the idea of the 'sublime'. I will later propose Constructivism as the last heroic attempt to cast the dream of revolution in concrete and glass. Ultimately the proclaimed revolutionary zeal was seen to have hardly any grip on architectural terms such as 'expressive' and 'formal'. The political conceptions of the left and right were stranded amongst the political and artistic violence that was Constructivism.

For a number of exhibitors at the 1988 exhibition in New York the exploration of the Russian experiments from the period 1918-1920, when the tormented form was tested, was extremely important for their work.

But these tests were made on paper, in drawings, and not with actual buildings. Only now, six to seven decades later, is there room for experiments with buildings. For Koolhaas the situation was different right from the start. His work is linked more with modernistic machine aesthetics, in which *the formal* is redefined. For the Deconstructivist the machine aesthetic means that the struggle for the free form has been lost, and that the design process is an automatic process which proceeds from cell and chain. In my view the machine of the modernistic concept has always malfunctioned. It is precisely the malfunctions and failures intrinsic to these kinds of perfect orders that need to be tracked down. This doesn't lead us to a 'free form', but it does increase the experiences that are evoked by this malfunctioning machine – and then in relation to the user's experience of time and space. The users – those seeking temporary accommodation, and the homeless – do not provide any kind of social guarantee that architecture will be able to leave its boudoir.[11]

↑ OMA Rem Koolhaas, Apartment Building and Observation Tower 1982, axonometric

↗ Ivan Leonidov, Narkomtiazhprom, detail of tower, 1934

The concept of temporary accommodation depends entirely on *transformation*, the ultimate molding of the world of the user's experience into the architectural concept. Only in this manner can a result be achieved that, as far as architecture is concerned, might still be called 'modern': the relationship between architecture and society. Nowhere has this relationship been examined so explicitly as in the experiments with Russian Constructivism and Formalism by architects such as Ginzburg, Melnikov and Leonidov. An act passed in October 1917 gave the communes the right to confiscate all empty apartments and distribute them amongst the homeless and impoverished. The later work was restricted to a series of proposals for new communal housing for the proletariat, as the homeless had left the scene once again.

If these experiments are reviewed in the light of the current situation in New York and Tokyo then it is not impossible that they might give cause for a new experiment. The intention of such an experiment is not to restore 'old' values; it is a question of the *differentiation*, the differences in the many possible links in the time-space experience – a relationship that modernism tried to capture with a single concept. Since there is no longer a connection between the architectural design and the developments in society *as a whole* the projects I present here can be described as *postmodern*. This doesn't involve 'the' emancipation of man, as the question is much more specific: the architecture of a shelter for the homeless, the processing of a modernist urban plan and a hiring hall for Tokyo's day laborers.

Until now Constructivism was mostly used as autonomous architectural material, as in Bernard Tschumi's *Parc de la Villette* in Paris. Tschumi's follies look like caricatures of Constructivism. They form a montage of the modernistic heritage, but now as a cheerful collection of garbage.[12]

The projects presented here are of a different order. I don't think it is possible to review Constructivism without discussing the political bankruptcy of Marxism. To a great extent it is an *anamnesis* of both; but another not unimportant element is that it contains the construction of a new aesthetic effect of a non-autonomous architecture. For the successful completion of the theoretical project it transpired that three designs needed to be made in parallel with the analysis. These were not intended to function as practical applications of the theory; they were needed for an investigation of the spatial consequences of these meanings. This architecture possesses its own relative autonomy and dynamism. The architectural result can never be explained entirely by a theoretical proj-

↙ Bernard Tschumi, La Case Vide
↓ La Villette 1985, Architectural
Association Folio VIII

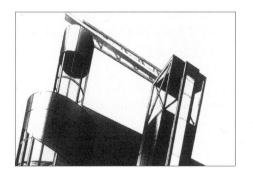

ect. In this book the designs are a second theme that develops relatively independently of the analysis. The text and the designs are intended to *bring back the social element* in the discussions about contemporary architecture. Deconstructivism and postmodernism dealt with this question rather too briefly when they were on their way to the fiction of an autonomous architecture and street culture.

If architecture and society cannot be linked to each other by political concepts then we need to find other terms for this purpose. For this reason I propose that the category of the 'sublime' should be used, a concept which refers to the aesthetic ideology of our experience. I will elaborate on this concept in a manner such that it acquires a relationship with society. This argument will enable me to make some significant statements about the relationship between architecture, (the perception of) beauty, and society. This is not possible using Kant's meaning for the concept of 'sublime', since a judgement of taste is not based on concepts and consequently is not a judgement of knowledge. For Kant it was a contemplative judgement that was indifferent to the existence of the object. This is emphatically not the case for the meaning of the concept of sublime as related to society, since in this situation aesthetic knowledge is not 'disinterested', as it was for Kant. The perceptions of beauty as distinguished by Kant were reason for me to introduce new terms and experiences.

I shall therefore attempt to explicate an *architecture of the sublime*. Sublime must be thought of in terms of the infinite; it is an absolute quantity that cannot be expressed in terms of time and space. The term sublime has a long history as an aesthetic category. Kant (*das Erhabene*) and Burke (*the Sublime*) are the most important analysts of this phenomenon. A threat can emanate from certain objects or certain impressions; Burke called this *terror*. Such feelings can never be evoked by a design drawing. Every drawing is an attempt to achieve an effect, a jump. Nevertheless, we may not exclude the possibility that this threat may be felt when the shelter for the homeless as shown in the drawing is actually built.

The sublime experience in architecture

In the past ten to fifteen years time and space have undergone a tremendous compression. Telecommunications and the increasing speed of transport have shrunk our space to a 'global village'. David Harvey's analysis of city politics has clearly shown their disruptive effect on the politico-economic climate. The three cities discussed in this book – New York, Amsterdam and Tokyo – are now all part of the 'global city', a term invented by Saskia Sassen, who investigated the effect of telecommunications and transport on New York, London and Tokyo. The flow of information makes these cities the 'informational cities' of Manuel Castells. Rapid movement is in the interests of capital, so rapid, according to Paul Virilio, that we lose our memory. Today the home is both the intersection of this compression of time and space and the last bastion against the outside world.

Not everyone has undergone this development in the same manner. A structural difference can be identified in the ways in which time and space are perceived. The homeless and vagrant have undergone a development in the reverse direction. At the turn of the century they were more mobile than anyone else: the American *tramp* and *hobo* migrated from one city to the next. Today their movements have largely ceased, and their space has become restricted to 'skid row'. Their space has become increasingly fixed – and time is a thing of *our* postmodern order. The question is then what effect this has had on the proposed shelter designed for Manhattan.

The postmodern eclectic aesthetics didn't wish to continue to be 'elitist'. Elements such as pop culture and kitsch from the 'lower' culture began to play a role in architecture and art. One effect of this was that cultural production moved closer to the consumer, another was that populism became the new value of this production.

Art and architecture are clearly very different from each other. For example architecture, unlike art, doesn't have its own group of consumers. It would seem to me that architecture also has less opportunity to establish a rapport with the consumer. Which doesn't mean that the street is a very popular source of imagery amongst architects. On the contrary: they appear to compete with each other in their aim for perfection, not in the least in their presentation techniques. The question I wish to explore here is to what extent the building can be mimetic in its design. In other words: to what extent is architecture able to reflect our society using the specific means it has at its disposal. Mimesis is a Greek word derived from the verb *mimestai*, which means to copy, imitate, portray, reproduce or represent. This can relate to the theater, literature or the plastic arts. Plato regarded mimetic art as sham and deceit. He was of the opinion that poets and storytellers should be barred from the ideal state;[13] since they replace reality with words and pictures, they make the world a *cave*. Plato attributed philosophy with the power to interrupt the narrative and to inquire after the true nature of things.

We have now left this conception behind us. Mimetic and anti-mimetic now function more as critical categories. Hegel was of the opinion that art should not copy life exactly. There should always be room for commentary about the image. The anti-mimetic view is focused on the *difference*, on the disagreement. This is actually implied by the very word mimesis. Mimesis is associated with a non-identity, a contrast. Various philosophers such as Deleuze, Derrida and Adorno all strongly emphasize the non-identical. It is this very aspect of the non-identical that I am searching for in architecture.

Branson, Coates Architecture, Metropole café, Tokyo

Architecture, like art, is a mediator: it reproduces social issues. Nigel Coates's former café *Metropole* in Tokyo is a good example. Coates's *Metropole* was mimetic. It appears to have absorbed its context into its architecture. Unlike Charles Jencks's architectural video clips, Coates's architecture really is directed towards the street – and not only its entrance, but also its interior, with a form of punk-pomo furnishings. The photograph reproduced here was taken by Coates himself.

The street has an important role. The untidy foreground is no coincidence; it has been staged in the photograph. Mimetics always raises the question of the original and the copy. The café now exists only in the form of a photograph, as a staged production. The café itself has since been demolished and replaced by DJ's, an Italian restaurant.

According to Baudrillard there are no more 'originals'. Everything has become simulacrum, an imitation, even the human body. We now consume only the meaning of the café. And in this case it is the meaning of the street. In this respect Coates's architecture differs from the pop architecture of architects like Charles Moore or the Dutchman Sjoerd Soeters, who create an aesthetic, perfect version of 'the street' in the *Piazza* and the *Circus*. It would seem to be obvious to use Coates's concept for the shelter; the location in Washington Street certainly gives every occasion to do so.

Ethics and social consciousness are displaced by the aesthetics of the simulation when the street is presented as an architectural concept. But the return to an unspoiled world is also impossible. The location for the shelter shown in this book is an urban area that has become characteristic of our large cities. They seem to be worlds that exist only in films or in cartoons, but anyone walking around Manhattan, Tokyo, Frankfurt or the Amsterdam harbors will be confronted with the same images. Of the 650,000 residents of Frankfurt, the financial center of Germany, 15% or 97,500 persons receive welfare benefits. The city actually has twice as many poor people. The report *Armut in Deutschland* concludes that 7.05 million Germans live on or below the poverty line. 180,000 live on the street, 700,000 have no home and are accommodated in communal residences or hotels at the State's expense, a situation very reminiscent of that in the USA.

However great the differences between these cities, in this respect they are all alike. The homeless and paupers confine themselves to the desolate no man's lands of the large cities, or to large public facilities such as railroad stations, subterranean corridors, or subway stations. In this respect Tokyo's Shinjuku Station is no different from Manhattan's Grand Central Station, Amsterdam's Centraal Station or Waterloo Station in London. The homeless bivouac in cardboard boxes under the railroad arches. Nor do the articles in the newspapers differ greatly from each other. The papers make a brief mention of actions to sweep public areas clean when the homeless have become too much of a nuisance to the public. For example, the homeless who were driven out of Shinjuku Station occupied the Station Manager's office and demanded accommodation and food. 'A group of about 50 homeless people protested Friday at Tokyo's Shinjuku Ward Office for allegedly breaking its promise when it evicted them from underground passages near J.R. Shinjuku Station's west exit last month', the *Japan Times* reported on Saturday 5 March 1994. As we shall see later, the reports in the *New York Times* are often literally the same.

This never results in anything more than a temporary solution to the problem. After a few days the homeless return, and the situation is the same as before. The provincial bus service's planned subterranean bus and subway terminus at Amsterdam's Centraal Station is going to suffer from the same problem. The homeless and the tramps who already live in the station will occupy these subterranean areas. They will regularly become a nuisance and the platforms, corridors and halls will be swept clean, without actually getting to grips with the problem itself. Rotterdam's Centraal Station suffers from the same problem, with its ebb and flow of the city's drug addicts and homeless: and no prospect of any definitive solution. There are few problems when the homeless simply stay put in the city's desolate areas, such as under Manhattan's Roosevelt Drive. These urban *wastelands* are virtually identical in any city.

The Meat Market under New York's 14th Street, Tsukiji in Tokyo, and the Westerdoksdijk in Amsterdam are all symbols of our imperfect world. They are sites characteristic of today's large cities. The many reviews of the non-elitist populist architecture that has replaced Modernism are blind to this reality. They go no deeper than the new fashion of a polished and readily-consumable pop architecture. The most noticeable feature of this architecture is its ridiculous degree of perfection. The

architect's drawings and presentation techniques emphasize the very thing that can never be realized in society; control over the process and the object. They actually have only one goal, that of a polished beauty. Of course this is made easier by the 'democratization' of presentation techniques, from CD-I to advanced photocopiers. Computer technology provides the most inane drawing with a compelling aura, the word processor does the rest. The tasks that are easiest to control seem to

↑↑ Tsukiji, Tokyo
↑   Meat Market District Manhattan, New York
←   Westerdok, Amsterdam

receive all the attention: the drawing programs, the photographic technology and the most improbable models.

Charles Jencks's books about postmodern architecture are nothing more than an apotheosis of this aesthetic ideal; the entire world, on file in the form of sleek color photographs. Architectural photography seems to have replaced the reality of the building. It is as though the general public's increasing interest in architecture is primarily focused on beautiful pictures of buildings – and then on the quality of the photographs as such. Jencks uses buildings like models on a catwalk. The professional architectural press is continually searching for photographs that have not been published before. In this respect the buildings can be compared with models. Architectural photography has itself become a subject of discussion, in which the 'effect' is debated at great length.[14] Of course this is nothing new. Photographers have been searching for the 'essence' of the building ever since Lucien Hervé's photographs of Le Corbusier's architecture, right up to Hans Werlemann's photographs of Koolhaas's work, and Hélène Binet's of Raoul Bunschoten's. A frequently-encountered problem is that the photographer's attempt to capture the more recalcitrant feeling of the beauty of a building's sublimity usually results in it changing into a tamed beauty. In my opinion sublimity in architecture is both cognitive and tactile. The latter can only be experienced from the building in reality. Photographs of buildings that actually possess architectural sublimity often portray only Kant's 'beauty'. The photographer while intuitively grasping this distinction, attempts to counter this by introducing an element of 'alienation' into his photograph; in fact he attempts to force beauty to accede to sublimity. Binet's photographs unmistakably touch on this theme. Although there may be something like sublimity in artistic photography, it is rare in architectural photography, which always aims to portray (part of) a building. Further, the building fundamentally acquires meaning in relation to its use – and here again many different perspectives are involved, as we shall see later. The actual use of a building will only very rarely tally with the ideas of its architect, and even less with the perfect photograph the photographer constructed of it. In this respect there is no real difference between the photograph of a model, a drawing, or a photograph of the actual building.

No single reproduction can be considered to be significantly more real than the others. In my view the most important task of a photograph is not to portray the 'essence' of the building – which, after all, doesn't exist – but to stimulate curiosity about the building itself. The photographer can't actually do much more than that.

The architects of the sublime, such as the Dutchman Koolhaas, have a different task. It is not a question of their work being 'uglier', merely that they endeavor to achieve this other perception of beauty in their work. The difference can be seen in the details. Koolhaas is of the opinion that he doesn't design details, while his critics think that he is sloppy, or that he has no interest in details. But details seem to me to be an essential characteristic of architecture, as they are linked with our tactile perceptions. And of course Koolhaas does design details, only not in the sense of 'beauty', but in the sense of the 'sublime'. Which usually means that expressive elements that please the viewer are omitted. In other words precisely the opposite of, say, the buildings of the firm Morphosis. The reason why Morphosis do something is never comprehensible. According to them their work reflects their interest in dead technology, but it isn't clear why one layer has to be rewound into another (the 'feedback-loop'). At a first glance these appear to be inventive drawings, but the idea that this feedback is related to the destructive side of our society seems far-fetched to me.[15] Thom Mayne actually designs attractive, very metaphoric architecture. Anyone who sees this architecture for the first time cannot fail to be impressed, although the metaphor of dead technology does wear off quickly.

However I cannot help feeling that the wrong images are being used when this architecture is imparted with serious social connotations. An example of this is Lebbeus Woods's design for war-torn Sarajevo. Woods believes that his mechanical monsters – which happen to be identical in all his designs – belong in the ruins of Sarajevo. He thinks that they could make a contribution to a possible post-war reconstruction of the city. There is no reason to doubt his intentions, but he didn't make any changes to his earlier sculptural designs. He sees a great deal of similarity between the destruction of the city and his architecture.[16] In his view the bomb craters have a kind of morbid beauty that is related to his architecture, an architecture that is truly mimetic when seen amidst the ruins of Sarajevo. Woods seeks legitimacy for this mimesis by explicitly referring to Burke's sublime. In my opinion it fails to survive in its location on a former battleground, and all tension between the architecture and its surroundings is lost in an analogous morphology. This entirely sculptural and completely uninhabitable architecture mimics the destroyed city in the smallest details. But Lebbeus Woods's work is undeniably much more interesting than Morphosis' 'techno-morphism'. This contemporary Piranesi, architect, cartoonist and postmodern philosopher, lets us see the world after a cataclysmic disaster. Woods's universe exhibits similarities with Enki Bilal's *Lady in Blue*. As an architect, he portrays the post-apocalyptic survival after a disaster. Like Ridley Scott with B*lade Runner*, Bilal, a cartoonist, designs a very likely scenario. It is, in Celeste Olalquiaga's terms, a culture-scape made of old images, junk, and debris. Woods has left this phase. The design for *Underground Berlin* (1988) is based on the idea of construction – but in the reverse direction, below ground level. His writings are also characterized by an unshakable confidence in 'methodology' and 'science'.[17]

His work certainly looks good, but in relation to our day-to-day problems it remains utopia. What we need is not 'simplicity' or 'functionality', but an architecture that stimulates not only our senses, but also our reason. It doesn't necessarily have to be 'ugly', but it does represent a different kind of beauty; a beauty which is founded on structure and detail. The detail doesn't need to be as ostentatious as in Morphosis' architecture. Modernistic architecture is 'plainer', but it certainly does have very evident details. Nowhere can this be seen better than in Pierre Chareau's *Maison de Verre* (in which, incidentally, Bijvoet's influence can be discerned).

Chareau was a perfectionist. He preferred to work for clients he knew well. *Maison de Verre* was commissioned by the Dalsace family, who were close friends of Chareau. Like Wittgenstein, he was completely engrossed with the idea of *perfection*. The partly built-in furniture, the sliding walls, the panels, the glass bricks and the steel frame make the house a perfectly-organized machine in all its parts. In this house everything, including the smallest details, appears to be in its place. Not only is the house a perfect machine showing the progress of modernity, it also gives the feeling that everything works as it should.

The *Kunsthal* of OMA in Rotterdam is a good example of an architecture which has left modernism behind. The unfinished floors have a meaning, the 'entrance' is nothing more than a simple sliding door, and where floors and walls meet they join seamlessly. The glass balustrade above the exhibition hall is completely devoid of ornament and has only a 'function', to separate space. This has nothing to do with imperfection, since everything functions as well as it does in buildings designed by Chareau, Hollein or Stirling. The only difference is that the details have another meaning. What isn't possible in society must not be achieved at all costs in architecture. We, as consumers of architecture, are not perfect – and consequently nor is the architecture of the sublime, a premise that I shall explain in Chapter 3. For Jencks the opposite is the case. Perfection and control may be unattainable in our world, but they certainly can be achieved in the selection and representation of architecture.

The *Kunsthal* can be considered to be an emblematic example of contemporary sublimity in architecture. The building is a modernistic box, which due to its location against the bank of a dike is transected by a descending internal walkway connecting the dike and the park. The building is also transected by a road, parallel to the dike. The auditorium follows the opposite direction to the internal street. The 'bank' returns in the form of a steeply ascending floor, on which rows of uncomfortable plastic chairs have been placed for the audience. They look out over the steel conference table: if that doesn't appeal to them then they can also choose from the rather boring dike or the banality of the road. The descending street outside the building leading to the main entrance is mirrored by the ascending floor of the auditorium. The 'invisible' entrance consists of a sliding door with a horizontal concrete 'step' in front of it for access to the door. An exhibition hall is above the auditorium. This hall is reached by agonizingly slowly-ascending stairs which then continue along the outside of the building towards the terrace.

Koolhaas is a practiced modernist who creates a number of spaces in which the difference between inside and outside is virtually eliminated. The building refers to the heyday of modernism. Mies van der Rohe is especially in evidence on the side of the building facing the park, the Constructivists are to be found in the combined elevator and installations tower, and the publicity billboard serves as the agitprop. If we go past the exhibition hall then we approach the most fascinating space in the whole building. It is an homage to Mies. In architecture space is demarcated by the *boundaries* and the *materials* used to create them. As such, space is a meaningless and infinitely pliable concept. *All space is enclosed space.* The same is true for the meaning of *empty*, which has acquired an almost religious significance for many contemporary architects. This is not incomprehensible in a country like the Netherlands where empty space no longer exists, and everywhere you look you will see some kind of man-made object. But, like space, emptiness is a term without meaning if the essential element in their definition, the *boundary* and the *enclosure*, is not included. And boundaries are not the same. The one space is 'emptier' than the other.

In his building Koolhaas comments on this central theme in architecture. The total height of the box is divided into two spaces; the lower area is intended for studios, and the upper space for use as an exhibition area. The intermediate floor consists of an open, industrial grid. The lighting for the lower space is attached to the steel beams. Here nothing provides any kind of visual hold. The exhibition area can be reached via the steel stairs at the ends of the box. They are made of the same material as the intermediate floor. The grids and the stairs can be negotiated by people wearing flat-soled shoes. Women in high-heels can't even use the stairs, let alone walk over the grids. The architect probably assumed that American and Japanese tourists all wear Nikes. The immense industrial wall of glass strips allows light to pass through, but doesn't offer a view (of the park). Where Chareau used glass bricks, Koolhaas uses strips intended for industrial applications. The wall is closed on one side, and transparent on the other. A slit next to the stair offers a glimpse of the outside. Then there is another outside grid; and right in the line of the slit a debarked trunk has been placed horizontally to act as a railing for the outside grid. In the background can be seen the decor of the existing buildings. Walking over the grid inside the building you have the feeling that you are floating. Every haptic or tactile sensation is eliminated in favor of a continual search for a visual focal point.

This space touches upon all the major emotions of the modernists, both negative and positive. This space is sublime, and not only in the usual sense of the word. As I will hope to make clear later in this book, a sensory vacuum also evokes a form of fear. This is because we are no Cassiels or Damiels as in Wenders's film *Der Himmel Über Berlin* (Wings of Desire, 1987), past or contemporary angels who see everything from a distance; on the contrary, we are people of flesh and blood. Our sense of touch might be classified as having less prestige by reason, but nonetheless it is of paramount importance for architecture.

Every perception of this space is related to the major themes of modernity. Its beauty is a form of the sublime; it is abstract, without orna-

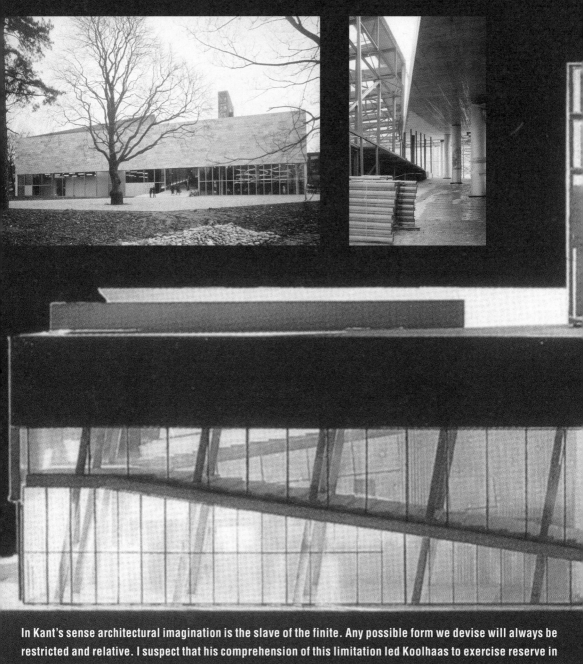

In Kant's sense architectural imagination is the slave of the finite. Any possible form we devise will always be restricted and relative. I suspect that his comprehension of this limitation led Koolhaas to exercise reserve in the form of his KUNSTHAL.

ment, empty, and at the same time associated with fear, pain, and distance. The space also confronts us with what Kant called *Ernst*, which plays a role in the imagination (*Einbildungskraft*): an almost melancholy feeling, a nostalgia for the form that will always remain form, i.e. *limitations*. In my view Mies van der Rohe's work was greatly influenced by this concept. Every form we devise constitutes a temporary enclosure, a perspective, and adds something new to an already existing repertoire.

In Kant's sense architectural imagination is the slave of the finite. Any possible form we devise will always be restricted and relative. I suspect that his comprehension of this limitation led Koolhaas to exercise reserve in the form of his *Kunsthal*. However this stance is usually associated with his pragmatism. But this is very much more the case for the Italian Rationalists of the Tendenza – only for them the principle of autonomy risks an unequivocal and sober *stylization*, from which no deviations are allowed. Koolhaas saw the chance to combine both Kant's Ernst and the postmodern *blockage* in one and the same building: Lite-architecture (Koolhaas's own term for the above) versus Mies-like *Ernst*.

The question then arises as to why this building makes such a powerful impression. After all there are more modernists who are masters of this métier, both at home and abroad. The difference is that Koolhaas uses reserve as a *means*, whilst other architects such as Richard Meier or Wim Quist become engrossed in it. This standpoint can result in beautiful architecture from all three, but Koolhaas's work has something extra. His architecture is *sublime*, not as a superlative of beauty, but as a simultaneous reference both to Mies's modern perfection and to our *flawed* world. The spaces in the *Kunsthal* are also postmodern. The covering of the columns in the main hall with debarked trees, the somewhat squat stairs – which in part come to a dead-end at a wall – leading to the hall and the toilets (themselves once again perfect), the oversized tube of the handrail of the stairs, the finish of the sloping concrete floors; in the modernistic context of the box these are all thoroughly postmodern.

The 'intensities' of our postmodern order are those of the unmanageable confusion of today's world. Consciousness in the sense of the Modernists has become a problematic subject in a world in which experience may just as well be an XTC trip or virtual reality, or in which you can switch from the one performance to the next as on MTV.[18] The slit offering a glimpse of the outside world from the Mies-like space is of significance. What you see is the peeled trunk, placed just next to the imaginary line. Modernity and postmodernity are linked to each other in a subtle manner. Like Koolhaas most of today's architects make grateful use of the *significance* of visually cheap materials such as untreated ply- wood, chipboard, concrete blocks, unfinished steel, industrial light-fit- tings, conduit in full view, steel grid floors, etc. But what we consume is not concrete, steel, or grids, but their meaning. Liane Lefaivre has used a term to describe this which she borrowed from contemporary American literature: 'dirty realism'.[19] My subject is related to her criticism, and I shall show how this theme can be examined in more depth from a philo- sophical point of view, as well as how it plays a far greater role in archi- tecture than she has suggested.

In the *Kunsthal* the intellectual significance of the Modernists is also *blocked*. It offers resistance to their intellectual dominance by the signifi- cance of the unfinished concrete surfaces, the crudeness of tree-trunks, the ambivalence of slanting columns, the stairs and even by the cheap chairs – of different colors – in the auditorium. It should not be conclud- ed however that sublime architecture should be swallowed up in a multi- tude of different materials, comparable with the demand made by Deconstructivism in which the geometry and the straight line had to be abolished at absolutely every level of the design. On the contrary, the suc- cess of such a design depends entirely on the *control* of the geometry, abstraction, and transparency, but equally on the disharmony and the disturbance of this order. In this respect Koolhaas is certainly not a Deconstructivist. His expertise is the very control of modernity set against the seeming playfulness of postmodernity.

Of course both the *Kunsthal* and Chareau's *Maison de Verre* can be compared with Japanese architecture. (The architect responsible for the *Kunsthal* project was Japanese.) But such a comparison will not yield anything of use unless we compare both creations with *today's* Tokyo, the prototype of the postmodern world. Deconstructivism is engrossed in tearing up Modernistic codes, for which Eisenman has a penchant for the German verb *reissen*. Koolhaas for his part *paraphrases*. This means the use of significant details, just like Modernism. Usually detail is understood to be the 'finishing' of the building, which according to its supporters must above all be done neatly. However, in my opinion *significant* detail has a different meaning. For me the significance of a building lies both in the concept and the details. With Koolhaas the details are essential for an understanding of the building as a whole.

Of course our sensory and perceptual impressions of the details touch on the more intellectual or conceptual aspects of the building. The details refer not so much to the building itself as to *the idea* of it. Details easily become decoration, which is also possible with exposed ductwork and unfinished concrete. With most buildings it is not even remotely possible to discover the concept on which they were based. With them details always serve a decorative function. The concept of a building is never just a question of its architecture, although many rationalists and other guardians of the profession would have us believe otherwise.

Architecture is not an isolated phenomenon, but a social product. It can blend in perfectly with the world of consumer goods, like Hollein's architecture: or it can offer resistance. However resistance requires an insight into the relationship between architecture and society, which is anything but the best-developed query in the field of architecture. Much resistance therefore stays on the drawing board, and is restricted to the easily-controlled medium of the CAD program. Is it a coincidence that today's most interesting architects have all been intellectually 'moonlighting', either as an artist (Libeskind) or as a scriptwriter (Koolhaas)? Or am I, a wanderer between architecture, sociology, and philosophy, the only person to have that idea?

One thing is certain. The architect's training certainly doesn't help him to show our society's faults. I am not arguing in favor of imperfect buildings; there are more than enough of those. But I am making a plea for a more intellectual architecture, an architecture able to use perfection and imperfection as conceptual tools.

An example of perfection can be seen in Koolhaas's Kunsthal. In some places the lighting is installed *in* the column, rather than on it. The light-fitting is hidden, as is the wiring. The opening is finished crudely and has no brass bezel or other decoration. It appears unfinished but in fact it is a difficult detail. The light is literally in the way, because of the steel reinforcement. It seems as though the light has been fitted into the column more or less randomly, without much attention. But nothing could be further from the truth: quite a lot is involved in its construction.

The converse of this form of detail is decorative detail. An example of this latter form can be seen in the work of Morphosis. The restaurant on Market Street in Venice, California, designed by this firm of architects has a column fitted with a symbolic seismic-registration ring. According to Aaron Betsky this portrays destruction, and the means we now have at

↗ OMA, Art Hall, column
↓ Morphosis Architects,
72 Market Street Restaurant,
Venice California, 1983, column

our disposal to register it in good time. It isn't going to be difficult for the restaurant's guests to understand the signification of the column with the ring in this city, where the threat of an earthquake is continually present. Moreover this restaurant was the first of a whole series to be liberally sprinkled with seismic symbols. But I am not happy when Jencks and Betsky extend the meaning of these symbols to a relationship with the *social* destruction of Los Angeles. I think that is too noncommittal. When Koolhaas uses detail it has a deep significance; here it is nothing more than a banal ornament. With Chareau it is different again. Little in his house is standard. Everything is of significance, because it refers to the perfection of the Modernists. Koolhaas's light can be regarded in almost the same way. It is an 'invisible' solution, without ornament: the only difference with Chareau is that the edge of the concrete is chipped, something you are not likely to find in Chareau's work. Most architects would mount the light *on* the column. This 'unfinished' appearance is not just a question of funds, as is commonly assumed; it is more a question of meaning. The *Nederlands Architectuurinstituut* (Netherlands Architecture Institute) is located opposite Koolhaas's *Kunsthal*. Unlike the *Kunsthal*, all the materials used for the Institute have no significance since the building lacks a concept of the relationship between architecture and society. Koolhaas's building does *not* come to life due to a *dialogue* between Modernity and Postmodernity, but as a successful attempt to create what Jameson would call a spatial equivalent of our world, a world in which we long ago took our leave of Modernity. Nowadays we are left wondering what use there is in *wrapping* one in the other.[20]

ARCHITECTURE
Constructivism

No face

The question we first need to answer is whether there can actually be such a thing as an architecture of the sublime. Kant compiled a ranking of the arts in his *Kritik der Urteilskraft*, in which he classified architecture amongst the figurative arts. According to Kant architecture is an art falling under the category of 'sensuous truth'. Use is in fact decisive, and results in a restriction of aesthetic ideas. However architecture does have a unique ability to evoke the sublime. Large buildings can evoke this sensation, in that the observer feels lost when confronted with such a building. Kant uses the example of the pyramid of Cheops, where the structure doesn't just inspire awe, it seems to overwhelm the senses. It is as though the observer is absorbed by the object, an effect the painter Barnett Newman also sought to achieve with his paintings (which he said should be seen from close by and not from a distance, because 'large' at once reverts to 'small').

One of the first architects to work with this idea was Etienne Boullée, who wished to achieve Kant's mathematical sublime in Isaac Newton's cenotaph.[1] Traces of Kant's (and probably also Burke's) sublime are to be found in his *Traité sur l'Architecture*. According to Boullée, large representations have an influence on our senses such that although they repel they still evoke admiration. The Constructivists never explicitly referred to the concept of the sublime; nonetheless a continuity in sensibility could be argued, even though this doesn't relate to the representation of an awe-inspiring size. Lyotard's comment about the sublime nature of Modernism has also had an influence on the presentation of my question, even though he didn't elaborate on this specifically for architecture. Perhaps a first comparison can be made using the paintings of Barnett Newman.

Some ten years ago in an essay written on his work I was fascinated by the fact that he was a painter who wanted to express himself solely by means of abstract art. He was so intensely involved with his material that he made his own paints, so passionate about his work that he made canvases of unsaleable dimensions. Moreover he often needed a long period of preparation before starting work on a painting. In one painting he retained the adhesive tape used to make the 'zip', as though he wished to emphasize precisely the fabricated nature of the object. The areas of similarly uniform color are never consistent, but vary in hue. At the time I brought this necessity for abstraction into relationship with his Jewish identity and his interest in the Kabbalah. Judaism, after all, forbids idolatry. Lyotard's articles about Newman, which I only read later, not only corroborated this interpretation but also made an important point with regard to the nature of modern aesthetic feeling. He drew attention to *absence*, actually a variant of Walter Benjamin's new poverty of experience. Newman's paintings are not abstract in the sense of being without tension. On the contrary, they evoke a sensation which, in a 20th century variant of the sublime, combines a feeling of unease with beauty. This tension is caused by an impulse which counteracts itself; something is to be portrayed, whilst this intention is simultaneously withdrawn. It is illustration and non-illustration in one and the same motion. This is the tension which can be felt in Newman's paintings.

Comparisons with Malevich and Lissitzky's Suprematism would seem obvious. Malevich's abstract paintings from the years 1915-1930 seem to wrestle with a similar theme. *Black Square* (1929), *Red Square* (1915), and *Black Circle and Cross*, for example, touch on Newman's theme. However, Malevich's work is more 'classical' than that of Newman, who often tried to disturb the balance in his paintings. Malevich's paintings, at least the ones I mentioned above, are also characterized by being enclosed images within themselves, a characteristic which Newman objected to in Mondrian's work. Their 'objectlessness' is an unmistakable similarity. Actually not all Malevich's work was formal, his paintings alternated between an abstract social-realistic and strictly formal style. The architecture of the time was not very different. Formalism, Futurism and Expressionism were to be found alongside each other. Social Realism was also already in existence in 1917, though at the time the state did not yet interfere with art. The contrasts remained latently present in the very first years after the Revolution.[2]

The question is whether this condition of absence is possible in architecture. The fact that the Modernists refrain from the use of ornamentation, or eliminate ornamentation, as the German art historian Michael Müller says, is an important step towards absence, but it is not the only one. I am of the opinion that we should concentrate on what I see as a result, the *aesthetic effect* of architecture. I shall try to make clear that *no 'face' is present* in Kant's aesthetic perception of the sublime. The significance of this 'facelessness' should not be underestimated.

It is striking that the texts of Deconstructivist architects such as Eisenman and Libeskind refer to a form of beauty that is very akin to Kant's sublimity. Frequently used terms such as shifts, fragmentation, and emptiness implicitly refer to the sublime. Eisenman redesignates the sublime with the term *grotesque*. In architectural terms this means disharmony. The British aesthete Roger Scruton uses this word in connection with the only building he rejects in his book: Shaw's *Piccadilly Hotel*.[3] Conversely, Eisenman uses it as the guideline for his work.[4]

Eisenman makes an appeal to Kant's complex understanding of beauty, which enables him to understand beauty other than as something good, or as something natural. Beauty harbors something Kant calls the sublime. The sublime is actually Kant's second aesthetic category, and he treats the sublime in relation to beauty. The sublime, like beauty, is subjective, and like beauty it refers to a feeling. So, it is certainly not a *logic-based* judgement in connection with the descriptive properties of an object. It should be realized that sublimity is not a property of an object – there is no sublime architecture – it is instead a reflexive judgement, linked with pleasure. A number of faculties are involved in that judgement. The capacities of the sublime are the imagination and *reason*, whilst the judgement of beauty mobilizes the imagination and *understanding*. For Kant reason is the faculty par excellence which surpasses our sensoriness: the *noumenal*. In fact in the sublime, imagination and reason *cannot be brought in harmony* with each other, because the noumenal always surpasses the sensory.

The architectural meaning of the sublime refers to this disharmony – although of a different nature. Its transposition from philosophy to architecture continues to be problematic since in philosophy the sublime involves a form of 'knowing', whilst in architecture it is a property of the object that can evoke this feeling. In architecture it is not a *pure*, but an *empirical* aesthetic judgement. It is not a pure judgement of taste, which is independent from external stimuli and from emotion. According to Eisenman the grotesque is usually considered to be the negative of sublime; but this is not absolutely true for architecture, where the sublime is associated with the qualities of the ethereal, while architecture involves a physical presence. Until recently the grotesque always referred to decoration: gargoyles and frescos. According to Eisenman the ugly was accepted as ornament.

The Romantic Movement, in particular, propagated the grotesque. In Romantic literature we see it in fairy tales, in horror stories and in Gothic novels. Famous examples are Edgar Allan Poe's *The Fall of the House of Usher* and Horace Walpole's *The Castle of Otranto*.[5]

However my understanding of sublimity differs from that of Eisenman. I am not concerned with Eisenman's ethereal qualities, but with apparently obvious and definitive terms, meaning and architectural forms, which when examined more closely are found to be anything but obvious and rational. Nor am I searching for the romantic significance of the sublime. I am interested in Kant's sublime in relation to the formal in architecture. Kant stated that the sublime is formless. In my view this consequently means that it doesn't permit decoration or ornamentation. My hypothesis is that Eisenman's Deconstructivism hasn't prevented his architecture from acquiring a face. What in the first instance was a significant *transgression* of Modernism has, despite itself, become a style. It has acquired a face in the work of the epigones who used his method as nothing more than a gimmick on the principle that anything that is lop-sided and deformed will be marketable and 'interesting'.

I shall attempt to bring Kant's formlessness into relationship with the now-obsolete Constructivism, which I consider to be my critical paraphrasing of the ideology of progress. Ultimately I shall relinquish the Kantian meaning and describe the perception of the sublime as a function of the ideological. This implies a different perception of our knowledge. The reason is that I am not convinced of the absolute autonomy of reason in the manner that is ultimately implied by the sublime. It should be realized that the feeling of pleasure resulting from the supremacy of the noumenal vanquishes the feeling of unease. In this sense Kant called our taste barbaric. The meaning of the sublime in architecture is always a gamble, an experiment. It is always uncertain whether the designs can actually generate a sensation of the sublime. We may not exclude the possibility that my interpretation of the sublime is equivalent to what is proposed by Lampugnani, who for that matter disposes of Deconstructivism in a very blunt fashion.[6]

A considerably more interesting commentary from a German source comes from Klaus Jürgen Bauer, who analyzed the aesthetics of the banal in architecture on the basis of the work of architects including the Swiss

← Herzog & de Meuron,
Tate Gallery of Modern Art,
Bankside, London, United
Kingdom, 1994-1995/1998
↓ Adolf Krischanitz, Art Hall,
Vienna, 1992

Adolf Krischanitz, Pilotengasse Housing Estate (Siedlung Pilotengasse), Vienna, 1992, with Herzog & de Meuron and Otto Steidle (photos Margherita Splittini)

Herzog & de Meuron, Diener & Diener and Marques & Zukirchen.[7] Bauer is also interested not so much in their architecture as in a specific interpretation. Banality is a thing without properties, it is invisible.

Bauer, like Lyotard, makes a relationship with *Arte povera*, in particular the theorist Germano Celant. It appears to be a question of the everyday, the ordinary, the non-dramatic – but then utilized as a sophisticated architectural tool. Bauer demonstrates that all the usual terms in the architectural press, such as 'minimalism', 'neo-functionalism', 'neo-modernism' and 'honest pragmatism' are inadequate as soon as we examine the question in a little more depth.

Moreover, these designers are not immediately visible for the journals; they are so ordinary and so banal that they are hardly noticed. This is 'b architecture' with a small 'a' until, as with Herzog & de Meuron, they are discovered, and then it is written in capitals. Bauer's analysis is interesting since he gives priority to an understanding of empiricism. His analysis of the Austrian Adolf Krischanitz's Art Hall in Vienna is in broad agreement with that of Koolhaas's Kunsthal in Rotterdam as discussed earlier. Krischanitz doesn't even take the trouble to refer to the great masters. Loos and Hollein in Vienna seem to be of no significance for his Art Hall; it is a container for art, nothing more, nothing less.

It has since become the most popular Art Hall in Vienna. The building's message is 'I am only temporary', and as Bauer rightly says, a temporary building should not behave all that hysterically. As a result of its banal, almost 'autistic quality', many colleague architects will consider it to be an 'ugly' building.[8] The same can be said of his houses in the Siedlung Pilotengasse, a project Krischanitz did with Herzog and de Meuron and Otto Steidle. Although this architecture finds itself on the opposite side of 'beautiful' it is precisely the kind of complex interaction between simplicity, paraphrasing and rigorous 'non-detailing' of the buildings that makes this architecture so worthwhile. It appears to be the major counterpart of Deconstructivism; Eisenman calls it 'fascist', according to Bauer. However I don't think that for instance Koolhaas's Kunsthal is so diametrically opposed to the *ideas* of Deconstructivism. Only his *architecture* is different, and, more importantly, its ability to achieve the desired architectural effects is greater than that possessed by Deconstructivism, which has ultimately become 'beautiful'.

My understanding of the sublime uses the same references as Deconstructivism, but searches for the specific effects of linearity, regularity and order, and their critical paraphrasing. It also assumes a nuanced view towards the consumers of this architecture. The undifferentiated view of Constructivism and Modernism can be broken down into a spectrum of perceptions, of which the one cannot be reduced to the other. The specialist views of the architect and the critic are not the same as that of the man in the street.

The bareness or the facelessness of this kind of architecture is the basis of my study; it is certainly not its ultimate destination. The obsolete architecture of Modernism is no longer of use in our times. All depends on the quality of the paraphrasing. However, one thing is certain: the sublime is no longer bound to deconstructions, which have since become patterns. They have become the innocent spouts and gargoyles on the flying buttresses of our present architectural images. I am searching for the vacuity of Modernism or, what Burke calls privation. It is not impossible that this actually constitutes the formal in architecture. My first step towards absence will be an analysis of the drawings of Leonidov. The question is whether such a tension is to be found in the drawing.

The elimination of the ornament

For an answer we need to go back to the Constructivists, in particular to Ivan Leonidov's 1927 design for a film studio. At a first glance what we see is a formal *drawn program*. On the face of it this is not architectural design: we see no detail. It suggests space more than it represents it. What causes a zealous architect like Leonidov to be so frugal with his illustrative material? Furthermore, not all his designs are like this. In other designs, albeit utopian ones, the representation of the building is different, it is much clearer. The film studio has something of Newman's sublime.

To some extent, this method of drawing can be explained by the economic vacuum in which these drawings were made. In spite of the explosion of expression and creativity, and in spite of its political defiance, Constructivism was actually able to realize very little. The traces of this are to be seen in the designs. Much was possible at the time, but primarily in the drawings. But there is more. There is also a great degree of *reserve* about decorative 'beauty' as referred to by Kant. Kant's other perception of beauty, which he called the sublime, is much more prominent. The sublime, the elimination of ornament, and modernity are related to each other. The jump is much less great than it would seem at first sight. Not unjustifiably, Starr relates the Russian proposals to the abstract geometry of the late 18th century classicism of Etienne-Louis Boullée and Claude-Nicolas Ledoux, who were both oriented towards Kant's sublime in their architecture. Both were intrigued by pure Platonic forms, such as cylinders, pyramids and cones. In their view architecture was not possible without this abstraction.[9] This tradition constitutes the roots of the Constructivists architects Melnikov and Leonidov. According to the Stalinists their proposals left absolutely no room whatsoever for the social element. However this deficiency has nothing to do with their political beliefs. Social functions and political agendas are never sufficient to generate meaningful architecture: not in Modernism, and not for the Constructivists. It involves the exhibition of functions, the demonstration of functionality. It is not the glass, steel and geometry that are of importance, but the experiences which are brought into play and which ultimately result in a certain experience of beauty. This was the beauty Wittgenstein aimed to achieve when he designed a villa for his sister (Vienna, 1928), and the same was also true for Loos, Mies van der Rohe, van Doesburg and most of all for Hilberseimer, who embraced Constructivism. And it is also true today. The Stalinists wanted to see the return of Kant's other experience of beauty. For them the tension of the sublime was unbearable. After 1933 the aesthetics of ornament and imagery were once again manifest in the Soviet Union. The sublime was driven back by imagery, or rather the portrayal of an *architecture parlante*. Of course this doesn't mean that all Soviet experiments were formal, and as a consequence essentially sublime.

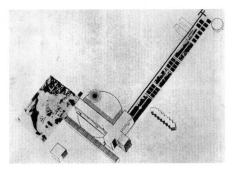

Ivan Leonidov, Sov Kino Film Production Complex, Moscow 1927, Competition Project
(Sovremennaya Arkhitektura, 1928, 5-8)

From the Revolution to the time of Lenin's death in 1924 there was tension between the expressionist and the formal, or between symbolism and purism. The expressionist characteristics were always concerned with

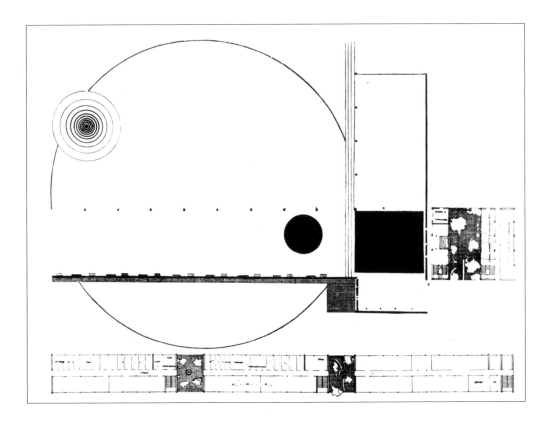

Constructivism **The elimination of the ornament**

the portrayal of power, especially with the future of the proletariat. Propaganda was a permanent ingredient in this architecture. The political climate began to change as early as 1927, and was quickly followed by the first purges and political trials.

And this was the very time at which Leonidov designed his film studio. His design is far removed from the architecture of expressionism and of social realism with their positive ideologies.[10] The expressionism of the Russians was related to the expressionism of German architects such as Hans Poelzig and Bruno Taut. Berlage's *Pantheon van de Mensheid* should also be understood in this sense. The ideas may have been different, but the dramatic expression was the same. This expression could be omitted in the housing projects, which is why we often say that the housing projects are more formal.

The designs of the two most formal architects Melnikov and Leonidov ultimately amounted to an *aesthetics*. Not an aesthetics in the sense of 19th century ideas about beauty, but a step towards what I here refer to as the sublime. If this is true, then the next question is whether this is also the case for all similar typologies. In my opinion this is not the case. The effect of the sublime is seen particularly in situations which aimed at the essence of Marx's theory, i.e. *collectivization*. In these experiments, which Ginzburg has described as the mechanized hell of the machines, the designs acquire something of the sublime. Melnikov's architecture always tended towards expressionism, whilst the ASNOVA architectural group and Ginzburg were more formal. The housing projects were more similar to the experiments in Western Europe.[11] But however different they may be, a similar effect is seen with them all. Since this effect is a result we shall need to analyze it using an actual example. Philosophy can describe this effect in general terms. That is its strength, but at the same its weakness. A more specific architectural analysis of the drawings will be required in order to understand the precise manner in which this effect is realized.

The poetry of the machine

The Soviet proposals for collective housing were modern. New means of communication and transport shrank distances. 'Space is now measured in terms of time' according to *Sovremennaya Arkhitektura* (SA), the leading journal of the time.

In effect, the Constructivists designed a perfect example of Le Corbusier's machine for living: the achievement of standardized and stream-lined human behavior in a mechanical process of a normalized life. The new relationships in production were condensed in Ginzburg's *dom-kommuna*. The dynamic organization of the machine served as an example for the organization of space in architecture. Ginzburg was one of the very few Constructivists who had lived and studied outside Russia. After a short period at the École des Beaux Arts in Paris and the Academy in Toulouse he had traveled to Milan to study under Moretti. Back in Russia he never renounced his affinity with Modernism, in particular with Le Corbusier. Nor did he after 1932. For him the machine was the example for the architecture of the future, the working and components of which needed to be defined just as accurately as those of machines. Everything that was super-fluous was to be eliminated. The concept of a machine must be detailed very precisely. According to Ginzburg it is a chain of dependencies that may not be disturbed, and in which each element has its own place. The machine compels us to be clear and precise when we formulate an architectural idea.

The image of Modernity as sketched by Ginzburg signifies a definitive break with the agrarian past. The machinery is represented as a living organism, as a thousand hands working on a new future.[12] Machines are well-trained monsters, in which the drive belts constitute an efficient link with all the moving parts. The image evoked by this is at the very least poetic. The light shining though the severe film-like screen of glass and steel imparts the machinery with an indefinable glow.

Every component of the machine has a function; unnecessary 'non-working' parts are unimaginable. In architecture this means relinquishing every form of ornament. Contrary to Loos, the elimination of ornament by the Constructivists was without moral significance.

The 'mechanized hell' of the machines didn't mean the end of Romanticism or poetry: on the contrary, it actually integrated them. A new poetry made its entrance, that of the noise and bustle of the new city with its busy streets, a poetry linked to modern city life. Constructivism had become a permanent part of modern life. It is linked to the impressions of the street, with the hectic pace, with day-to-day worries, with the posters, and with the Palace of Labor.[13]

European Surrealism and Dada were very remote from Russian Constructivism, which was based on the partial assimilation of Western culture and the rationalist values of Positivism. After 1924 Constructivism was typified by a utilitarian view of nature and society. Its aesthetics were those of the machine, a concept of the machine that is also to be seen in the German Functionalism of Hilberseimer. The concept of the machine was used to make an example of the capitalist method of production. However Ginzburg was of the opinion that Constructivism or Functionalism could only be achieved in accordance with the cultural or ideologically-determined definition of the *function* of architecture. Architecture can only be assessed in relation to specific needs, needs that are always local. This is still applicable seventy years later, and consequently it also applies to the designs shown in this book.

The ties with Western Modernism resulted in major problems. Until the turn of the century Russia hadn't had anything resembling a modern culture. Industrial production only began to develop around 1890, but then grew faster than anywhere else. The question was whether it was possible to transplant Western ideas to the Russian situation, a question that remained valid even after the Russian Revolution. This situation inspired the experimental work referred to by Wigley. This is comprised of designs that would be impossible to build. The still primarily agrarian society of the time could not absorb these designs. Lunacharsky put this into the following words: it would be more in the interests of the proletariat if the architect were to take account of the local conditions, of the farmer and his landscape. The metropolis is the very confirmation of alienation and the values of consumption. So Lunacharsky was repeating the Western contrast between the city and the countryside as described by Simmel and others.

Around 1922 the Berlin avant-garde merged with the Russian Formalists and Constructivists. Ehrenburg, Lissitzky and Gabó stayed in Berlin in 1921, and in the following year the famous exhibition of Soviet Art was held in the van Diemen exhibition halls on Unter den Linden.

Ivan Puni and his wife Zhenia Bogoslavskaya had already settled in Berlin in 1920. Inspired by the work of Malevich and Lissitzky, Puni organized an exhibition in *Der Sturm* exhibition hall in February 1921. In the same year Lissitzky moved to Berlin and became an important exponent of the ideas of Constructivism. He could speak German, and he was able to build a bridge between the Russian avant-gardists and Western purism and De Stijl using the journal *Object*, which was published in three languages (Russian, German and French). Theo van Doesburg, Le Corbusier and Ozenfant all wrote articles for *Object*. This doesn't imply that the journal was a mouthpiece for Constructivism. However, it certainly was of very great use in the propagation of the Berlin exhibition and of Soviet ideas. The Party had its suspicions about the exhibition. Lunacharsky criticized the exhibition held on Unter den Linden. His criticism was in part based on that of the anti-Soviet critic Stahl in the German press, who compared the USSR with the Empire under Kaiser Wilhelm. (Tafuri establishes a relationship between the ideas of Lunacharsky and those of Lukács, which insightfully explains Lunacharsky's criticism of the exhibition).[14]

To some extent the entire history of the Russian experiment is reflected in the development of the *Vkhutemas*, the most important institute for the development and teaching of architectural ideas and artistic experiments (Vkhutemas: *Vysshie Khudozhestvennotekhnicheskie Masterskie*). The Vkhutemas or studios were created in 1918 as a kind of workshop (*Svomas*). They were officially established in 1920, and were reorganized in 1922. The school existed until 1930. The *Vkhutemas* were supported and protected by the State. Lunacharsky considered the appointment of El Lissitzky, Moisei Ginzburg, Ilya Golosov and Nikolai Ladovsky as lecturers at the institute to be the pinnacle of the *Vkhutemas*. The architectural Section was established in 1920, some seven years before the Bauhaus in Dessau.

Ladovsky was responsible for most of the curriculum, and he devoted a great deal of attention to a new aesthetics that contrasted sharply with Russia's vernacular architecture. In this context Starr's comment about Melnikov is of interest. Melnikov was searching for a certain aesthetics that I shall here describe as the sublime. He endeavored to dissociate this from architectural problems more associated with engineering, which wasn't well received by all the students. As such this is quite understandable, since the *Vkhutemas* had not been established solely to stimulate artistic development. They were a part of much more comprehensive measures that had been taken by the State: the improvement of the quality of industrial production.[15] A number of production workshops which accepted commissions from industry became operational in 1923. In 1926, under Novitsky, a substantial part of the curriculum was aimed at providing an engineering training. Starr states that both Melnikov and Ilya Golosov were searching for an aesthetics that distinguished itself from one focused on the creation of objects in good taste.[16]

For Melnikov the objective of architecture and art was more a question of arousing passions by the manipulation of elements linked with the unconscious. Starr speaks of a strongly romantic approach to architecture. And not incorrectly, since the sublime has an explicit relationship with this, as we shall see later. Melnikov's roots lay in the world of Romantic Classicism. He believed that architecture should be dramatic and emotional. This was precisely what distinguished him from the sober and pragmatic nature of New Economical Politics, and from the more pragmatic than expressionistic architecture of his colleague Moisei Ginzburg, which equally strove for sublimity. With all the differences there is also a similarity. Ginzburg was very familiar with the classical orders in the architecture of the Enlightenment. So he was already acquainted with this style when the Revolutionary tide turned and Classicism came into vogue.

Architecture and the new society

The Russian prototypes extended considerably further than Functionalism. In the Soviet Union collectivization was regarded as a means to stem the influence of capitalism. Collective dining rooms, schools for children, dormitories, collective laundries and maintenance units were to break with the family structure of the pre-Revolutionary collective Russia and the West, which was focused on private property. The ultimate objective was the disappearance of the family as an economic unit. Intimate human relationships were to be separated from associations with property. [17]

The intention was, slowly but surely, to come to a situation in which Man was no longer dependent on property. Milyutin adopts an intermediate position with respect to this standpoint. In contrast to the Productivists, he wanted to equip the living cell with minimal furnishings in the form of chairs, a working area and a bed. His ideas are in agreement with those of his friend Ginzburg. In 1928, as Minister of Finance of the Russian Republic, he granted Ginzburg the commission to design one of his most important buildings, the Narkomfin building for the civil servants of his ministry. The building was designed in accordance with the collective socialist principles. However, the spirit of Le Corbusier was explicitly present. Starr didn't have a very favorable opinion of Ginzburg. He describes him as a Jew from the western region of Russia who a few years previously had cited Spengler and even the Pan-Slavonic nationalist Danilevsky in order to make clear how vacuous the Western world really was, and who now sent copies of his drawings to Le Corbusier. Starr's sympathies lay with Melnikov, an individual amidst the Russian masses. In fact Ginzburg had the same attitude as Le Corbusier: modernity on all fronts and by all possible means. The 'social condensers' were to transform the individual who was focused on himself into a whole person who offered up his individual interests for the benefit of those of the collective. [18]

Hilberseimer's idea of the cell, the cell in the social condenser, the studies for the Existenzminimum home, and Le Corbusier's design for Algiers were all imbued with the spirit of the times. The dom-kommuna was the socialist answer to a social development that was to result in the abolition of private property. The building itself played a pioneering role in the realization of communism. The conditions for admission were stringent. Ninety percent of the residents were active as workers either outside the building in industry, or inside the building in the communal facilities.

The social condenser was assigned an active role in the Revolution. It was to change the behavior of its residents. The architectural asceticism that characterized the work of the Constructivists found a parallel in the views on a sober life. The designs of this time were the precise answer to the creation of a new social order. In anticipation of this new society the residents were to expunge every trace of the old family structure. The bourgeois family was considered to be a remnant from the capitalist past. Rules for the dom-kommunas were drawn up by the Central Committee. The residents were forbidden to bring attributes reminiscent of the old way of life with them. Kitchen appliances for individual use were not permitted, nor were 'unhygienic objects'. Everyone was to show disapproval of drunkards, vulgarity, ignorance and other remnants from the old lifestyle. Anyone reading Kuzmin's time schedule is confronted with the regime of a work camp. Get up at six o'clock, five minutes' gymnastics, ten minutes for the toilet, five minutes for a shower, five minutes to dress, three minutes to go to the dining room, a quarter of an hour for breakfast.[19] The adult members of the commune sleep in groups of six, men and women separated from each other, or the former 'husband' with the former 'wife'. However, Kuzmin's ideas remained a minority point of view.

According to Kopp, Kuzmin and his associates really were convinced of their plans to improve the way of life. The promiscuity in Kuzmin's plan would probably not have differed much from the usual situation in overfull flats in which various families had to share the kitchen and the bathroom that were actually intended for a single family. The origins of the dom-kommuna are rooted not in the October Revolution, but in the ideas of the Utopians.

The similarity between Ginzburg and Le Corbusier is deceptive. The economical and political conditions in which they operated were utterly different. The effect intended with the dom-kommuna was a collectivization that was focused on day-to-day life, in particular the lightening of the domestic duties of the woman. The ultimate objective was the total transformation of Man and society. This 'new architectural organism' was the result of the Constructivists' study of the years 1927-1928, of the OSA competition and the Stroikem study.

In many aspects the OSA architects were the opposite of the ASNOVA (Association of New Architects). Around 1925 a number of architects switched over from ASNOVA to the much more pragmatically minded OSA (Association of Contemporary Architects). While ASNOVA was searching for unique and expressive forms, OSA was interested in mass production. Engineering was a side issue for one group, but the main issue for the other. One group attempted to make a science of art, the other was searching for a science of craftsmanship. Between 1928 and 1930 OSA carried out experiments with the way in which the housing cells could be incorporated in the entire building. The Stroikem plenum that met in 1928 to examine the results of Ginzburg's study wanted to organize an exhibition similar to that of the Weissenhofsiedlung in 1927, so that a number of the experimental homes based on the Stroikem study could be built.

This plan was never executed, although in the period between 1930 and 1932 architects who were affiliated with the Constructivist movement completed six experimental buildings in Moscow, Sverdlovsk and Saratov. They were conceived of as the 'doma-perechodnogo tipa', a transitional type in the development of a more advanced typology. Ginzburg and Milinis's Narkomfin building on the Boulevard Gogol is a good example of this.[20] In 1931 Leonidov and his family moved to the F-type. The Narkomfin building was a combination of two types, the previously-mentioned F-type developed by Stroikem intended for small families or for married couples without children, and the K-type which consisted of three rooms at two different levels. The F-type was provided with a small kitchen in a recess, whilst the K-type had a kitchen of 4 square meters. The presence of a rudimentary kitchen meant that there was little reason for the residents to make use of the communal facilities. The rudimentary kitchen would later disappear from the collective blocks.

In order to stimulate communal life, buildings of the Narkomfin type contained a large number of collective facilities such as a shared kitchen, dining rooms, laundries, crèche, sports accommodation, a library, and rooms for study. All these communal facilities were accommodated in a separate building that was linked to the main building via a walkway on the second floor. A new feature was the 'factory kitchen' (*fabriki-kuchni*).

Narkomfin, Moscow, Novinsky Boulevard, architects
Milinis and Ginzburg, 1928-1930

Architects derived its layout and execution from industrial architecture. They used enormous glass walls, simple saw-tooth roofs, and designs based on the manufacture of goods using the production line. The intention was not so much to simply repeat the language of industrial forms, but more to *reinforce the symbolic image*. The design was an important stage on the way to the total reconstruction of daily life. Since the construction methods were of a low technological level the form was primarily a reference. The refinement of the Modernists was never achieved.

The symbolic meaning referred to *industrialization*, which was in full swing at the time. In contrast to Hilbersheimer and Le Corbusier Milyutin was an advocate of the linear city. Arthur Spraque points out the similarity between Nikolai Milyutin's linear city and production line manufacture in the USA, in which he was very interested. Fordism was in fashion, in particular during the 1920s. Both Ginzburg and Milyutin had been directly influenced by Ford's ideas. They were familiar with his biography, *My life and Work*, which had been published in Leipzig in 1923. They also knew of the work of Frederick Taylor, the American pioneer of labor efficiency. His book, *The Principles of Scientific Management*, was translated into Russian in 1924.

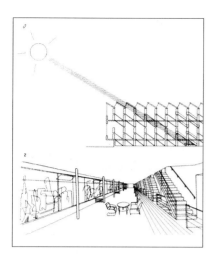
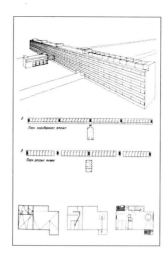

Narkomfin, Moscow, Novinsky
Boulevard, 1928-1930
←← E-type, plans
← F-type, plans

The uselessness of political categories in architecture

After 1930, the ideological struggle took on grotesque forms. Capitalism had always been an interesting example in view of its productivity. The question as to which communist ideology was most suited to this capitalist model resulted in continual switches in the architecture. Constructivists combated Formalists, and vice-versa: Classicism fought Formalism. In 1933 Milyutin, who in the first instance had supported Melnikov, was of the opinion that the 'extremists' and the 'formalistic parasites' should be banished. In December 1930 Arkadi Mordvinov's actions resulted in Leonidov losing his lectureship at the Vkhutein, by which time the Vkhutemas had now come into being. The poetry of his drawings, or more accurately their formal nature, no longer rhymed with the ideology of the mass movement. 1930 was also the year in which the SA journal ceased publication, of which he had been one of the editors since 1928. The Vkhutein closed in the same year.

From now on, formalists were regarded as right-wing, and Melnikov was associated with the design ideas of ASNOVA, which were contested by the OSA architects. The OSA Constructivists were in turn attacked by the vulgar-Marxist sociology of the VOPRA (All-Russian Association of Proletarian Architects). The Constructivism of the OSA was seen as left-wing. Ginzburg's ideas, in particular, were the reason for this. But how can you call a building, or a design for a building, left-wing? Is Melnikov's Palace of the Soviets of 1932 or his Narkomtiazhprom of 1934 still left-wing, or conversely, should these works be classified as examples of 'socialist realism' or 'socialist classicism'? Did Leonidov lose his powers as an architect in the 1930s? Khan-Magomedov and Aleksandrov thought that this was so, but Andrei Gozak disagreed entirely. Starr was of the same opinion as the latter. Both emphasize the continuity exhibited by the two architects. This is certainly correct from a biographical point of view, but not from an aesthetic perspective. The formal nature of their work changed dramatically after 1930. Leonidov's submission for the Narkomtiazhprom on Red Square is still formal, but this is no longer true for the Narkomtiazhprom Sanatorium in Kislovodsk of 1938, however attractively it may be situated in the landscape. Gozak's discussion of Leonidov's work remains just within architectural terminology. He talks only in terms of 'Euclidean spaces', 'linearity', 'suprematist influences' and 'pure elementary forms'.

This is essentially a process of registration and omission. The question is: what is actually organized by the lines on the paper? How much meaning does it convey and what, exactly, is omitted? What does this imply for the attitude and the architectural perception? What is prescribed and what is left free? 'That is all', Gozak concludes in his discussion of Leonidov's *Centrosojuz* design.[21]

This might well be the key to this almost intangible architecture. Leonidov's son Andrei says that the architecture of his father was focused on the majestic and on the sublime. This was supposedly manifested by his penchant for the pyramids, which touches on Kant's concept of the sublime. Political categories cloud the view of architecture. I am not interested in an 'architecture for architecture's sake', but in the question as to where we can find the terms we need to assess and analyze architecture, and to assign it with a social significance. The use of Marx's theory of the classes is unavoidable in dealing with this question.

The Russian interpretative struggle is never-ending, as Formalism, Functionalism, Constructivism and Expressionism – insofar as they function

Ivan Leonidov, Palace of Culture for the Proletarskii District of Moscow, 1930

as architectural categories – can never be left- or right-wing. Discussions in the Soviet Union at the end of the 1920s between Rationalists and Formalists, or between Constructivists and Functionalists all show evidence of the impossibility of relating lines on paper to politics.

Rationalists such as Ladovsky and El Lissitzky were convinced that architecture also possesses an aesthetic aspect, but this in no way coincides with the aesthetic effect I refer to here. Rationalism was oriented towards an analytical and scientific understanding. It attempted to derive abstract definitions of the social and historical conditions by the development of a psychological aesthetics. As with Purism, for the Rationalists the origins of the aesthetic judgement lay in biological and physiological facts.[22] They attempted to change the art of the future in a scientific manner according to the rules of the 'artistic material' of architecture: space and form. Like Le Corbusier, Ladovsky is a prisoner of these scientific references. To this very day they still play a role in discussions.

The conclusion must be that political concepts such as left and right cannot be related to architectural concepts such as space, mass, and construction. It is not even possible to establish the function in this fashion. For the time being, the only way to relate architecture and society with each other is by defining the philosophical and aesthetic category of the sublime in a way such that it also refers to our society. Here an important role is played by the formal, which may not be equated with the effect the sublime has in architecture. Ultimately this depends on the critical paraphrasing of the formal: in other words the question as to which disruptions we will permit, which disruptions will be present without us so wishing, the extent to which we shall include the muddle of the world in the architecture, and where we shall exclude it. The fact that this is a 'paraphrasing' is the result of Kant's concept of the ultimate 'formlessness'. In this context it is entirely relevant to 'the formal'. This approach makes it possible to say something about the relationship between architecture, society and politics.

ARCHITECTURE The Sublime

Burke and Kant

Isn't it paradoxical to treat Modernism — and certainly Constructivism — as an aesthetic? After all, both Modernism and forms of functionalism such as Russian Constructivism reject every aesthetic. What they attempted to create was an explicit, rational, and above all functional building, certainly not something to be judged in terms of 19th century beauty. And it is this very aesthetic which constitutes an obstruction to a rational and functional building. It was certainly unthinkable for the Russians to base their work on the teachings of a philosopher such as Immanuel Kant. After all, Kant's philosophy laid the foundation of what would later be the positive sciences. In this sense Max Weber's sociology is similar to Kant's philosophy. Positive sociology would ultimately be the major opponent of the Russians' historical materialism. The German 'Positivismusstreit' made the irreconcilable differences clear.

The construction of a Kantian feeling of beauty for architecture seems doomed from the very beginning. Yet I don't believe that it is. In the first place we must avoid an aesthetic which constitutes a goal as such. For this does indeed lead to purposeless decoration. (This kind of beauty has in fact already returned in what I have earlier called pop architecture.) We should realize that there is no science of the beautiful and the ugly, unless in the form of Ladovsky's doctrine. It is something that is created more or less coincidentally in architecture, as a result of a functional and spatial problem. It is a beauty which is not deliberately incorporated in the building. It is the result of a building project in which the formation of space, materials, use, light and air and their meaning all play a role. In other words instead of an aesthetic I shall speak of a result, the aesthetic *effect*. It will be obvious that this is not something that can be analyzed simply in scientific terms. In that respect I concur with Roger Scruton's analysis of architecture.[1] Although I have criticisms of important parts of his work I do agree with his view on philosophy in that we should endeavor to argue as clearly as possible at an abstract and general level, without losing sight of the object of the architecture. But this is not the complete answer.

The issue we now need to address is whether Kant's ideas about beauty and sublimity are still valid. This question is not one that can easily be answered. I think that Kant introduced a critical distinction in regards to our perception of things that we find beautiful. And we can certainly learn much from him when these perceptions relate to things that are not entirely pleasant. My intention is to link these kinds of perceptions to something that is intrinsic to all our perceptions, thoughts and feelings: namely ideology. Not an ideology in the meaning it was given by the Russians, of something which would disappear in a classless society, but ideology in the sense of a characteristic of the human organism, as something which will be eternal, albeit continually changing in form and content. Philosophy is indispensable if we are to make this link. My analysis is based on Kant's description of the *Erhabene* (the sublime). In practice this meaning proves to be of great use for a study of architecture in our postmodern society.

The perception of the sublime is not entirely pleasant; for Kant it also encompasses fear (*Furcht*), although this is displaced by a feeling of relief. Here Kant was influenced by Edmund Burke's essay about the sublime, which he wrote in 1757.[2] Burke described the perception of the sublime as the fear that is experienced when seeing an immense object, accompanied by the feeling of relief when it is realized that there is no reason to be afraid. However this doesn't mean that Burke is of the opinion that pain and pleasure are direct opposites. Pleasure is not directly related to the elimination of pain.[3] Burke uses the word *delight* to express the feeling associated with the elimination of pain or fear. The sublime is now linked to our strongest emotion, the feeling of pain or danger. When danger or pain come too close, as for Damiens during the French Revolution, then there can be no question of delight; the experience is nothing less than horrific (in Elaine Scarry's sense, which I will discuss later). (On 5 January 1757 Robert Francis Damiens attempted to kill Louis XV and was put to death, after being viciously tortured, on 28 March). In comparison with the pleasure beauty gives us, that of the sublime has an unfavorable association in the sense of Burke's 'delight'. The unfavorable associations of this pleasure are brought in relation with admiration (*Bewunderung*) or respect (*Achtung*).[4]

Kant's earlier essay *Beobachtungen über das Gefühl des Schönen und Erhabenen* (Observations on the Feeling of the Beautiful and the Sublime) is in broad agreement with his later *Kritik der Urteilskraft* from 1790.[5]

John Goldtwait, who translated the *Beobachtungen* into English, is convinced that Kant had this book open before him when he wrote his treatise on aesthetics. Many passages are actually literally identical. His conceptions of the beautiful and the sublime remain unchanged. The philosopher Paul Crowther discusses this in detail, and shows that Kant was primarily descriptive in his *Beobachtungen*. He is more of an observer than a philosopher.[6] Both feelings are described as pleasant, although in different ways. Kant cites scenes from nature not all of which he had experienced personally. He describes mountains whose eternally snow-covered peaks reach into the clouds, the pyramids, an ocean storm, and he cites Milton's description of hell in *Paradise Lost*. All these scenes arouse a certain feeling. They give rise to enjoyment, but combined with horror.

The feeling of the beautiful is associated with the sight of a calm, blossoming nature. The primary sensation is a feeling of joy; here horror is absent. In Kant's and Burke's sense day and light are beautiful while night and darkness are sublime.

In his *Traité* the 18th century French architect and architectural theorist Boullée describes how he was impressed by his own shadow in a field at night. Prompted by his melancholic feelings he decided to elaborate on this experience from nature by making use of it in his architecture. He attempted to find a whole which would be built up of silhouettes. The sublime goes deeper, or in Burke's words, all edifices calculated to produce an idea of the sublime ought to be dark and gloomy. For Kant and Burke the sublime is always great, while the beautiful can also be aroused by something small. The sublime always involves forces beyond those of man (the *dynamic* sublime) or is very large (the *mathematical* sublime), while the beautiful is often ornamental. In architecture the distinction between the beautiful and the sublime is related not only to the magnitude of a building, but also to its *harmony* or *disharmony*. This is to be seen in the work of Roger Scruton.[7]

Scruton characterizes Palladio's *Palazzo Valmarana* as an elegantly-ordered facade. However at the corner of the building Palladio departs from the classical order on which he based his design. He creates a very fragile image at the very point where we would expect a powerful effect. Ultimately the entire effect is not disrupted, the building remains in harmony. In Scruton's opinion the disturbance of the classical order is meaningful, provided that the order is maintained.

Architects are continually searching for the rules which govern design – not to follow them slavishly, but to change and break them. The consequence of this can be a mixture of styles. An example is Cockerell's *Ashmolean Museum* in Oxford, which is a mixture of Greek, Roman and Renaissance styles. Ultimately here, too, the harmony is preserved. But it is a completely different story with Norman Shaw's *Piccadilly Hotel*, which is an example of Edwardian baroque. This building also exhibits a mixture of styles, but now Scruton's judgement is unfavorable. In his view the classical references have become *grotesque*. The screen of columns actually hides nothing. It gives no protection, it supports nothing, it is much too great in relation to the building behind it, and it seems to have been erected in front of it more or less by chance. According to Scruton this building shows a disregard for the underlying principle of harmony. *Harmony becomes disharmony*. For him disharmony is associated with an erroneous conception of the effect of details and ornamentation, both of which offer an opportunity for architectural organization. This was not only the case for the Renaissance and Baroque styles, but also for Modernism. The Bauhaus still exhibited a mastery of this métier, but architecture rapidly went downhill afterwards. In fact, as far as Scruton is concerned the entire profession has ceased to exist. Our modern-day architecture is nothing more than grammarless anti-architecture without significant detailing. He views the development of architecture purely as a matter of style. He situates his conception of style in his criticism of Marx's concept of base and superstructure. Where, according to Scruton, there is no better evidence of the autonomous life of the superstructure than architecture itself, in which styles, buildings, towns and cities have risen and perpetuated themselves independently of their fluctuating economic circumstances. Gropius's rejection of ornament is to him a stylistic principle, a form of ornament. The entire socio-political content of Gropius's 'neue Baugedanke' is erased here in favor of an autonomous notion of style that in Scruton's view is immutably decorative by nature. Scruton shows a complete lack of understanding of the present architectural culture, even if we disregard his ridiculous misconception that Modernism's elimination of ornamentation was in itself a form of ornamentation. But his usually analytical and clear line of argument becomes completely out of tune once he begins to discuss the question of *disharmony* in architecture.

With the disappearance of Modernism there is in fact no longer any style, nor any kind of ordered design system. Anyone looking for principles of style or order in drawings will be disappointed. They simply no longer exist. Not only do buildings no longer acquire their look from their decorations or ornaments – they have no embellishments at all. This has, of course, also had its repercussions on the critics. There is little else to criticize other than methods, procedures and intentions, whether realized or not. It is not without reason that Roger Scruton's book makes such a 19th century impression. His philosophy is completely untenable for today's architects. Come to that, he doesn't consider contemporary buildings to be architecture, since they fall outside the decorative tradition. This is where his conservatism is fully exposed. Actually he fully appreciates this fact. His book is justifiably critical, i.e. it sets a standard for architectural actions. I have no argument with him about that, but I do disagree with his ultimate assessment of the relationship between architecture and society. Properly speaking, architecture is anti-individualistic. Nowadays however the 'personal' is dominant.

With my criticism, I have something else in mind. I am disturbed by the architectural criticism of today when it is made completely without obligation, and is entirely separate from the architectural object. Since design rules and styles have ceased to exist, the critic no longer has to occupy himself with the actual architectural object. It says enough that style is understood to be the architect's personal style, which is an oxymoron. In my view the great strength of Scruton's analysis is his refined and rich understanding of style. Although he is ill-disposed to Hegelian and Marxist dialectic his understanding of style immediately refers to the relationship between Man and his world, a relation I will develop in the last section of this chapter: Man manifests himself by his products, which are essentially social in a fundamentally social world. I prefer not to call that 'style' or 'disharmony'. The relationship between Man and Nature would appear more suitable than style, which in our times has lost its critical meaning.

Deconstructivism is obsessed with disharmony, but it has now developed into an overruling template within this movement. I am looking for another way to explain something of disharmony. This might be possible by using the sublime in an architectural context. It would seem that the sublime confronts our powers of imagination with its own limits, as happened in the *Kunsthal* exhibition area. When we are confronted with a sublime object we initially ascribe the immense nature to the object itself. Burke was of the opinion that our senses are occupied by the object to such an extent that there is no longer any room for any other feeling. In other words, we are dumbfounded with astonishment.

Kant's explanation of this feeling was that reason compels us to unify the immensity of the sensory world into a whole. The sublime confronts us with an immediate subjective relationship between imagination and reason, which are not in tune with one another. We experience a contrast between the demands made by reason and the limited capacity of our powers of imagination.[8] When confronted by the sublime we realize that the imagination cannot accommodate the extrasensory. And thus we find this feeling of shortcoming uncomfortable. Nevertheless this discomfort, this pain and euphoria, becomes pleasure; the pain makes the feeling of pleasure possible. The imagination is confronted with its limits; but this confrontation is unfavorable, in the sense of a negative presentation: the sublime is 'formless'.

Lyotard has characterized this interpretation of the sublime as the first step towards Modernity. He gives most attention to what Kant refers to as the *grotesque*.

Another sublimity: our concepts are never comprehensive

Modernism and Cubism are non-mimetic. They do not imitate nature. Like the architecture of the shelter they refer to a world of mechanized hell, and to the non-decorative. After all, this world encompasses the possibility of the sublime. In contrast with Kant's and Burke's ideas, this doesn't mean an immense size in the sense of a mountain range or an ocean storm. Here I shall join Adorno, whose understanding of the sublime is characterized by its distance from the classical meaning. Nonetheless, my interpretation of the sublime differs to some extent from Adorno's. For example for Adorno the perspective of the technological advance of modernism is absent and the malfunctioning machine of our shelter project focuses on a specific group of people, i.e. tramps and the homeless.

With Kant, not only was the attraction to an object of importance; repulsion also had a role to play. The classical scenes referred to by Kant are approached with too great a respect for their power and size. Less imposing objects can also result in images of great intensity.[9] The often bombastic images summoned up by Kant belong to the past. In its spatial context the shelter is not particularly large. It only seems to be so when seen from the perspective of the street. When seen from the street it appears to resemble a horizontal skyscraper. The building is infinite. In the first instance this would seem to be related to what Rem Koolhaas calls 'bigness'. Koolhaas also sees that this meaning is past its prime. Actually he gives it a slightly different meaning to mine. For him 'big' really does mean 'large', as his designs for *Yokohama*, *Lille* or the *Zeebrugge Sea Terminal* prove. This scale results in specific problems which cause the 'artistic' actions of the architect to be retarded and ultimately eliminated. After all, these designs can only be realized using a team. Many architects are at a loss to cope with this, they cannot 'get to grips with space'. According to Koolhaas 'bigness' lies 'beyond good and evil',[10] though in relation to today's size.

Nietzsche's criticism of the German idealistic philosophy of Kant, Fichte, Schelling and Hegel was that it was half theology. An echo of this theological side to their philosophy is to be found in Kant's *Achtung* for the sublime. This element needs to be eliminated from the meaning of the sublime. The sublime should no longer be understood merely in Kant's sense, with all its reminiscences of respect for power and size; an interpretation that is in fact readily made due to the associations with 'big'. In fact, in Kant's terms it would be possible to use the term 'magnitudo'. In *Delirious New York* the skyscrapers always seem to disappear majestically into the heavens, whilst the sublime 'disenchanted mountain' of the shelter always remains close to the ground, close to the perspective of the street.

For Kant the sublime was an experience associated with nature. This doesn't mean that nature can only be considered in terms of the sublime, since we can equally justifiably talk of the beauties of nature. In the *Kritik der Urteilskraft* he says that 'the sublime ... cannot be contained in any sensuous form, but rather concerns ideas of reason'.[11] The sublime mobilizes imagination and reason (*Vernunft*). The idea of reason is a totalizing movement that will always transcend the sensory. It would be possible to say that the imagination falls short of the transcendental or the noumenal. We live in the worlds of the sensory, and of reason. There is not an adequate form of sense for the sublime. A sense of inappropriateness (*Unangemessenheit*) remains.

Lyotard transposes this idea to modern philosophy. He wonders to what extent our concepts reflect reality. And that brings me back to the question as to the degree to which these abstract ideas are capable of representation. In a discussion of the sublime, Terry Eagleton has reproached Lyotard for his neglect of ideas such as the class struggle and the proletariat, while he does refer to Burke's reactionary ideas. (Although it all depends on what you understand by reactionary.) Burke was the leader of the English Whigs, and a liberal. He rejected the French Revolution, which he predicted would culminate in terror, yet he supported the American War of Independence.

Lyotard's answer was that an idea such as the proletariat should be seen as a regulative idea, as *Vernunft*. After all, no one has ever seen a proletariat. In Marx's sense this concept is a part of the perceptible society. According to Lyotard it is impossible to substantiate the argument that this part of society is the embodiment of a 'proletariat', as a general Idea cannot be represented. For Lyotard this is the very essence of the sublime.[12]

The same can also be said of attempts to develop a theory for the meaning of homelessness, as discussed in the last chapter. Classifications such as social stratification, low incomes, proletariat or unemployment rapidly lose all meaning due to the frequently changing *composition* of the group described as the homeless. This group has a floating composition. It is eminently possible to be homeless during one period of time, and in the next to be housed in temporary accommodation, and then be admitted to a psychiatric clinic. It is often barely possible to establish what is objective, i.e. caused by the social process, and what is subjective. It is obvious that this is an entity, but not how it is structured. I shall not follow in Lyotard's footsteps, although I do agree with his criticism of enlightened spearhead pretensions.

Derrida's 'question' to Eisenman discussed earlier in this book poses, albeit in other words, Lyotard's idea of *non-representability*. The term *homeless* cannot be reduced to a category or classification, and the earlier definitions of marginality or social stratification such as low incomes, the proletariat as a class, the unemployed, etc., are not sufficient to provide an explanation of the phenomenon. This is also apparent in the literature I shall refer to in Chapter 6. None of the descriptions covers the totality of the problem, let alone explains it. The sociologist Peter Rossi argues along Eagleton's lines. Homelessness is primarily a capitalist problem, caused by housing and real-estate politics. Cohen and Sokolovsky name the three most important reasons for homelessness as being poverty, alcohol and 'idiosyncratic factors', i.e. human and social factors and occurrences which push someone over the edge and cause him to adopt a nomadic existence on the streets. Kim Hopper and Ellen Baxter's *Private lives/public spaces* is the report of an action-study with a clear political intention and result. They themselves describe it as an impressionist action-study. A large number of contributions to Jon Ericson and Charles Wilhelm's *Housing the Homeless* follow the same lines. Both reports give a good idea of this world, which they view from the inside. In spite of the restrictions and risks that are associated with social mimicry these reports constitute the most interesting studies of the environment of the homeless. In the usa psychiatric problems are often the cause of homelessness, as has been shown in a penetrating description and analysis made by Fuller Torrey. Joel Blau gives a well-documented description of the problem in the usa. His books constitute the most comprehensive studies of the subject, and draw on Poulantzas and Miliband's insights into the theory of the State.

A universal theory of homelessness cannot be devised, and such intentions should be abandoned. It would undoubtedly lead us astray, towards schematism, illusions of totality and causality – whilst particularization, differentiation and non-simultaneity are more suitable categories of investigation.

Studies of homelessness in the Netherlands reveal a similar picture. Heydendael and Nuy, who charted the homelessness in great detail, state that we shall not live to see a situation in which this phenomenon in all its multiformity has become completely transparent. In each case we are again forced to reconstruct the individual's life,[13] of which the ingredients are failed or completely absent socialization, poverty, alcohol abuse, and so on. The ingredients may be the same, but the structure in which they are to be found is always different. The *Marmot project* made an analysis of the mechanisms of marginalization on the way towards homelessness. In this project 47 cases from the period 1988-1990 were reviewed. In all these cases the problems encountered during the course of the person's life finally resulted in their homelessness – but in 47 different ways. The only thing these people have in common is their ultimate status as homeless persons. How this came about differed from person to person. Cause and effect can no longer be distinguished from each other. Heydendael and Nuy refer to their subordinate economic position, but this is not usually the main reason in the Netherlands. In this instance the economy doesn't explain very much.

If seen in relation to a universal theory, for example for the classes, then the phenomenon can be compared with what Deleuze calls a *line of flight*. This means that as soon as we try to define the meaning of homelessness – which at the first glance would appear to be a very simple term – then it slips through our fingers due to the ultimately immense complexity of the factors involved. However this doesn't mean that economic contrasts no longer play a role. Obviously these continue to be of importance at a general level, but from a micro-political perspective 'molecular' relationships have a much greater influence on homelessness.

There is no unambiguous definition of homelessness. Anyone who studies the history of the homeless will see that the phenomenon continually adopts a new form. The problem is certainly very tangible, but an explanation simultaneously acts as a projection screen showing one's own views, ideologies and theories about society. In *political* terms the problem appears to be virtually unsolvable. Homeless people no longer organize themselves. Since they don't join together in the sense of Deleuze's 'molar' (political) organizations the phenomenon remains a line of flight. It is difficult enough just to establish the number of people involved. The homeless are relatively elusive participants in a census. The distinction between molecular and molar isn't merely a question of size or scale, but primarily of the differences in the specific nature of the systems which bind them together. The entire question of the designation of the phenomenon becomes a problem, and on a more abstract level this would appear to be true of all our terminology.

Joel Blau uses the definition of the *United States General Accounting Office*, which states that a homeless person is a person who has insufficient means of support and lacks the social contacts needed to provide for accommodation in an adequate manner. *Accommodation* is central to this definition, but at the very beginning of his book Blau points out the enormous differences in living conditions.[14] The Policy Documents of the Netherlands' *Landelijke Stichting voor Thuislozenzorg en Onderzoek* (National Foundation for the Care and Study of the Homeless) from 1986 and 1990 emphasize the social, personal and relational vulnerability of the homeless, as a result of which functional and human relationships in the usual forms of society become practically impossible. One of the first American sociologists to study the homeless in the 1920s, Nels Anderson, drew attention to the temporary nature of their work, their inability to work due to a handicap, personality disorders, crises, discrimination and *Wanderlust*. Today this last factor would be called nomadism. So for the time being, an unambiguous definition is out of the question.

Lyotard's comments make the real problem very clear: our categories and concepts will never correspond with our social and psychic reality. Not one term can offer a sufficient explanation, which also includes the theories of Marx and Freud. Theories are provisional and incomplete, and at most explain only part of reality. Yet this need not be considered as detrimental, for they give us an insight into phenomena that until then had remained outside our field of view. For Adorno and Benjamin Kantian subdivisions are nothing more than signs that are a reminder of the discontinuous structure of the world of ideas.[15] Concepts are used to reproduce ideas by means of empiricism. The reproduction of ideas in terms of concepts makes use of specific theoretical configurations which do not correspond with empiricism, but in fact frame the empirical. I think that Benjamin was right in this. Our ideas are related to things in the same way that the constellations are related to the stars. They are neither their definitive meaning, nor their order. We can at best search for other, possibly more accurate, meanings in other constellations.

Lyotard rejects Hegelian dialectics. He makes a distinction between the phrase regimens which order sentences (*régimes des phrases*) and kinds of discourses (*genres des discours*). The latter are to some extent comparable to Habermas's discourse analysis. Examples of phrase regimens are argumentation, knowing, describing, showing, or asking a question. The knowledge of reality contains the transition from an event to structure; in a narration this is precisely what is not possible. Lyotard understands a discourse to be maintaining a dialogue, giving education, evaluating, or administering justice. In fact this means that a discourse is more complete than phrase regimens. An essential feature is that the various kinds of dialogue are heterogeneous in comparison with each other. The one sort can never replace the other. In actual fact there is no regulative principle, no longer any set of rules that regulates this heterogeneity of discourses.

Nonetheless, as I wrote earlier, the universal nature of our pronouncements continues to exist. This constitutes more than just a personal preference in our appreciation of beauty. However, the universal is a limit which we can only approach, but never achieve. The heterogeneity of our world with its various kinds of discourse makes a harmonious and comprehensive order impossible, but *as an idea* this order certainly does exist.[16] The notion of a just division is not abandoned. It continues to exist as an idea. As long as we realize that this is a philosophical idea then there is nothing amiss, but it was very different during the Russian Revolution.

Lyotard points out that Kant, and possibly also Burke, recognized the danger of what he calls putting the politics of the sublime into practice, i.e. the pretension of representing reason in political practice in the way that the French or the Russian Revolution wished. In other words, it is never possible to claim: we are the proletariat or we are the embodiment of liberalism's or communism's free people or humanity. For Lyotard criticism of Modernity means an anamnesis of criticism itself, it means the disruption of the idea that one represents reason. For example the Constructivists believed in the idea of being the vanguard of the proletariat; the VOPRA group believed the same, and on similar grounds. 'We are in favor of a proletarian class architecture' they stated in their manifesto.[17] Around 1930 Leonidovism was regarded as a dangerous ideology, to be combated by all possible means.[18] I think that Lyotard's notion is applicable here. According to Kant the images of the sublime from Romanticism could not be illustrated either. In his view the vast storm-swept oceans could not be called sublime. For the judgement of nature's beauty we need to look outside ourselves to find a suitable basis. We must search for the sublime in ourselves, and in our way of thinking. The sublime makes each of us his own 'psychologist'.

The sublime often acts as a dividing line between an aesthetics which is located in consciousness, as with Scruton, and one which primarily emphasizes the unconsciousness. Of course we should exercise care with explanations that use the unconscious. Unlike Scruton, for whom this meaning plays no role whatsoever, Weiskel does in fact accept the intra-psychic meaning of the sublime. In the poetry and literature of the 18th century the sublime is associated with something that is both vague and obscure. It wouldn't allow itself to be clearly distinguished. It is ultimately traced back to the plumbless depths of our psyche and passion.

If we follow Kant's theory to its logical conclusion then little remains of an *aesthetic* judgement, since this judgement is not necessarily based on an object.[19] As such the sublime does not refer to nature; it is primarily applicable to our ideas about nature.[20] Kant's 'knowing I' is not 'substance', but a formal perspective of reality without there being an unequivocal way of moving from transcendental perception to day-to-day reality. Knowing I and known reality do not belong to the same order, although knowledge does make this seem plausible.[21] Moreover, we should realize that the third criticism is concerned not with pure scientific knowledge but with a pseudo-knowledge which we designate as aesthetic knowledge. The aesthetic is non-cognitive. It only appears to resemble the rationality of science. The system is on a more affective level.

Eagleton contends that the forms of Kant's rationality exhibit similarities with the commodity form, which is in agreement with Adorno's ideas. The concept is comparable with the commodity. It gives rise to a formal equivalent exchange between isolated individuals, and it evens out the differences between their needs and desires. For Eagleton both beauty and the sublime are characteristics of the ideology. The sublime is responsible for the subject being perceived in its finiteness. Lyotard called this the now, which he analyzed in Barnett Newman's paintings.[22] In Eagleton's opinion the subject of the sublime is decentralized. It is confronted with loss and pain, and it experiences a crisis which threatens to allow its identity to crumble. At the same time this experience is a condition for the subject to come into action. Philosophical Deconstructionism uses this meaning: here the sublime is a break with, and undermining of, metaphysical certainties. Eagleton considers this to be a favorable aspect. In this he is in agreement with Lyotard and Adorno.[23]

The theoreticians of architectural Deconstructivism emphasize the *disintegrational* side of the sublime, Anthony Vidler being the most explicit in this.[24] The theme of the sublime has also given rise to a large number of interpretations in a wide range of areas. Neil Hertz has associated the sublime with psychoanalysis. Lyotard investigates the possibilities Kant's philosophy offers for the interpretation of abstract art, in particular Newman's works. Paul Crowther's remark and his motivation for writing his book, i.e. that in one way or another sublimity is in fashion, seems very plausible.[25] Nonetheless the potential of the sublime in architecture is far from exhausted. Unlike much eclectic Postmodernism which leads a comfortable life in architectural photography, our buildings in Tokyo and New York are linked to the fragmented experiences of its users. This also says something of the relationship between architecture and philosophy. Architecture cannot be reduced to ideas in terms of the sublime. They did play a role in its conception, but the project designs in this book are no echo of these ideas. After all, the buildings would then be nothing more than carriers of philosophical reflections. Supplemented by 'engineering' and 'surroundings', the narration would then be complete. However this means that the meaning of the building is dismembered into one for the expert and another for the constructor. Once again the user ends up on the sidelines.

Nor are the surroundings of the buildings neutral. The buildings and the surroundings are one. The Manhattan building is anchored in its morphology. In New York the building *is* the Amtrak railroad. It has become one and the same construction. In Tsukiji the building blends in with the fishmarket area; we didn't aim for extravaganza. Facades are actually assemblages of existing types in Tokyo. This results in tactile and visual perceptions that have no need of exploded or bird's-eye views. We should really give precedence to examining the perspective of the homeless and day laborers in the streets in more detail.

With our Tsukiji and Manhattan projects we aim to offer a bed, nothing more, but also nothing less. In 1929 Melnikov designed a hotel which he called a 'sleeping laboratory'. The intention of this design was to realize at a collective level what we are now attempting to achieve for individual homeless persons. His design was comprised of two buildings, both of which were slightly elevated on one side, with a symmetrical middle block which served as the access. All beds were built in, like tables in a laboratory. The entire building was run from a central command post. Sleep was regarded as a *scientifically-responsible form of rest*: SONNaia SONata. The technicians in the control room worked according to 'scientific principles'. As necessary, or as desired, they could generate the noise of rustling leaves, the song of a nightingale, or the sound of waves on the sea-shore. If that didn't help, then machinery could move the beds slowly from side to side, so that the occupants could finally fall asleep. We had no desire to copy the SONNaia SONata. We needed a different kind of com-mand post, even though we were working on the same problem: the cre-ation of a place to sleep after a long and tiring stay on the streets. In our Postmodern variant, sleep has the same *curative* function as it did in Melnikov's hotel. Undisturbed rest is a luxury if you are used to sleeping in a doorway or under a bridge. However the building has a more modest significance. It is closer to life on the streets.

The meaning of the sublime involved in these projects is very close to that of Adorno. For Adorno, like Benjamin, the sublime acquires the meaning of the experiences contained in the personal history as 'nature', as opposed to freedom. Adorno's concept of the sublime constitutes a good basis for the interpretation of architecture (and art). At the end of his book Crowther comes close to such an interpretation as he investi-gates the possibilities of the sublime in art. As an example he cites Zola's *Germinal*, in which capitalism plays the hidden leading role.[26] Capitalism presumes order and chaos in one and the same movement. In a society structured along these lines we can perceive something which touches on the sublime.

Man-nature instead of 'style'

We need a more detailed meaning for the sublime. What that will look like depends on the philosophical perspective. Is it critical in the sense of Kant's Reason, or is it related to a Marxist perspective of economy and society? These are the two most important traditions in Western thought that attach great significance to the concept of criticism. With Kant this criticism is primarily directed towards our knowledge, with Marx towards knowledge and society.

A Critical sublime

I began this chapter with the sublime from Kant's point of view. In this section I shall attempt to link this approach with the other form of criticism: Marxism. Marxist thought actually relates to the human body; it injures itself with its own product, society and technology, and so destroys its own sensuousness. This narrative has already been told by several philosophers inspired by Marx, but it is seldom brought into relation with the aesthetic, one of the central subjects in this book. Terry Eagleton has made an in-depth and interesting analysis of this aspect. In a continuation of Kant's work Eagleton attempts to reconstruct a 'Marxist sublime' by connecting Marx's early work with his later criticism of the political economy. His study therefore deals with cultural expressions at a more abstract level than architecture. In this the body plays an important role. The body was a central theme in architecture from the Renaissance until Modernism, just like engineering, and nowadays technology. We have already seen the great importance the Russians and Le Corbusier attached to machine-aesthetics.

The question that now has to be dealt with is: which terms are eligible for use in a description of the relationship between man and nature (and technology), and which are ineligible? This question doesn't only imply that one term is better than another, but that many terms are less innocent than they seem initially. Here Eagleton gives language a special significance. Human history can be read from language. This gives individuals the opportunity to push back frontiers. At the same time the body is trapped in a web of abstractions which cause injury to its sensory capacities. One of Marx's most important concepts, commodity, is understood by Eagleton as such. The abstract and the tangible come together in commodity. It is a relationship of form and content, of sensory perception and concept, it is an object and at the same time it is not an object, in short it is a relationship. Eagleton links his concept of a Marxist sublime with the dynamism of the social relationships in which commodity plays the leading role. The 'evil sublime' is encapsulated in the dynamism of capitalism – just as Zola describes it in *Germinal*, or Marshall Berman shows in his analysis of modernity in Paris, New York, and Petersburg.[27] Like Kant's mathematical sublime this endless accumulation of pure quantity, of which money is the most important parameter, undermines all permanent forms.

This *Unform* links both critical philosophers. It is both negative and positive. Negative, inasfar as formlessness always possesses something monstrous, and positive in an aesthetic and historical sense. It is literally impossible to illustrate or project the future. Marxism is not a theory of the future; it is more a theory and a practice which make a future possible. In fact this concerns the old question of human powers. Which can indeed lead to nuclear warfare, concentration camps, and the destruction of the environment.

If we descend to the dungeons of physical torture, as does Elaine Scarry, then we can establish an analogy with the sublime. However this is no longer an aesthetic experience in which fear and terror are vanquished by the ethical, as with Kant, but a literally speechless and irrational terror. Scarry points out that physical pain is something special amongst the mental, somatic and perceptual phenomena. Pain is the only sensation that is not answered by any object outside us. Although the experience of physical pain is just as human as the ability to hear, to feel, to desire, or to be hungry, it differs from every other physical and mental sensation since it has no object outside us.[28] This lack of an object, the absence of a referential context, makes it almost impossible to express it in language.

Scarry shows how pain and imagination are each other's missing intentional antitheses, they are not opposites but mutually exclusive – the existence of the one requires the elimination of the other. Together they form the framework of our identity as a creative being, within which all other intimate perceptual, mental, emotional and somatic sensations are to be found. In many languages the term which comes closest to the term pain is *work*, a term that always refers to a created object. In addition to its associations with physical pain this term is also associated with pleasure, art, imagination and civilization, words which express the creative power of man. Imagination, art and culture are directly related to the opportunities we have to make use of our creative abilities, and transform them into objects. Conversely, reduced chances to use these abilities to actually produce an object will be experienced as unpleasant, which will ultimately closely approach pain conditions. We use the term work to describe our artistic products, such as paintings, books and buildings. The opposite of this is work in the sense of suffering, a situation in which man is alienated from his product. In the 19th century factory the term work was associated with pain and suffering; not only by Marx, but also in the official reports from the British Parliament which he used in his studies. The relationship between work and pain was manifested by the omnipresent hunger, misery, and illness, in the lack of light and fresh air and in the exhaustion of the working classes, who were alienated from the products of their labor.[29]

The question is whether we can still describe our reality by making use of Marx's terms. Eagleton sees hardly any reason to revise Marxism. It is true that a 'certain sexism' is to be seen in Marxist theory, and Marx's thoughts might possibly be masculine and ethnocentric, but this is not detrimental to his theory. Nonetheless I think that Eagleton's attempt to come to a theory and a history of sensuousness is doomed to failure. While completely ignoring the highly relevant work of the philosopher Louis Althusser, he relates Marx's early philosophical *Economic and Philosophical Manuscripts (EPM)* to his later economic work in *Grundrisse* and *Das Kapital*. Althusser demonstrated that Marx's thoughts underwent a development, which means that his 'early' texts such as the *EPM* are greatly different from his later work such as *Das Kapital*. Not only has the tone changed, the way in which the terms are organized is also different. Althusser was convinced that there is a definitive break between his earlier and later work. Subsequently, what Eagleton is trying to do is impossible.

The two manners of thought and formulation cannot so easily be reconciled. Scarry also remarks on this difference in Marx's tone. In her analysis of Marx's theory she places the emphasis on terms associated with the body, its experiences and its products. She borrows practically all terms such as creative ability, creator, body, object, work, maker, etc., from Marx. She explains the discrepancy in the tone of Marx's work from the general and barely political nature of the body in relation to machines, materials and objects. The abstract terms from his later work, such as commodity, money and productive capital have no specific place, unlike the terms cited above that are related to the body and the objects it makes.[30]

It is these latter terms which Scarry uses in her own analysis. Vidler also tries to describe the architecture of Tschumi, Coop Himmelblau and Libeskind using these terms.[31] Both make use of a terminology related to the body and its objects.[32] However Vidler's analysis is too simple. He considers Deconstructivism, with its fragmented architecture, to be fully compatible with what Eisenman himself proposes. But my analysis takes a completely different course. The sublime is *not* present in fragmentation, but in the vacuum of the 'formal'. This can only be made visible by bringing this 'formal' under tension by means of architectural paraphrasing. The terms may well be identical, but the direction of the analysis is completely different.

Scarry derives much of her book from the archives of *Amnesty International*. She attempts to develop a theoretical framework in order to understand the terror described in the *Amnesty* reports. This terror cannot be linked to Marx's later work, which is primarily concerned with terms such as commodity, money, and classes. Political terror was very much present under the communist regimes, which claimed to have abolished class distinctions. The only way to combat terror is with openness and democratic controls.

In other words, if we wish to discuss this problem in theoretical terms then this will only be possible with the terms that Scarry developed, and not with those proper to Marx's *Das Kapital*. In my view the difference in tone is related to the private nature of physical experiences, which in fact rarely remain private. They are transmitted and shared via culture. The language in which they are expressed still bears the traces of their intimate genesis. Pleasure, effort, or pain can still be seen as an aesthetic component in language. For Burke, terror directed towards the body was the regulating principle of the sublime. In this aspect Scarry is unmistakably influenced by Burke. Burke had already pointed out that the Greek language has one single word for surprise, admiration, and terror. Scarry's use of the term 'work' has similar connotations.

The Body without Organs

In the occasionally hallucinatory prose of the French philosophers Deleuze and Guattari pain and desire are situated in the *Body without Organs* (BwO), the translation of *Corps sans Organes*, CsO.[33] Even though there seems to be a resemblance to Scarry's analysis, the Body without Organs is not an object in a material sense; it is not a concept, not even a condition that can be achieved. At best it can be touched on when stage-managed.[34]

For Scarry pain is inflicted by brute violence and oppression, but in Deleuze and Guattari pain is a physical and mental condition. It concerns the body as a desiring object. Nor do they refer to the dungeon of political violence. Their intention is to unlock mental dungeons such as psycho-analysis using the ecstasy of the BwO. The comparison here remains dubious, and in the end falls short. The pain Scarry describes is so extreme that relating it to philosophical concepts is hardly possible. Torture is such an extreme event that it seems inappropriate to generalize from it to anything else or from anything else to it, as she remarks in her book. I put them next to each other with an explicit aim: a better understanding of Deleuze and Guattari's extreme set of practices (no concept is involved) of the BwO. Like Scarry, they are indebted to Burke. Their BwO shows some rudimentary resemblance to Burke's ideas about the sublime of which Adam Philips rightly says that it is the drift of the erotic that sabotages method and by the same token makes it imperative. They borrowed the concept of the BwO from Antonin Artaud's *Héliogabale* and William Burroughs's *Naked Lunch*. In their view pain is not something which is imposed from outside, but is instead accepted voluntarily. This gives the term a meaning which is completely different from Burke's and Kant's. The masochistic experience, which the writers consider to be poorly understood, plays an important role in this meaning of pain. Deleuze and Guattari use the definitely physical experiences of hypochondriac, schizophrenic paranoid patients to arrive at a description of the body without organs, a description which has little to do with a phantasm and nothing whatsoever with a spatial metaphor. It is in fact a program for handling ecstasy, the enlargement of Burke's delight, a sort of delightful horror (Part Four, section VII).

Eagleton's and Scarry's ideas are related to a body with organs (organism); but Deleuze's BwO is the complete opposite of such a construction. The organs are not the enemy of the BwO – it is the *organism* itself, i.e. the organization of the organs. The desiring machine makes us an organism; 'but at the very heart of this production, within the very production of this production, the body suffers from being organized in this way, from not having some other sort of organization, or no organization at all'.[35] The BwO cannot be compared with a fragmented body as illustrated by Hans Bellmer, nor with architecture designed by Coop Himmelblau, Hadid, or Libeskind. Every spatial comparison falls short. The BwO is desire itself, but as the unproductive, the sterile, the genderless and the unconsumable. It has nothing whatsoever to do with the body, according to Deleuze and Guattari. It is in fact the body without an image. 'The body without organs, the unproductive, the unconsumable, serves as a surface for the recording of the entire process of the production of desire, so that desiring-machines seem to emanate from it in the apparent objective movement that establishes a relationship between the machines and the body without organs'.[36] If there is a BwO, then it does not involve ideology, only matter. The BwO is a phenomenon comprised of physical, biological, mental, social, and cosmic matter. Deleuze and Guattari bring the BwO into the field against psychoanalysis. Where the latter says: 'Stop, refind yourself', the authors call out to us: 'Let's press on because we have a long way to go before we reach the BwO.' With the masochistic experience, the BwO can be inhabited by nothing other than pain and lust; similarly Deleuze and Guattari's *plateaux* consist of intensities that accept no external interference. In fact this 'plateau-thinking' is used against the three major strata which we constitute as 'subject': the *organism*, *meaning* and the *invocation of subject* by psychoanalysis. The BwO of Deleuze and Guattari is a metropolis, held together by the whip of the mistress. The streets of lust are inhabited by 'intensities' with neither name nor identity.

This image is obviously far removed from the politico-social orientation of Scarry's book. It would seem to me that the architecture of Deconstructivism has primarily been searching for the Deleuzian meaning. I think that Eisenman's more recent work, from about *House X* onwards, can be characterized by this search. The lustful shredding of systems of architectural rules and codes is typical of this.[37]

PART TWO

Cities

Project credits

Urban Plan The Nieuwe Reael, IJ-bank, Westerdok, Amsterdam Architects Arie Graaf-land, Harry Kerssen Model Limited Editions, Rotterdam Digital Assemblings Arie Graaf-land, Hans Schouten and Bureau Piet Gerards Project Photography Hans Schouten, Photographic Department, Faculty of Architecture TU Delft **Tsukiji project, hiring hall with living accommodation for day laborers, Tokyo** Architects Diana Juranovic-Ishida, Toshikazu Ishida/KID Conceptual Research & Development Arie Graafland Design team at Kyushu Institute of Design/Ishida Studio Toshikazu Ishida, Fumio Ohkubo, Kazutoshi Sakaguchi, Toyofumi Nakashima, Yasuhiro Yamada, Christian Ricart (CAD preliminary studies, study models, site model, site research) 3D Graphics Shuhei Nemuto Model Limited Editions, Rotterdam Digital Assemblings Arie Graafland, Hans Schouten and Bureau Piet Gerards Model Photography Photographic Department Faculty of Architecture, TU Delft, Hans Schouten **Prototype Manhattan Transfer Shelter System (MTSS), Washington Street, Manhattan, New York** Architects Arie Graafland, Harry Kerssen Model Limited Editions, Rotterdam Digital Assemblings Arie Graaf-land, Hans Schouten and Bureau Piet Gerards Project Photography Hans Schouten, Photographic Department, Faculty of Architecture TU Delft

CITIES Amsterdam

Rhizome City

Amsterdam Westerdok, morphology and modernity

Amsterdam, rhizome city, the Venice of the North. A network of canals, waterways, locks, alleys and embankments, held together by the 'stem-canals' formed by the ring of canals, the Kloveniersburgwal, Oude Schans and Amstel, a folly linked to a commercial machine.[1]

At the beginning of their book *Mille Plateaux* Deleuze and Guattari call Amsterdam the rhizome city. Do the book and the city resemble each other? Is it actually possible to write a thousand plateaus about Amsterdam? It wouldn't surprise me if it were possible, and in fact it's already been done. Anyone who enters the library of the *Amsterdams Historisch Museum* will find it difficult to leave again. The building seems to imprison you; and the permanent exhibition keeps on drawing you back to the diamond cutters, the hydraulic engineering works, and the rebellious citizens of the Wallen and of the Jordaan.

Today's commercial machinery had a forerunner in the trading and shipping of hundreds of years ago. If there is anywhere where the word 'tissue' is applicable, then it has to be here. Every more major spatial intervention or intensification, be it the office blocks on the Rokin or the never-ending traffic congestion, is perceived as 'alien'. The 'body' of the city doesn't permit the traffic to function as the circulatory system for its blood.

Deleuze and Guattari compare the rhizome to a map with an infinite number of entrances. In this map power bases, centers of art, science, social struggle, politics and commerce are linked to each other. The rhizome is above all a figure of thought; it extends beyond the pluralism of a decade ago. It renders every line of thought based on a structural or generative model impossible. According to Deleuze and Guattari one consequence resulting from this is the end of Freudian psychoanalysis with its Oedipal theater; but it also signifies the end of state Marxism – where the state plants a 'tree structure' in both our soul and body, but also in space, where it uses grids and axes to create these divisions.

Misunderstandings are commonplace when a philosophical figure of thought such as the rhizome is introduced into thinking about architec-

Amsterdam, Oude Zijds Kolk, 1999

ture and urban planning. 'Tree structure', 'tissue' and 'urban body' found their way into this field long ago.

For Deleuze 'tree' has a different meaning. The metaphor 'tree structure' is misleading, as it doesn't embody the remotest analogy with space. Deleuze sees the tree as a *logical* tree, as revered by the philosophy of the Enlightenment. But this doesn't imply an abstract negation of this philosophy. Although, in his opinion, the philosophers of the Enlightenment always expressed their thoughts in the shadow of a despot and legitimized a given form of the state, he still considers them to be philosophical friends who should be criticized. In our ideas the tree constitutes the shadow of the state; we also find the latter in the systematics of Kant's and Hegel's philosophy, a criticism which we had already seen in Benjamin and Adorno. The terms tissue and urban body lead to associations with healthy and unhealthy, so they easily result in normative thinking; a body in equilibrium should not be disturbed. That is certainly a risk with these terms, and a degree of caution should be exercised in their use.

Versailles, with the perspectives offered by its axes and lakes, can be characterized as a state-like order; but the Oudezijds Kolk, with the curve between the Oudezijds Voorburgwal and the Achterburgwal, is rhizomatic. The view extends no further than the next curve one hundred meters away. Unlike a tree the rhizome links any given point to any other point. Dissimilar elements can also be linked together in this manner. The rhizome cannot be reduced to a number of discrete components as it consists not of units but of dimensions, or more accurately of dimensions in motion. There is no beginning and no end, but there is always a certain environment in which the rhizome thrives. Unlike a structure with given fixed points the rhizome consists solely of temporary characteristics and provisional ideas, ideas that are still in development. These can result in a 'deterritorialization', which in turn leads to other developments. Insofar as the rhizome is applicable to the old Amsterdam, Bickerseiland, the Westerdok or the Eastern harbor area, it always involves varying connections in our perceptions, or more accurately different 'plateaux' in our perceptions, which cannot be compressed into a tour of the city using a guidebook.

There is certainly some room for criticism of the rhizome as a mental model – and here the meaning of 'model' as such is a problem – but with the necessary qualifications the concept of the rhizome can be used to describe the problem of the meaning of space. It has many similarities with Benjamin's conception of a large city as a labyrinth. Moreover, in my view the meaning of rhizome in a philosophical sense is similar to Bataille's labyrinth of language. In effect his labyrinth breaks open lexical prisons; it prevents words from finding a definitive anchorage, a permanent meaning. Words become metaphors which change their meaning. According to Hollier, at the very least they lose their original meaning. The words become drunk. Bataille associates the feeling 'of wanting to get out again' with the labyrinth, but in his labyrinth the thread of knowledge needed to escape from it has long since disappeared. Bataille rejects the 'Icarus' solution; according to him a solution no longer exists, neither scientific, nor in the form of an artistic-utopian solution as a dream of escape. The very will to escape makes the labyrinth a voluntary prison. As Hollier says, the problem is that one never knows whether one is inside or outside.[2]

Deleuze and Guattari's rhizome no longer differentiates between the various forms of knowledge (ideological, scientific, and philosophical), and is akin to the labyrinth. For them there is no longer a difference between philosophy, science, literature and poetry. The Body without Organs (BwO) is a literary figure which now plays a part in their philosophy. This ambiguous spatial metaphor of rhizome is comprised mainly of openings; it is not known whether these openings provide access to an inside or an outside, or whether they are an entrance or an exit. If I walk from my home to my favorite restaurant on the Oudezijds Voorburgwal in the manner of Richard Sennett, then I never know whether I am walking through the Bloedstraat or through the Koestraat. And in fact I don't really want to know. What makes the labyrinth simultaneously numbing and surprising is the ensemble of the water, the architecture of the banks and the alleys, the prostitutes and the porn industry.

Perhaps the rhizome as a spatial and social structure can be associated with what Sennett calls *narrative space*.[3] Narrative space involves a much more restricted relationship between time and space than for the large unit Sigfried Giedion isolated in Manhattan (which in the Netherlands was advocated by, for example, de 8 en Opbouw). Sennett regards his narrative space as a place in which something unexpected can occur, where change and transition is possible. The form follows the function in the linear space of modernism, but narrative space is characterized by its very indefiniteness – it provides the opportunity to start something new. Sennett explains this with an example. Battery Park City and Roosevelt

Island on Manhattan are both neighborhoods for the upper-middle class, with a balance between housing and parks. Both are enclaves; the former is enclosed by a freeway, the latter is surrounded by the East River. The children living in these neighborhoods seem to have little or no interest in the playgrounds that have been provided for them – they prefer to play in the 'hotspots', the basketball fields in the midst of Manhattan's busy traffic. Anyone thinking back to his or her childhood will recognize this: did anyone ever want to play under their mother's watchful eye? It is no different in Amsterdam; it is particularly the open spaces of de 8 en Opbouw that are avoided, and the playgrounds that have been laid out in our new neighborhoods remain untouched. Only very small children still play there. Nothing unexpected can happen in these spaces. The same is true for architecture. An architect wishing to design a narrative space is going to have to depend on the indefiniteness of its use – and not use the concept that *form follows function*.

Such a design requires overlapping rather than segmentation, and complexity rather than clarity and unambiguity. The same is true for the rhizome. As a spatial structure the rhizome can never be viewed separately from the sections of society that thrive in its midst. In my view Amsterdam is the perfect territory for Deleuze and Guattari's ideal schizophrenic – a term which, it should be realized, has nothing to do with the psychiatric condition with which it is normally associated. On the contrary, their schizophrenic is able to live a number of coordinated lives at the same time.[4]

Modernity

Modernism only ever had one answer to the rhizome, and that was clearance. Hygienic motivations camouflaged other more subjective motives; the chaos of the rhizome causes fear, the fear of being absorbed by it. The grid helped overcome this fear. Le Corbusier proposed the grid for Paris. The Algemeen Uitbreidings Plan (the General Expansion Plan for Amsterdam or AUP) used the grid to control the use of the land and its ownership. A closed entity was brought into action to combat the specter of the unrestrained growth of the metropolis.[5] Stabilization appears to have been an important motive for the AUP; it endeavored to control society using a spatial plan. The maximum population of 1 million residents would have been reached in about the year 2000. According to the plan the definitive form of the city would have been a more or less self-contained entity – and not a map with many entrances, but a tree, homogeneous and articulated.[6]

Amsterdam could be described in the way that Richard Sennett described Manhattan. It would certainly differ considerably from the route in the architectural guide, in which the grid acts as the space for economic competition, and is used as though it were being played, like a chessboard. It is the space of neutrality; it is rational in the sense of abstract Cartesian space.[7] The AUP was designed to provide social and spatial control, but Manhattan's grid primarily controls the economy and the traffic. Only the old Amsterdam on the banks of the IJ would appear to have its own rhizomatic dynamism, which in my view is broader than Sennett's narrative space. It is also characterized by the different histories associated with this space; and perhaps not so much the 'official' history as recorded in the history books, but more the history of the city as handed-down stories that haven't been verified scientifically. The Westerdok unmistakably acquires an extra significance when we learn that it once housed the Public Baths for the children living in the Jordaan neighborhood. We also learn of this story from the rhizome.

Shouldn't a spatial intervention in such an area always be described as 'modern'? Modernity was characterized by the shock caused by the new when it was literally implanted into the old tissue. 'Old' and 'new' are part of the modernist sensitivity that had already been anticipated by Aloïs Riegl. In his opinion old buildings should have the chance to grow old with dignity by allowing them to decay 'naturally'. In this Alan Colquhoun sees an analogy with Nature. He also speaks of 'the onslaught on the fabric of the past' that characterized the plans of the 1920s and '30s. For him the difference between modernity and postmodernity does not depend on an assessment of the relation to the historical culture, as it did for Riegl, but is primarily the result of the fact that in modernist ethics the new was given an explicitly positive meaning and, moreover, was attributed with a compelling aesthetic power. In the last decades this has often been viewed as a form of reductionism.[8] Marshall Berman gave an impressive and literary description of this context in his book *All That Is Solid Melts Into Air* (1982). The dynamism of modernism aims at merging all solid forms and structures, both social and spatial. Everything 'of value' disappears in the course of 'progress'. A satisfactory analysis of the consequences of this has been made by Fredric Jameson. Our postmodernity is characterized by the uniform developments under the dictatorship of curtain-wall standardization and the imposition of the concrete-skeleton order. Further, while this has been taking place the traditional ideas about 'urbanization' have been changed completely.

This dynamism is also seen in all the older means of production; and consequently also in the agricultural industry, which is becoming mechanized and is focused on maximum yields, and in the mechanization of stockbreeding into a bio-industry. It can also be seen in spatial interventions such as the construction of shopping centers and the laying out of 'public spaces' in which the difference between public and private has disappeared. Spaces in which a foreshadowing of the end of Hegel's civil society can be perceived.

The IJ-bank project and Koolhaas's interventions

The IJ-bank project differs from the other developments of *boom-town* Amsterdam because it is sited atop the medieval city of old Amsterdam, the area I refer to as rhizomatic. The South-East lobe of the city and the peripheral development of Sloterdijk are here considered as postmodern. This is not, however, because the various architectural practices involved in these developments made desperate attempts to formally give each building a 'postmodern' appearance. On the contrary, these office districts are postmodern because they derive from the *uniform* development of yet another commercial enclave that contains nothing but 'more of the same' character of expected corporate identity. This is not merely architecture 'without a context'; above all, it is architecture without a concept. Ill-considered left-wing critiques have given the 'blame' for the 'social failures' of these developments to 'capital' – or more precisely to the influence of capitalist developmental strategies. However, it can no more be convincingly argued that the urban design motives behind the South-East lobe and Sloterdijk or 'the plankton' around Schiphol airport are motivated as capitalist developments than in the case of, say, civic developments like Canary Wharf. Such political distinctions do not intend to subsequently dismiss the important influence of economic feasibility on these areas, for in truth, there are no longer any enclaves which are not to a great degree governed by capitalist laws. Architectural differences, if they can be found, are due primarily to the conceptual abilities, entrepreneurial vision, and persistence (or lack thereof) of the various architects commissioned and involved. Conditioned, in fact, by their ability to incorporate or resist the 'bottom line' economic leveling of such capital concerns.

The essential difference between the major capitalist economies lies in the relationship between public and private funding, which in Europe differs from that in the us and Japan. With the IJ-bank project the architect has opportunities to program and conceptualize the public-private relationship in design terms in two ways. First, he can use the difference between European and American developmental motivations as his basis. In other words, the distinction between public funding flows and civic-minded concerns which still retain some influence in the European arena, and the bottom-line strategies and profit margin determinants which dominate American growth and development. Second, he can use existing architectural design and urban planning differences between Sloterdijk and the IJ axis. The former being a recent office district built at the periphery of the city and designed much like the ring road or suburban corporate park type of developments in America. The latter is a central and critical area of old Amsterdam with historic precedents of narrow alleyways and high density planning.

Elsewhere I have described Koolhaas's manner of design as 'Faustian'. This term refers to his interpretation of the dynamism of our Western capitalist society and its effects in the sense of our loss of orientation. In that same contribution I also discussed in more detail the book Koolhaas wrote at the beginning of his career, *Delirious New York*. This 'retroactive manifesto for Manhattan', as stated in the sub-title, has become the most explicit manifesto for the *Office for Metropolitan Architecture*.[9] If what Marshall Berman says is true, i.e. that in its unprecedented and *unscrupulous* development capitalism melts all that is solid into air, then this is also true for Koolhaas's designs.

Of course there are differences between Koolhaas's first designs and his later work, which can be characterized as the differences between modernist montages and postmodern assemblies: for example the IJ-bank project in the north of Amsterdam representing the former and the Fukuoka housing project in Japan the latter. Here postmodern doesn't refer just to stylistic characteristics, but moreover to the postmodern nature of our society and capital's penetration into society's last enclaves. *Delirious New York*, published in 1978, should be seen as an essay driven by an anti-mimetic impulse. Although the book does bear similarities to Deleuze and Guattari's description of 'technonarcissism' in their *Mille Plateaux* of 1980, the mimetic impulse I intend bears a greater likeness to Adorno's and Horkheimer's understanding of it as a natural impulse in man to deliver himself up to his surroundings.[10] Further, the content of Koolhaas's book has little to do with Deleuze and Guattari's project, which addresses, as its subtitle indicates, 'capitalism and schizophrenia'.[11] Of course attempts to manipulate direct comparisons between the works of an architect and the writings of philosophers such as these very often result in dubious analyses. Of more interest is the question as to whether the ideas of these two thinkers can be used to describe Koolhaas's architecture. I shall endeavor to make clear that this is *not* possible (even if they do have some theoretical characteristics in common). On the contrary, a plan such as the IJ-bank project will ultimately constitute a postmodern (architectural) transplantation in the rhizomatic body (urban condition) of the IJ axis, irrespective of whether it is carried out by Koolhaas or by another architect. Postmodern in the sense that the municipal council won't allow for any dominant control of the plan (at least not in the sense of Le Corbusier's Obus plan for Algiers). The council will ensure that it has no identity by propagating a pluralism of influences which will ultimately result in a piecemeal character with too many architects assuming the part of the virtuoso. Especially the Oosterdok, one of the single most critical small islands just behind the central station, has no guarantee as yet that it won't be developed with the same indifferent office buildings as can be found in the contextless sites such as Sloterdijk.

Perhaps the only way to prevent such an urban indifference from being developed here is for the municipality to impose a strict definition of the architecture, a delineation of what is possible versus what is not permissible. The Oosterdock Island, for instance, should be treated as a space without front or rear. The architecture must be defined in relation to the urban space, the rhizomatic space. Of course differences in architectural expressions can be accommodated, but they should not be as great as the piecemeal model above would generate, nor should they be used to express hierarchical differences on which the 'front/back' scenario depends. The plan should be treated more in the spirit of La Defence in Paris than that of Sloterdijk.

I wish to focus my comments on the perceptions introduced by this transplantation, i.e. the perception of modernity and the pre-modern level of perception that sometimes can still be found in the city and which is brought into relationship with the rhizome. Koolhaas's IJ-bank plan is modernist (although certainly not in the absolute sense as understood by Carel Weeber; local urban characteristics play an important part in Koolhaas's plan), whilst the Old City and the islands appeal to other perceptions. An analysis of Koolhaas's design concept in relation to the city is required to avoid ending up in the position of someone who is merely defending a conservationist ideology.

Design strategy, the avoidance of a master plan

I don't think that Alejandro Zaera Polo's description of Koolhaas's designs as 'rhizomatic' is correct. Moreover, this contradicts Koolhaas's own remarks in an interview in the same issue of the journal *El Croquis*.[12] But another observation is certainly correct, when he states that Koolhaas is fully aware of an important characteristic of our society, i.e. its continually increasing differentiation, often with disastrous results, such as the fragmentation of both consciousness and spatial configurations.

Zaera Polo cites the 1987 plan for Melun Sénart near Paris as being typical of the rhizomatic strategy, since the definitive valuation of the components of the plan is delayed for as long as possible. There is certainly no 'umbrella' idea behind this plan. This strategy aims to create a given design system that is geared more towards development than towards the registration of formal results. Melun Sénart's entire urban system is designed as a series of strips, each with its own specific kind of activity and its own specific speed.[13] This entire combination of lines, strips, sectors and fields ultimately results in connections at insignificant places in the plan. In my view a similar strategy had been used previously in the design of the Parc de la Villette, which at the time was attributed to Bernard Tschumi.[14] Koolhaas, although the same is also true for Tschumi, is focused not so much on the architecturally significant characteristics in the plan as on its operational and pragmatic possibilities – where time is an essential characteristic. Melun Sénart would appear to be a plea for a rhizomatic randomness. Nonetheless it does possess a structure. Koolhaas criticizes Coop Himmelblau's proposals for Melun Sénart in no uncertain terms. In my view Koolhaas's pragmatism is determined more by the tensions between standardization and homogeneity versus the wish to allow relatively random 'streams' to flow freely. It is certainly not his intention to design a 'master plan'. The architect has long since lost control over the future of his design. The fortunes of Le Corbusier's plan for Algiers are illustrative of such megalomaniac aspirations. Koolhaas fully understood Le Corbusier's defeat in Algiers.[15] The various interests of capital and the local political interests will result in a master plan disinte-

The distribution of mass is such that you can never achieve any kind of density. Except for maybe the Oosterdokseiland. Within the plan, this is a machine that indicated how the rest of the plan was beginning to find a somewhat bizarre definition. We hoped that we could use the old city center as an argument for a typological renewal of the exhausted arsenal of Dutch architecture. (Rem Koolhaas, in Appendix)

IJ Bank Project, Amsterdam,
supervision OMA

grating into sub-interests and irreconcilable contradictions. The master plan will be submerged amongst the confusion of the sub-interests.

The outcome of the IJ-bank plan was hardly surprising in view of the highly complex issues of the financing, the willingness to invest, the phasing of housing, work and the infrastructure, and the unpredictable tribal decision-making in Amsterdam. Moreover, the office developers will take over the sites. What that means can already be seen in the South-East lobe and in Sloterdijk – where for such developers the term 'original' is little more than a marketing phrase which in actuality means that everything looks the same because the market has somehow borne out a 'desirability' for such design schemes. The urban planning concept in such development strategies is reduced to civil engineering – infrastructure and accessibility.

Those who consider Koolhaas's design to be a rhizome allow themselves to be overly influenced by a ready-made mental picture and fail to see the *specific* nature of Koolhaas's design concept. The elevator, the rigid structure – a condition often too loosely interpreted metaphorically as a 'tree structure' – of the Downtown Athletic Club, and the free, not definitively specified movements of the athletes on the various floors continue to guarantee the structure of many of OMA's designs. The Sea Terminal in Zeebrugge and the Bibliothèque de France are the social condensers of our time. They share the same abstract principle as the Club: a rigid, undifferentiated tree structure, combined with the unobstructed flows of traffic, accelerations, undefined spaces and imagery.[16] This is in fact the same pattern as in the *City of the Captive Globe*, with its grid of modernity and the uncontrolled growth of the imagery. He stated this problem concisely in the speech he held on the occasion of his departure as Professor at the TU in Delft: 'Possibly the question that for me best describes the difference between Rietveld and Mies is as follows: is there such a thing as a freedom that captures, and conversely a thing which captures that liberates? The former would be Rietveld, Mies would be the latter'.[17] In my view Nexus World, the housing complex he designed in Fukuoka in Japan, would seem to be his attempt to achieve the latter. This is also in agreement with Koolhaas's own remarks in the interview in *El Croquis*, in which he says that at this very point in time there are possibilities for an architecture which can withstand the social mimesis. This does not entail a repetition of the chaos that already exists, but a structuring, and then within that structure allowing the Deleuzian flows to merge into each other. For OMA the 'tree structure' in architecture is the *procedure of the envelope*.

The architecture of OMA is certainly not modernist in the sense that it aims to create a mega-structure – Melun Sénart even goes so far as to explore chaos – but nor are its designs rhizomatic.

The problem of time was also indicated by process planning a decade ago. Nowadays only a very few urban planners would deny that urban planning means making scenarios for the future. Nonetheless Koolhaas's position is different. In my view he is one of the 'modernists' of our time, which nowadays also means 'postmodern'. OMA is filling the last enclaves in our society with architectural objects which accelerate, bind, and merge social life. That cannot be achieved by a rhizome in which, according to Deleuze, the primary flow is one of desire. OMA's social condensers combine a rigid structure (the 'tree structure') with barely defined and fragmented spaces. That is not the same as an 'architectural structuralism' which is comprised of Deleuzian fixed 'units' structured according to the more or less regular pattern of a 'tree' aimed at infusing the scale with 'human proportions'. It should be realized that this doesn't imply that one architect creates 'human spaces' and another 'inhuman' spaces. Neither of these ideas can be of further assistance to us. Here we are confronted with a theoretical definition, i.e. the definition of human subjectivity. In the one instance this is centralized, in the other decentralized. Humanism puts Man at the center, postmodernism displaces Man from the center. Every idea of topos, place or of genius loci that is so fundamental to structuralism (compare, for example, van Eyck's Orphanage) has disappeared in Koolhaas's work and has been absorbed by the acceleration of our society, in which the primary flows are capital and culture.

In the IJ-bank plan the Centraal Station has the function of a condenser. The station is not merely an accelerator because of the expansion of its infrastructure (high-speed train, North-South and East-West subway links), but also as a result of the architectural treatment of the space. The inverted roof (analogous to the roofs over the platforms) no longer forms a barrier between the city and the water, but instead becomes the 'interface' between them.[18] As a result of the 'boardwalk' (Coney Island?) the station no longer has a rear. 'The acceptance of the scale of the functional 19th century roofs over the railroad platforms is demonstrated by their "transformation" in the form of a third inverted floating "roof" above the boardwalk housing the public facilities. The station is therefore

Amsterdam **Design strategy, the avoidance of a master plan** emphatically regarded as an ideal contribution to a new urban culture. It has a positive role to play.'[19] Anyone who – like the Greenberg Guidance Committee supervising the plan – views this transformation as a *possible* illustration has understood little of Koolhaas's design ideology. In this instance the roof isn't just an accelerator of the circulation of capital, but of culture. The linear tree structure of the roof is accepted and is put to typological use; within it the 'flows' of the reading and shopping public, the music of the IJsbreker theater and the cinema programs merge into each other. No attempt is made to reduce the scale of Centraal Station – and rightly so, for a 'human' scale would have resulted in pseudo-security.

Koolhaas uses the same procedure in his design for the Japanese Nexus World. This design is not a montage, but an assembly. The black frame that wraps the homes as in a Christo project plays the part of the 'tree'. Here the 'topos' is the *repetition*. The homes have the same orientation towards the sun; the consequence of this for their ground plan and access means that most homes have an identical design. The repetition of section and ground plan is vaguely reminiscent of an assembly line. The degree of differentiation is limited since the homes are constructed in three layers, which once again is itself uniform. Differences are created by the rising and falling roofline, the details of the internal and external spaces, and by the force of the mold. Other than in architectural structuralism no attempt is made to create 'unique' spaces. The project is unique in its use of regular Mies-like spaces within the envelope, which serves as a plinth for Isozaki's 120-meter-high towers. The aspect that the architectural critic Norberg-Schulz once considered to be detrimental – the loss of the genius loci – is inextricably integrated in Koolhaas's design system. The design doesn't criticize Isozaki, but anticipates his increase in scale.

It is this very tension that his later work shows between the rigid, non-humane structure and the randomness of the spaces, the activities that may take place within them, and the trajectories right through the buildings – it is this tension that makes his architecture so worthwhile. And New York continues to be the inspiration for this line of thought. This configuration keeps on returning in his later work, whether it be the elevator in the Downtown Athletic Club contra the choreography of the athletes, or the rigid grid of Manhattan contra the flexibility of Coney Island. 'At the junction of the 19th and 20th centuries, Coney Island is the incubator for Manhattan's incipient themes and infant mythology. The strategies and mechanisms that later shape Manhattan are tested in the laboratory of Coney Island before they finally leap toward the larger island. Coney Island is a fetal Manhattan.'[20]

My ideas about the nature of Koolhaas's design concept were recently corroborated in an interview by Michael Speaks with Fredric Jameson. Jameson's attention had been drawn to this very envelope for all kinds of unprogrammed and differentiated activities. What makes Koolhaas's work original isn't that he simply advocates differentiation in what Jameson calls a conventional pluralistic ideology, but that he *relates this differentiation to some kind of rigid, undifferentiated form*. Without actually using the term, Jameson is in fact defining Koolhaas's work as *non-rhizomatic*.[21]

When, in 1982, the social geographer Heinemeijer suggested that an esplanade should be laid out along the banks of the IJ he was thinking of a special area, of a topos in which the public could promenade and get a breath of fresh air. It is impossible to find any trace of this suggestion in the plans drawn up by the Planning Development Department (DRO), or in the scenario commissioned by the Amsterdam Waterfront Financing Company (AWF).

For the sake of convenience Amsterdam's Burgomaster and Aldermen have neglected the consequences of the four-lane freeway along the IJ (the link between the A10 beltway and Centraal Station) for the number of automobiles in the rhizome of the Old City. This is because it must be possible to reach Centraal Station from the beltway within seven minutes. This acceleration in the OMA scenario actually repeats and intensifies the situation at the time when Centraal Station was built. At that time construction coincided with the dismantling of the fortifications and the abolition of the city's excise duties.

In his *Geschiedenis van Amsterdam* the historian Brugmans characterizes the railroad as an acceleration of social life. The railroad net was the physical expression of the position of Amsterdam as national and international traffic hub. The Westerdok and the Oosterdok were constructed between 1830 and 1840, but after only a few years they had lost their significance for ocean-going shipping. Nonetheless, in the second half of the 19th century these docks created the conditions needed to make it not only possible but also viable to lay the railroads and to construct Centraal Station. Brugmans notes that this was the beginning of the damage to the city's beauty. According to him the engineers couldn't keep their hands off things.[22]

Jacob Olie's photographs, pencil drawings and watercolors from the second half of the 19th century portray a world that has since been submerged in the maelstrom of progress. In fact Koolhaas reinforces a structure that is already present. The island pattern refers to the significance and specificity of the topos, and the 'critical mass' to the modernist ethics of the new, which is given a meaning in architectural terms.[23] The use of the island pattern makes Koolhaas's plan considerably more interesting, and more successful, than the proposals in the *Policy Document* published by the Municipality of Amsterdam. In this plan the Municipality (DRO) achieved little more than a crude mixture of Kevin Lynch and Manhattan-like architecture. Its 'land abutment model' was comprised of five new links between the rhizome and the IJ, with 75- to 100-meter-high towers projected on these very links. Koolhaas's rejection of this idiocy and his choice of the *specificity* of the morphology argues in his favor, even though his 'critical mass' will still swamp the rhizome.

Project: Westerdok, the Nieuwe Reael

Can Modernism's linear space be interpreted for use in a new development in urban planning? I believe it can. The rural 'organic neighborhood' provides such an opportunity, although it can only be used with a completely new plan. For this reason the concept plan should be drawn up so that it can be viewed in different ways. The scale of the Nieuwe Reael is determined by the Jordaan, and not by that of a neighborhood in a rural setting. The Nieuwe Reael is a plan located on the water's edge, with the IJ with its inland and sea-going shipping, and the Westerdok with its many houseboats. The original significance of the strip development has been lost in the hybridization of the plan with the Jordaan, one of Amsterdam's most densely-inhabited neighborhoods. The hygienic significance of Modernism is no longer central; the plan is focused on the smell of tar, the ships, the wind across the IJ, and the dynamism of the boats without a permanent fixed mooring-place, boats that are continually being shifted, that sail away or attempt to secure a new berth. And the houses try to break free from the strips in which they are built by virtue of their sheer numbers, and by their proximity to the small businesses interspersed amongst them. Here little is the same – an impression that is only reinforced by the juxtaposition of the different facades and the relationships with the water and the ships. The strip development of Modernism functions as no more than a shadow; it is a mold for the new multiplicity of the new Dock. A gully contains the traffic passing along the bank of the IJ; it is cut into the ground and linked to the access roads by traffic circles at the bridges. The dynamism of the IJ banks can only be recovered by the links with its history; the plan opens up to the water on both sides. The mooring places for the boats are just as important as the throughway cutting through the plan. The plan is characterized by its different speeds – those of the throughway linking up with the A10, the access roads for the neighborhood, the shipping, the houseboats, the pedestrians, and the IJ-rail.

Amsterdam **Project: Westerdok, the Nieuwe Reael**

Urban Plan The Nieuwe Reael

Amsterdam
IJ Bank Westerdok

Architects **Arie Graafland, Harry Kerssen**
Model **Limited Editions, Rotterdam**
Digital Assemblings **Arie Graafland, Hans Schouten and Bureau Piet Gerards**
Model Photography **Photographic Department, Faculty of Architecture, TU Delft, Hans Schouten**

The original significance of the strip development has been lost in the hybridization of the plan with the Jordaan, one of Amsterdam's most densely-inhabited neighborhoods. The hygienic significance of Modernism is no longer central; the plan is focused on the smell of tar, the ships, the wind across the IJ, and the dynamism of the boats without a permanent fixed mooring-place, boats that are continually being shifted, sail away, or attempt to secure a new berth. Here little is the same — an impression that is only reinforced by the juxtaposition of the different facades and the relationships with the water and the ships. The strip development of Modernism functions as no more than a shadow; it is a mold for the multiplicity of the new Dock.

Average dwelling space 1,290 sq.ft / 120 m² High-rise cluster I, dwelling 129,120 sq.ft / 12.000m² High-rise cluster II, offices 258,240 sq.ft / 24.000m² Density per hectare 58 units / acre / low rise housing or 145 units / hectare FAR 1.71 / low rise housing / total amount in low rise 740 units

Amsterdam, a city entirely without roots, a rhizome-city with its stem canals, where utility connects with the greatest folly in relation to a commercial war machine. Gilles Deleuze and Felix Guattari

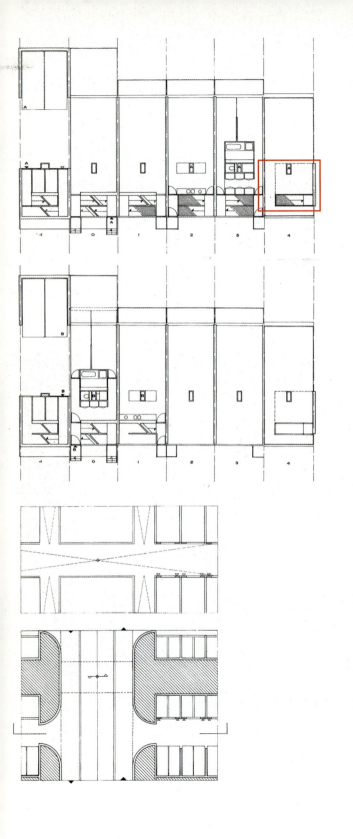

CITIES Tokyo

the Sugoroku Board

Tokyo, the city

Tokyo, like Amsterdam, has a history associated with water. That history is still clearly visible in Amsterdam, but in Tokyo it has become hidden, or has disappeared. In the same way that so much of its culture is not immediately apparent to us in the West. Tokyo is a city of opposites, of contrasts, of high and low: many times larger than Amsterdam, and considerably more difficult to comprehend. The city originally consisted of the Shitamachi district, the lower-lying area in which the ordinary folk lived in the days when it was called Edo (since 1868, Tokyo), and the Yamanote district, located higher in the hills, where the Samurai lived.

Shitamachi's history is associated with water, the waterfront of Tokyo Bay and the Sumida River amongst a network of canals; a city of water, comparable to the Old City of Amsterdam. Teeming with merchants and craftsman, it spawned many *sakariba* (entertainment centers), urban spaces in a continuous state of festivity, lending the city excitement and life.[1] Yamanote, on the other hand, was always more a city of parks, a quiet and rather elegant neighborhood – although the contrast has continually decreased in the past few years as a result of Tokyo's tempestuous growth. *Low city* and *high city* Edward Seidensticker calls the area, his affinity unmistakably lying with the *low city*; Nihombashi and Kyobashi.[2] Towards the end of the Meiji government (1868-1912) the upper class had already left Nihombashi in favor of the city of the parks in the hills. Nihombashi was a mixture of rich and poor, of those with power and those without; it was in fact the heart of the commercial city of Edo. This was where the rich merchants lived and where the big stores were, Mitsui and Daimaru, according to Seidensticker. In a certain sense Nihombashi and Ginza represent two sides of the Japanese culture at the time of the Meiji, modern and traditional at the same time.

In the 1880s Nihombashi was comparable with what I called the *rhizome* of Amsterdam in the previous chapter. Just like the Old City of Amsterdam and its ring of canals it was the focus of trade, transport over water, and culture. The water was not just of importance as a waterway; the large squares with their crowds of people coexisted with the city's waterways – most of the theaters in Edo and early Meiji Tokyo were located near the water.[3] But that was not just the case with the theaters. A restricted scale, hordes of people, trade, shipping and water seem to create a more liberal climate, and offer entertainment and prostitution a place to flourish. Both cities are similar in this respect. Ryōgoku Hirokōji became popular as an entertainment center where people could enjoy the cool breeze blowing across the river, according to Jinnai. An almost medieval, carnivalesque atmosphere could be found near Eko-in with bands of play actors and jesters offering an escape through the antics of theatrical irony and exotic expose. This area, on the eastern side of the river, was moreover the site where cheap and unsanctioned prostitutes dubbed 'golden and silver cats' could be found.[4] The eastern side of the river at Ryōgoku acquired the character of a 'city of darkness', comparable to the Wallen of Amsterdam, the oldest part of the city. As in Amsterdam social life was much more free and relaxed in this district where residents might evade the duress of their institutionalized society by indulging in erotic adventure or voyeuristic escape.[5]

Edward Soja's enthusiastic description of the center of Amsterdam raises an aspect that I consider to be a characteristic of the rhizome, a spatial structure related to a 'libertarian and participatory structure' (Soja) that can flourish there. The populated spaces of the Center are popularly designed to make density beautiful as well as accommodating, to flexibly enculturate and socialize without imprisoning, to make the strange familiar, and to add somehow to one's regular habits of thought that entertaining stimulus of a little confusion.[6] (I don't think that Amsterdam is libertarian, a typically American phenomenon; it seems to me to be more anarchistic, at least as far as Soja's example of the squatters' movement in Amsterdam is concerned). Tokyo's Shitamachi to me seems to be of the same order. Together with Sakai-machi and Fukiya-chō Kokiki-chō was a licensed red-light district that was directly related to the water. These are the districts that most closely resemble the harbor and the old Wallen areas of Amsterdam. The odors, sounds and flavors will have differed greatly, but nowhere else were they as obtrusive as at these waterfronts.

Conversely, Ginza was the district that was most open for modernization; it was a gate to the West. The development was a consequence of the construction of the railroad, and the fire of 1872. The wooden houses had already largely disappeared by 1874, after which 'The Bricktown' was built. A horse-trolley service opened in 1882 in the north-west, which passed straight through Nihombashi and was later extended to Asakusa, Nagai Kafū's favorite *sakariba*. In the same year the district was provided with street lighting. And, as in Paris, the flâneur had made his appearance. It is true that Seidensticker doesn't call him that as such, but the phenomenon he describes is equivalent to Baudelaire's flâneur. It was the time of the Gimbura. Gimbura is a contraction of Ginza and *burabura-suru*, a term which denotes the nomadic journey, as well as the roving motion of the Ginza itinerant whose only purpose lies in the chance encounter with delectation. Little effort is needed to see the similarity with Walter Benjamin's description of the Parisian *passages*. With a little imagination it might still be possible to feel a little of this atmosphere in Nihombashi, but there is absolutely nothing left of Ginza's Bricktown. At present Ginza is the area which shows the greatest resemblance to the cradle of realized Modernity, Manhattan.

Kyobashi was a poorer neighborhood and was more dependent on the patronage of the aristocracy, a place of shopkeepers and artisans. Like Amsterdam, Kyobashi was characterized by a web of waterways that were used for transport. At the time of the Meiji the wealthy part of the population left to move to the High City, taking their power with them. Culture tends to go where the money goes, as Seidensticker notes. In cultural terms the importance of the Low City gradually diminished; after the Meiji Restoration the city of water changed into a city on land. The Sumida River and Tokyo Bay increasingly acquired the character of an industrial belt. Slowly but surely, the population disappeared from the waterfront. Only in the 1960s with Tange's Bay Project did the water once again become of residential significance. Nagai Kafū wrote about the Low City with a great deal of passion, in particular the Shitaya ward. He lived in Tsukiji, the location where our project is planned, and moved to Azabu just before the earthquake. Nowadays the distinction between the High and Low Cities is much less apparent. The northern wards are often brought into conjunction with the Low City, as they are much poorer than the southern and western wards. But the Low City also contained prosperity in the time of Edo and the early Meiji period. By now that world belongs definitely to the past, continuing to exist only in the books of Nagai Kafū and Tanazaki Junichiro.[7] Little of the old morphology has survived, even though there is still a difference between high and low.

There is still something to be found in Tokyo that refers to small scale, locality and complexity. Behind the main roads with their high buildings lies an urban area that, in a certain sense, is comparable to Amsterdam's Old City. Often overshadowed by the high-rise buildings or sometimes literally roofed over by an expressway it is possible to find small houses, sometimes made of wood, small restaurants, a yakitori-under-the-track, a playground or a couple of small stores. Behind and under the new large-scale urban buildings the fine-meshed network of another Tokyo continues to exist. The Japanese are real experts in making use of every possible space. The Bonsai tree is a good example of that. The Bonsai (tree in a drawer: bon=tray, sai=vegetation) is not a small plant such as we understand it, but is a slowly-growing tree that is pruned in accordance with special rules and is associated with a symbolic urban space. In the absence of a private garden the tree represents urban greenery on the balcony.

Seidensticker quotes another, more historical example. Nihombashi's land was worth its weight in gold. Amongst the *godowns* (department stores), small gardens have been planted with meticulous effort and at considerable expense. 'Earth merchants', not brokers of land but peddlers of soil, can be found there to facilitate and profit from these forms of nature's reprieve. Late Meiji saw the exodus of the elite, yet the merchants, the middle class, often remained with their houses and gardens in Nihombashi though they still owned land in the High City.[8] The land has always been used to the utmost; there are still innumerable small enclosed spaces in use. Necessity is the mother of invention. Jinnai makes a comparison of the idea the Japanese have of their city with a Japanese game for two or more players; *Sugoroku*, vaguely resembling the game of snakes and ladders. The element of play is an integral part of Japanese culture, as Isozaki explains: Rules are strictly obeyed, or with Japanese behavior can be likened to the playing of a game where the rules of the game can not be usurped by rectitude, for it is in adherence to the rules alone that value can be assessed. The mastery of the game demands an alliance, an honoring of regulations that results in a precision of play that can only be seen as fervent devotion if not obsessive reflexivity.[9] This *Meisho Sugoroku* was played at the time of the Edo period; players moved over the board from one famous place to another (*meisho* means famous place). This is how the layout of the city became apparent.

Hidenobu considers the sum of these various places to be characteristic for Tokyo; one obtains a mental picture of the relationship when moving over the Sugoroku board of Tokyo. Nowadays this is only possible to a limited extent when moving around on foot, as will be obvious when it is realized that the population of the city amounts to twelve million inhabitants. (Greater Tokyo metropolitan area encompasses also the three adjoining prefectures of Saitama, Kanagawa, and Chiba, some 2300 square miles containing 28 million people.) Its dissociated nature is made very clear by the subway network that, like in any large city, leaves you at a loss as to your location in the city. Moreover the continued existence of Sugoroku is seriously threatened by the present urban development. As in many other Asian cities the past is rapidly being overrun by the present. Few wooden houses survived the great Kanto earthquake of 1923, and the bombing during the Second World War erased many of the rest. The few wooden houses that have survived are worth their weight in gold; the square yards of ground they occupy will soon accommodate a nine-story block of flats. But in spite of this the city is still a jumble of low-rise buildings, detached houses, stores, karaoke bars, yakitori cafés and the many – invariably specialized – restaurants, temples, and shrines. There are still a great number of people who work close by their homes, or live above their store. Everywhere neighborhoods with a local character are to be found, vernacular in their architecture and their small scale.

Tokyo was always characterized by its decentralized city layout. Edo had wooden gates that were closed at night, which included the larger thoroughfares. The city was compartmentalized at night-time. In a

Sugoroku Board,
Famous spots in Edo.
1860, painted by
Utagawa Hiroshige

certain sense this is still the case. The small-scale residential areas between the throughways possess an autonomous character. They are too small for an automobile, and moreover you have the feeling that you are trespassing on private property. Pots with plants are placed by the door, a ladder is left unsupervised, shopping still stands in front of the door and the dustpan and brush seem to have found a permanent place next to the immaculately swept alley. Small children can play here in safety, street crime is virtually unknown.

small-scale, Tokyo

The labyrinthine atmosphere of these neighborhoods creates something that de 8 en Opbouw paid no attention to at all in the Netherlands: an exciting and challenging environment to discover the world, and to develop the imagination. It seems an indestructible fabric in the midst of the avenues, the expressways, the high-rise and the flow of the traffic. It all comes to life, particularly at night: the many bars and restaurants open their doors – the supermarkets also stay open in the evening – and everyone is under way, or acting the flâneur. The city is a true beehive of activities. This is the picture of city life in many Asian cities such as Hong Kong, Kuala Lumpur or Seoul, and to a somewhat lesser extent Singapore, which has spread its neighborhoods amongst the island's vegetation. However the pressure of a new fabric on an older fabric is very great as a result of the high price of land. Not incorrectly, Jinnai states that for us Westerners the demolition of an old building or a monument is often experienced as a loss. But it is different in Tokyo. It is precisely because the old dimensions are used once again that it seems as though something of an ethnic continuity is passed on. The old layer of the city sometimes seems to peek through the gaps in the current urban fabric. While Tokyo is one of the world's most advanced cities its old ethnic elements live on in the vernacular, according to Jinnai, rendering it a mysterious place.

What is needed is to observe without any form of nostalgia for the old Edo. Edo is still present, but a search for temples or shrines or merely regarding the splendors of the Imperial Palace won't be enough. The image that will then remain will be that of Modernity, which has displaced the old Edo. What won't be noticed is how Edo has survived in the present fabric of the city. From the 15th century onwards Edo, a place of imperial residence, was planned primarily as a fortification town. The containment apparatus of moats and ramparts express this in a most obvious way. Yet another, more intriguing device was also conceived: the chaotic patterning of streets divisively laid out to confuse the uninitiated, a strategy leveled against the enemy in the form of disorientation and subsequent surprise tactics. It was an urban planning implementation that is clearly recalled today in the seemingly random organization of Tokyo's streets. In fact, this pattern has never been disturbed, unlike, for example, that of Haussmann's Paris. An important reason for this pattern was the existence of the various *daimyo* establishments and the three large Edo temples (Sensōji in Asakusa, Tōeisan Kan'eiji in Ueno and Zojoji in Shiba), which were in the form of enclaves distributed over the higher ground and the isolated hills. The farmers' ground was situated around the *daimyos*. As a result the urban development always had to be laid out around these cores. The inviolability of the daimyos and the temples resulted in the irregular layout. Everyone who stays a little longer in the city will be familiar with the impossible street plans and the house numbering related to the year of construction. It is a Sugoroku game, certainly for a Westerner. But not only for them; most taxi-drivers have to stop and ask the way in the different wards. The wards in the city often have their own very specific character. The cemetery and the brothel might well constitute a good example of a Japanese meisho.

In the West, until the end of the 18th century, cemeteries were sited in the middle of the city, usually next to the church. From the beginning of the 19th century most cemeteries were located outside the city. Death was associated with illness, the dead appeared to infect the living and were buried more towards the periphery of the city. A cemetery is a world of its own, it is characterized by its enclosed nature. Foucault, who made a study of this phenomenon of relatively isolated and significant spaces, calls it a *heterotopia*.[10] The term first appears in a lecture he gave in 1967 to a group of architects. This lecture, 'Des Espaces Autres' (Of Other Spaces) was never published, leaving numerous questions about the consistency of the idea. As it is not my intention to delve into these issues here, I will attempt to use the term less ambiguously. The term regained importance through its republication in Europe in Documenta X (1997) and especially in the American work of Edward W. Soja (1996) and Derek Gregory (1994). I use Foucault's heterotopia as enclosed space in contrast to modernity and urban utopia, and finally relate the idea to the rhizome, to which it shows some resemblance. The connection between Deleuze/Guattari and Foucault is not much of a stretch, since they worked together in 1972 at the Cerfi (Centre d'Etudes de Recherche et de Formation Industrielle). There are countless relations of both difference and resemblance between the authors. The term has become increasingly problematic in the West, but in Tokyo it still appears useful (for now). The similarity of both Tokyo's and Yokohama's waterfronts with the urban utopia is of great importance to my context.

Utopias are sites with no real place. Utopias present society itself in a perfected form, or otherwise a society turned upside-down. Heterotopias, like utopias, are to be found in all cultures. In primitive cultures they acquire the characteristics of a 'crisis' heterotopia, privileged or sacred places reserved for individuals in a state of crisis; adolescents, menstruating women, pregnant women, the elderly. They have all but disappeared in Western society. Foucault cites the example of the boarding school in its 19th century form, or of military service for young men. Their place was increasingly taken over by the heterotopias of deviation, the psychiatric hospitals and prisons, institutions that he analyzed in *Discipline and Punish*. Daniel Defert, who gives a description of the use of the term by critics and architects, emphasizes its *monadic* nature, the Leibnizian dimension of the heterotopias; each formally complete and referring to all the others.[11]

Foucault cites the same examples I use here: the cemetery, the brothel, and the garden. Sanshiro Pond is such a garden 'onto which the whole world comes to enact its

→   Heterotopia, Tokyo, Sanshiro Pond at Tokyo
     University, Hongo
↓   Heterotopia, Tokyo cemetery

symbolic perfection' (Foucault). The Yoshiwara also meets this description: it is 'one of those famous brothels of which we are now deprived' (Foucault). A characteristic of heterotopias is that they are not freely accessible, unlike a public space. A number of these spaces are wholly devoted to activities of purification, partly religious and partly hygienic, such as the hamman of the Moslems and the Japanese Public Baths, the Sen-toh, associated with the *Mizu wo abiru*, purification by means of the bath. Another example is the brothel, as mentioned above. At the time of Edo the pleasure quarters were central to the Edo culture. Nagai Kafū considered the new Tokyo to be above all a loss in comparison with the old Edo. Seidensticker regards his books as essentially nostalgic and elegiac. The Edo culture in the Kabuki theater and the pleasure quarters in which Kabuki's roots lie had a theatrical aspect, a favorite subject of Nagai's. The Yoshiwara was above all a brothel, but it was also more than that: it was also a theater, a sanctuary, and an inversion of the social hierarchies held in place by the Tokugawa Shogunate (1603-1867). The pleasure quarters were culture centers, according to Seidensticker.

That is undoubtedly what the visitors perceive; samurai, artists, rich merchants and kabuki-players. To the women it looked quite different. Prostitutes were often sold as children and imprisoned behind the great gate, the Omon. The mortality rate was high, and those who died were disposed of in a mass grave near the Jokanji temple. The temple primarily became known as a 'dump'-temple, the Nagekomidera. Behind their pristine facades, these sakaribas have nothing to do with Seidensticker's and Hidenobu's culture, but with power and exploitation. The most important reason to centralize prostitution in a single place was of course the possibility for surveillance, which the Shogunate could then optimize. The night-time compartmentalization of the city — traffic was forbidden at night beyond the quarters — served the same purpose. These places are comparable to execution sites, which in both Tokyo and Amsterdam were isolated from the residential districts. Amsterdam's Galgenveld (Hangman's Field) and Tokyo's Kotsukappara execution grounds resembled each other in this sense.

Analogous to Amsterdam, Edo was also known as the Venice of Japan. The best way to visit the Yoshiwara was by boat, for Foucault a heterotopia par excellence, a floating piece of space. The pleasure quarters were licensed quarters: they had an official status, were relatively isolated, and were certainly not accessible to all. The water has now disappeared from the Low City, and the older pleasure quarters have ceased to exist. In the 1930s there were still about six licensed quarters left, all within the city area. Alongside them were the unlicensed quarters, the 'dens of unlicensed whores' (Nagai), (the *shishōkutsu*, of which the most famous lay outside the city.) Tamanoi quarter was one: in 1932 it had already been incorporated in the urban pattern, when the city annexed a large number of surrounding wards. Kameido lay more to the south, contrary to Tamanoi that lay to the north-east. Tamanoi had about six hundred prostitutes, Kameido some seven hundred.[12] The Kabukichō Shinjuku quarter was one of the six licensed quarters; nowadays it is a sakariba that exhibits the greatest similarity with the Wallen in Amsterdam or 42nd Street in Manhattan. (The latter is already being revitalized in the gigantic Times Square redevelopment project.)

The brothels have returned in a new form, strongly westernized, but also very Japanese. The present 'love hotels' in Kabukichō have very little in common with the Yoshiwara, which was devastated during the last year of the war. The rooms in the love hotels can be rented by the hour, and a prostitute is normally picked up in a bar elsewhere. The love hotels seem to have their origins in the inns that appeared after the Second World War. They are sometimes called *doyagai*, a cheap place to spend the night. *Doya* is also used, a word that closest approaches a 'flophouse', a phenomenon I shall discuss in detail in the next chapter in connection with New York's homeless. Doya is a transformation of the more

A 1716 Map of Yoshiwara

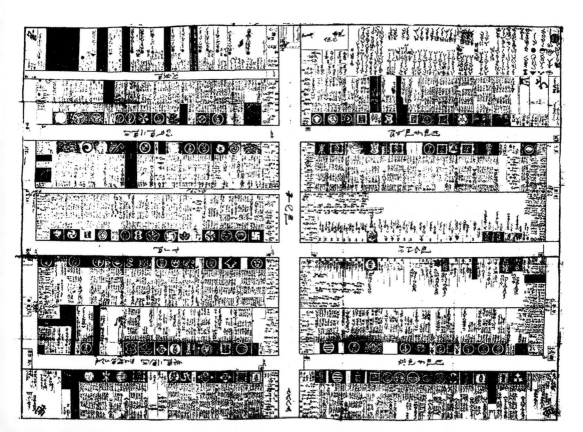

regular *yado* (tavern, inn); doyagai refers to the cheap laborer's quarters, a theme I will deal with at the end of this chapter in relation to Tsukiji. They also seem to be comparable with regard to their use, since in both Tokyo and New York they have rooms for a number of persons. The prices are relatively low, and the facilities are far from perfect and always collective. Some of the hotels were of a 'dubious' (*aimai*) nature; they were also called 'upside-down jellyfish', an analogy with the steam baths that were in use there. A more recent variant is the present 'soapland', a politically correct name for the former Turkish baths that could no longer be so called following protest from the Turks. The Japanese dream up the most exotic names for their brothels. As is the case in Amsterdam's red-light area many references are in English (everything that is 'blue' in English is 'pink' in Japanese). 'Peep shows' would seem to be a part of the globalization of the sex industry, but 'pantyless tea-rooms' will always remain something uniquely Japanese. The same is true for the call boxes where the ladies leave their telephone number on their visiting card. In Amsterdam or New York they would disappear within the hour, but in Tokyo everyone leaves them untouched. When the stock of cards is depleted they are meticulously replenished. The Yoshiwara was an open and social space demarcated within the city, but the present love hotel certainly is not. People went to the Yoshiwara to meet their equals, but in a love hotel people prefer to remain anonymous. The 'artistic quality' of today's prostitutes consists of listening and in particular confirming the customer's difficulties with his work and family.

After the war Tamanoi changed from a public into a private quarter, and the geishas were free to come and go as they pleased. In this period the women founded their own clinic for venereal diseases. They already had their own trade union at the time; something that only now, at the end of the 1990s, is happening in Amsterdam (the *Rode Draad*). A striking feature is how these heterotopias are related to urban life in Tokyo. The isolation that Foucault found to be so characteristic still exists, but now at the level of a couple of hotels, or a small cemetery, or a garden in the middle of the city. They seem to have shrunk to a smaller scale: the various *meishos* of Tokyo's Sugoroku board are small-distributed *heterotopias* that remain relatively isolated from other social life. To a certain extent that is also true for Tokyo as a whole. Although the doors to the West are open the inhabitants are certainly not ready for the pluralism of Amsterdam or New York. Everything that goes on in Kabukichō remains hidden to us. A

Edo Yoshiwara Courtesans wearing Shiromuku Kimono on the first day of the eighth month, painted by Utagawa Kunisada

Japanese guide is needed to be able to understand something of it. This closed nature makes Tokyo an insular city. In contrast with the rhizome which above all owes its productivity to the *connections* between dissimilar elements, the very pattern of the distributed heterotopias is *unconnected*. The Japanese city has neither the pattern of the European city nor a completed grid characteristic of a number of American and Chinese cities; it is mostly partial. The city is particularly regarded as 'additive texture', in which preference is given to the parts (or episodes) in a network of independent places.[13] This specific heterotopic nature seems to be found in other places. Sanshiro Pond is an example of such a place, but the many restaurants, bars and coffee shops are just as many contemporary heterotopias. In Europe social life still revolves largely around the street. I would think that Amsterdam's Old City is a good example of this kind of life. In Tokyo this social life has largely been transferred to the restaurants, bars and coffee shops located high in a building. Edo's Yoshiwara could only be visited on foot or by boat, and at present Amsterdam's red-light area is only visited on foot. A bar or love hotel in Tokyo is rarely situated on the ground floor. It is first necessary to take the step of getting into an elevator, or finding the way in the basement to reach the bar or restaurant. Heterotopia may be associated with the ground floor level, but much is above or behind it, and sometimes below it, and far removed from any daylight. The ground floor is increasingly occupied by the stores, the McDonald's and the sushi bars. The ground floor in those wards in which the economic pressures on the real estate market is the greatest has become, in spite of those pressures, nothing more than circulation room. In this it differs greatly from the rhizomatic space of Amsterdam's Old City. It is increasingly becoming a passage to that which lies behind or above it. The resemblance with a city like New York is continually increasing. In spite of its grid Manhattan is also the sum of discontinuous places, connected by flows of traffic and the subway. This fragmentation is generally favorably received in both Tokyo and Manhattan. For each fragment is designed with such care as to attract the observer's eye away from the dereliction of the space of the inbetween. M. Christine Boyer similarly views New York City as a chaotic composition and incongruous collation of city elements.[14] As in Tokyo the public space is subject to 'scenographic arrangements' that increasingly resemble each other. But this uniformity is most pronounced in the plans for new residential areas, and for business accommodation. This is where the nondescript *homotopias* arise, in which Tokyo's present complexity is definitely banished to the past. These homotopias, or invented environments, are not only in contrast with the heterotopias; they also reveal a difference in *thoughts* about *space*. Heterotopias are conceptualizations of spatiality that challenge the conventional modes of spatial homotopia. They are meant to detonate, to deconstruct, not to be poured back comfortably in the old containers, according to Soja. He considers them to be a necessary first step en route to what he calls *Thirdspace*, an inhabited space of radical openness and unlimited scope in which all histories and geographies, all times and places are immanently presented and represented, a strategic space of power and domination, empowerment and resistance.[15]

←← Call box
← Call box cards

Tokyo **Tokyo, the city**

The question is whether his *Thirdspace* is in agreement with the term *heterotopia* as I use it here. I don't believe that it is. Foucault's heterotopia can accommodate a world of difference in one and the same place, usually associated with different units of time. Museums and libraries have become heterotopias in which time never stops accumulating, according to Foucault. That is a similarity between the rhizome and heterotopia. Both in Amsterdam's Old City and in Tokyo's Meisho, history is accumulated in one and the same place. However Foucault's heterotopia is a system that *isolates*; a heterotopia, unlike a public space, is not freely accessible. Conversely a rhizome exists by virtue of an infinite number of *connections*, open, porous, reinforcing each other. Power and resistance play an important role in both the rhizome and heterotopia. In this sense the rhizome resembles *Thirdspace*, but not with the heterotopia that I consider to be much more characteristic of Tokyo, and not for Amsterdam, where Soja's *Thirdspace* is indeed much more in place as he suggests in 'Off Spuistraat', a comparison between Amsterdam and Los Angeles.

Economic growth and the Bay Project

As a result of the rapid growth of the Japanese economy in the 1960s the Japanese business community became concentrated, particularly in Tokyo. Despite the territorial dispersion of present economic activity the top-level control management of the industry is concentrated in Chiyoda (Marunouchi), Chūō (Ginza and Nihombashi), Minato (Roppongi and Akasaka) and more recently Shinjuku. Together with Shibuya and Ikebukuro, Shinjuku has become a sub-center (*fukutoshin*). Only after the earthquake of 1923 did it gain new opportunities to develop. Shinjuku station was built in 1885, on the Shinagawa Line. Ginza, Shinjuku, Ueno, Asakusa, Shibuya, Ningyō-chō and Kagurazaka are mentioned in a 1923 summary of Tokyo's sakariba's. Nowadays the last two no longer belong in this list. Ikebukuro and Roppongi have now taken their place as new entertainment centers.[16] At present Shibuya is one of the most popular and fashionable entertainment centers, close-knit and very busy. The station is a place of great significance for the residents of Tokyo. Appointments are made to meet each other under the statue of Hachikō the faithful dog that died in March 1935, where every evening he came to meet his owner at the station. After his owner died the dog continued to come to meet him, and no one could convince him that this would never happen again. A statute of Hachikō was erected in front of the station about a year before the dog died. It is now a place where the young meet each other, a place of significance with a story to tell. Whether or not the story is true (in other versions it is said that the dog always hung around the station) it is something that is becoming rare in today's Tokyo with its large-scale urban developments. The development of Shinjuku was tackled in this fashion in 1960, with the construction of a plaza of 49,000 square yards both above and below ground, and with a new street profile, parking spaces, etc. In 1964 a new floor-area ratio (far) was introduced in order to limit the detrimental effects caused by the abolition of building restrictions on the heights of buildings, which resulted in many buildings being deprived of sunlight. The economy continued to grow and the demand for offices increased. In 1982 the present multi-core structure

→   Shibuya
→→ Shinjuku

was adopted, with the intention of decentralizing administrative tasks. However the concentration of labor and capital in the metropolitan area was much greater than had been anticipated. Some industry withdrew from the city and the resultant vacant space was taken over by high-rise buildings. This ultimately resulted in one gigantic metropolitan area. The extremely high densities evident in these commercial districts constitute a spatial expression of our present economic language. The spatial answer to this congestion came, in particular, from the Japanese Metabolists. In 1961,

Tange Kenzo presented his design for Tokyo Bay, a large-scale plan in the bay comprised of a complex structure of superhighways to which residential areas were attached. Tafuri compares it with Tange's project for Boston that he drew up in conjunction with students from the MIT. In 1959 he was a guest at the last CIAM meeting in Otterlo. At this meeting he presented his Tokyo City Hall and Kagawa's Prefectural Office. He also showed a project of Kikutake Kiyonori's that had never been realized, which consisted of cylindrical residential towers in combination with floating platforms in the sea for heavy industry. Tange left Otterlo the day before the definitive end of the CIAM, as he had to go to the MIT. As a result he was the first to announce its closure (he had a telegram in his pocket) to Walter Gropius and Sigfried Giedion. Kikutake's plan played an important role in the assignment he presented to the students at MIT, a plan for the Bay of Boston for 25,000 inhabitants. In this assignment the residential areas were planned not on land but in the water, as in the later Tokyo Bay project.

Tange proposed with his Tokyo Bay project a decisive alternative to the official plan of 1956 for the Tokyo region which evidenced obvious affiliations with the Greater London plan designed by Abercrombie and Forshaw. Tange's argument was leveled against what he saw as an equalizing and reductionist tradition of planning that denied the promise of a city center through the dispersal of such centrality into peripheral satellite towns.[17] Tafuri links Tange's proposals to those of the English Archigram Team of Peter Cook, Ron Herron, Dennis Crompton and Michael Webb, for the Plug-In City from 1964 and Herron's later Walking City, a bestial macrostructure capable of both hovering motion and telescopic displacement. Since these lacked every socio-economic analysis, Tafuri considered Archigram to be nothing more than *graphic divertissement*, an *ironic nostalgia for the future*. It was the time of 'an academy of the utopian' that was then especially popular in architectural education. The resistance to the unimaginative bureaucratic planners resulted in a particularly graphical design that paid no attention to the rationale of a large-scale scheme, the local complexity or long-term planning. This is an assign-

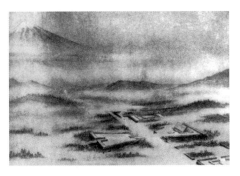

↑ Tange's entry to the Greater East Asia
  Co-prosperity Sphere, 1943
↑↑ Great Ise shrine
← Tange's Tokyo Bay Project, 1961
↘ Tokyo Bay, 1961

ment that was more successfully dealt with by OMA, as we saw in the previous chapter about Amsterdam. Tokyo Bay is a more final plan that hardly allows flexibility or conceptual changes in time. Tafuri rightly states that the plan exhibits great affinity with Le Corbusier's Obus Plan for Algiers, which was also a definitive plan that was revised several times by Le Corbusier because the socio-political context in Algiers was able to do nothing with it. However Tafuri's criticism is too one-sided, because Tange certainly did make a conscious attempt to integrate traditional Japanese culture in his plan. The form of the homes in the bay is more akin to a modern example of Hidenobu's ethnical continuity; the residential blocks are given a traditional form, but are executed in a contemporary manner.

Tange wrote a book about Ise, the most sacred of Shinto sanctuaries. He had played earlier with the idea of the shrine in a 'fascist' project of 1943, now detested by everyone. This was for the Greater East Asia Co-prosperity Sphere that was projected at the foot of Mount Fuji. He described his project as a representation of the

shrine of Ise combined with Michelangelo's reorganization of the Capitol in Rome, begun 1538. Though the Mount Fuji project won Tange first prize, it was never realized. Nor is it 'fascist', but at most an attempt to create something of classical sublime architecture. It was hopelessly monumental and quite suggestive of the Japanese wartime nationalism.[18] However it is striking that the theme of the Ise shrine resurfaces in the Bay. Ise is a holy place where Amaterasu, goddess of the Sun, is worshiped. Every twenty years the temple of Ise is completely destroyed in order that it may be rebuilt identically. This act of re-creation can be found in many primitive cultures; its basis lies in the belief that the act of creation isn't stagnant or absolute but must be perpetuated in action and continuous renewal. Such rituals necessitate that a class of carpentry artisans be maintained in order to preserve the ancient and arcane techniques of building. The site of Ise was once the destination of a pilgrimage

Tokyo **Economic growth and the Bay Project**

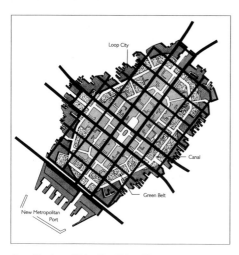

↑ Kurokawa Kisho, New Tokyo Plan, 2025, construction of the New Island in Tokyo Bay, proposal 5

↘ Kikutake Kiyonori, residential towers, 1958

that every Japanese was to undertake at least once in their lifetime. Yet the interior of the sanctuary was never entered for the pilgrimage was completed by visual proximity alone.[19]

Tange's homes exhibit some formal resemblance to Ise, although his roofs are curved like the Chinese. There may be continuity with the past, but everything is planned, drawn, designed. The ten million inhabitants seem to have found their definitive place. A development in time is rendered impossible. And that is very non-Japanese, and very much 1930s European Modernism. The temporary and the provisional in Japanese architecture are negated. As a result of the use of wood and paper whole neighborhoods were regularly consumed by fire; these were the *flowers of Edo*, which in spite of everything were appreciated as an event worth a visit. Houses were taken apart and rebuilt elsewhere; earthquakes ravaged Japanese cities. Shintoism and Buddhism emphasize the relativity of life, all is temporary and relative. But in the Bay Project everything is permanent in a trivial copy of the urbanism of the 1930s. Japanese architecture is 'floating on a sea of signs' and is less tailored to historical continuity and stability than is Western architecture.[20] Tange's implicit model is *utopia*, not heterotopia. The decision as to what should and should not be specified was decided to the advantage of a concrete utopia, rendering the plan analogous to the Obus Plan for Algiers. Tange's entreaty for stability within an apparently chaotic structure, though polemically disguised, can be easily read as a modernist appeal towards control through rationalization of highly populated urban areas. Equally however it contradicts such utopian strategies through its complicity with traditional Japanese city planning tactics such as those found in Kyoto (as opposed to Edo or Tokyo).

In Tokyo an orthogonal grid of infrastructure is overlaid upon the entire bay area, while at its center megastructures find their objective identities. Bordering, and set perpendicular to, the road system are the notable dwelling units conceived upon the shrine typology borrowed from the WHO scheme. This residential diagram based on the model of Ch'ang-an (Sian), China, thus imitates the plan repeatedly articulated in ancient Japanese capitals.[21] Ch'ang-an had the same pattern as the Western forti-

fied city, a regular grid of roads from east to west and north to south that was enclosed by fortifications. Actually there is no city in Japan with such a pattern; the layout is always comprised of a hybrid mixture of different patterns, of which the grid is just one. Although Tange recognizes the changing dynamism of Tokyo's real estate market the answer remains just as utopian as that of the Modernists. Kurokawa Kisho's new Tokyo Plan 2025 is of the same order; it consists of a gigantic island in Tokyo Bay. Kurokawa incorporates just about all of Japan in his plan; the island is plan 5 from a series of 12. His concentric city is the prototype of all utopian cities, and, in fact, runs contrary to his own notion of heterogeneity.[22]

In recent years Tange has done little else than construct enormous projects, of which the latest are in Tokyo's Waterfront Subcenter, the Tokyo Teleport Town. Both the Fuji Television Building and the Tokyo Fashion Town Building are the work of his firm. Both buildings are located in the new land reclamation area of Ariake, district 13. The first plan for this area consists of a landfill about 4 miles south of central Tokyo, and

Tokyo **Economic growth and the Bay Project**

dates from 1987. Since the end of 1989 and the burst of the 'bubble' economy the demand for office space has decreased dramatically. Moreover the 1996 Expo, which was precisely what was needed to vitalize the plan, failed to take place. In 1996 the Tokyo Metropolitan Government presented a revised plan. The budget has been cut back, and every five years every aspect of the plan will be subject to review. Although the *Japan Architect Yearbook* still describes the area as a 'lively environment' there is virtually no one to be seen. It is just one more desolate enclave, unassailable for pedestrians, and totally without character. Tange's stairs in his Fuji Building don't seem intended for pedestrians, and it is certainly impossible to imagine a dog waiting for his owner here. The whole area is strung together by the Yurikamome Line, the 7.5 mile elevated railroad connecting the Subcenter to the existing subway and train lines. The Yurikamome passes over the Rainbow Bridge and makes a loop through the area. The total system is reminiscent of the lines in amusement parks, such as Singapore's Sentosa, although these are on a smaller scale. It is also a residential area, with high-rise housing and stores in the Daiba area. Daiba Seaside Park is intended for residential complexes. It houses an elementary school and a secondary school, and a supermarket stocks the day-to-day necessities. Daniel Buren's *Twenty Five Porticos* rises from the inside area to the waterfront. Recently the Decks Tokyo Beach was opened, which is comprised of restaurants, bars, stores and the unavoidable amusement park. A bay-side walkway, the Waterfront Promenade, links the Daiba Seaside Park and the Nikko Hotel. Tange's Fuji Building

↑   Tange Kenzo, Fuji Television Building
←   Tange Kenzo, Fuji Television Building, stairs

stands in between. District 13 is an example of what Saskia Sassen calls a 'new form of locational concentration', which means not only concentration in the existing city, but also land reclamation projects such as Tokyo Teleport Town and Yokohama's Minato Mirai 21.

The increased mobility of capital brings about new forms of locational concentration, which are as much a part of this mobility as is geographic dispersal. According to Sassen they do not simply represent a persistence of older forms of agglomeration, but respond more to a new economic logic. The increase in land prices made it impossible to live in the commercial districts. Ten years ago one square foot of building ground in the Chiyoda Ward sold for about $4000, while developed property in Chuo went in the range of $13,000 per square foot. Prices were somewhat lower in Yokohama, but the difference was not that great. The Japanese government recognized the problem of the one-sided development and initiated new residential projects in these areas in order to prevent them being completely deserted at night-time. However residence in these wards has become considerably more expensive during the past decades. At present Roppongi, Aoyama and Akasaka closely resemble parts of New York and London. The gigantic Ark Hills redevelopment project (*Akasaka Roppongi Kaihatsu*, by Mori Taikichiro) which straddles the border between Akasaka and Roppongi consists of a series of skyscrapers containing the very latest communications and information technology. It has swept away complete hills and has eradicated all local residential forms in the area. Most Japanese cannot afford to live here. Most commute between home and work, usually a journey of an hour or more.

Narita Airport is about 40 miles from the city. For most Japanese this has become an acceptable distance from their home, located far outside the Tokyo wards. They cannot afford even the tiniest apartment in the city. The per capita floor space in the USA is twice that in Japan (USA 540 sq. ft., Japan 270 sq. ft. per capita dwelling floor space). In Tokyo the cost of a home is 12.9 times a person's annual income, in comparison to 2.9 in New York.[23] Usually about 20% of the income is devoted to residential

Akasaka Roppongi Kaihatsu, Ark Hills,
by Mori Taikichiro

Tokyo

Taito Ward

expenses, but the percentage is much greater in these areas. Cheaper homes are increasingly to be found far from the commercial districts. There are already mortgages on the market with a term of 99 years, so that whole generations are committed to their house. The picture that has continued to take shape over the past few years is exemplified in New York where increasing poverty and vagrancy (principally amongst the elderly who have been displaced by gentrification) becomes increasingly prominent when seen in contrast to the advent of stylish residential and conspicuous commercial development.[24] This is a theme that I shall discuss in the following chapter. Sassen shows that the poorest areas do not lie at the edge of the city, but adjoin the central business district. Arakawa, Taito and Sumida which border directly on the CBD are extremely impoverished. The demise of traditional manufacturing is the reason for the decline of Arakawa and Sumida. Taito, which is part of the old Asakusa Ward, had housed higher concentrations of the poor and those with lower incomes for a much longer period of time. The different areas are relatively autonomous – for example each has its own closing times for the stores – so that a kind of complex patchwork or mosaic is created. In spatial terms this is the opposite of Amsterdam, which fans out around the Old City to the ring of canals and the 19th and 20th century residential neighborhoods beyond. It is precisely because Tokyo is a city with many cores and without a 'city center' that most visitors regard it as a turmoil of cars and chaotic buildings.

Yokohama, urban planning during Meiji

About 140 years ago the Edo government decided to open Japan to Westerners. Until then Japan had been isolated (*sakoku*, closed door). Yokohama was a small fishing village. The history of Yokohama as a metropolis began with the opening of the port in 1859. Many of the new areas of the city, particularly its center, were situated on land that had been reclaimed in the Edo period after the port had been opened. The port was the result of a treaty between Japan and the United States, together with a number of other countries such as the UK, Russia, France, and the Netherlands. There was a great need for a new port, but it was almost impossible to reach agreement as to where it was to be located. The USA and her allies chose Kanagawa, but the Japanese Tokugawa Shogunate decided otherwise. Yokohama was awarded the port. However the real motive behind this decision was the Shogunate's fears of possible turmoil that might arise as a result of the presence of foreigners living on Kanagawa's Tokaido Road during times of domestic unrest. Another reason for opening the port in Yokohama was its topography, which consists of hills and the Bay of Tokyo. This topography had the same advantages in isolating the foreign community as that of Dejima in Nagasaki. The construction of the new port proceeded at a steady pace. The inhabitants of Yokohama village were all evacuated to Motomura while a customs house, two harbors and a checkpoint for trading goods were constructed.

The new port was divided into foreign and Japanese settlements. Both gradually came to prosper following the influx of merchants. Countries trading with Japan wanted an improved port, so the *Third Estate Regulation* came into force in 1866. Two years after that, the basis of the present Kannai district was in fact formed. Political swings had hardly any influence on the development of Yokohama. The transition from the Tokugawa Shogunate to the Meiji Restoration (*ishin*, which really means *revitalization* rather than *restoration*, although the latter term is always used) in 1868 passed unnoticed. The reason for this was the presence of foreign armies under the command of a British minister stationed in Yokohama. In fact the Meiji government continued the politics of the

Shogunate. Based on the slogan 'rich country; strong army' (*fukoku kyohei*) and a productive industrial policy, the Meiji government made aggressive attempts to introduce modern technology from the West. Yokohama was receptive to Western industrial influence on the principle of 'Japanese spirit to Western knowledge' (*Wakon yosai*). The port was greatly improved in the years between 1889 and 1902. The development of capitalism resulted in a rapid increase in the city's population, which flourished with its trade. The abolition of the foreign settlement under a revised treaty of 1900 further accelerated its development.

The fourth mayor of Yokohama, Morihiro Ichihara, introduced the *Future Urban Facilities*. This was a first form of integral city planning, which gave more room to the manufacturing industry. Ascendancy of the (rural) citizenry was enforced both in their homes and (industrial) workplaces by heightening the authority of the prefects, the dominion of the police as well as that of the supervisory warrant of landlord and business proprietors. Although freedom of religion had been granted under the Constitution, freedom of expression was little tolerated during the Meiji period. In spite of all restrictions, intellectual criticism could not be silenced and the concerns of the people were voiced with some semblance of a liberated society. Issues of political corruption, bureaucratic inflexibility, moral degeneration, and the rise of a society that based its values on material accumulation were rigorously scrutinized.[25] In 1918 Japan's first modern city planning act, the *Tokyo City District Improvement*

Act, was applied to Yokohama during the Taisho (1912-1926). After the great fire that broke out in the next year Yokohama began its city district improvement program in 1920. The emphasis was placed on road expansion in the area most affected by the disaster. This program was completed in 1922. However the improvement program on its own wasn't sufficient to deal with the industrialization and urbanization that accompanied the rapid growth of industrial capital following the First World War. *The City Planning Act* and the *Urban Buildings Act* were passed in 1919. In the next year, 1920, Yokohama announced *The General Principles for the Construction of Greater Yokohama* and it established its basic city planning policy. In 1921, a City Planning District was set up to this end and in 1923 land use zones were established to designate the various commercial, industrial and residential zones. The various districts acquired a more clear-cut form. Matomachi, Isezakaki-chō and Hancho-dori each acquired their own characteristic nature.

However, the major Kanto earthquake of 1923 (7.9 on the Richter scale) devastated a large part of Yokohama and Tokyo. This was one of the worst natural disasters in recorded history. There had been earthquakes earlier, in 1855 and 1894, but this surpassed everything. Even the seismographic equipment was unable to withstand the shock, and only that of Tokyo Imperial University was able to register the series of shocks in the days that followed. Nearly 100,000 people lost their lives, and some 2 million were made homeless. The first shock came when the midday meal was being prepared, mostly on open charcoal braziers (*hibachi*), so the conflagration that followed was instantaneous and devastating. At least, this is the explanation that is usually given. Seidensticker provides another: chemicals have been identified as the major cause, followed by electricity cables and burners. This suggests that the earthquake would have been equally disastrous at any time of the day. The earthquake of 1855 took place in the middle of the night, but the results were similar. It, too, devastated a major part of the Low City. The firestorm and the tidal wave that followed the earthquake utterly destroyed most of Yokohama and much of central Tokyo. On the first and second of September most of Tokyo's Low City was engulfed in the flames. At first Shitamachi had appeared to have survived the shocks, but the fire that followed destroyed it. Just one ward in the High City escaped the flames. The fire reduced immense areas of the city to cinders and rubble while the death toll of victims either consumed by flames or asphyxiated by smoke and debris was incalculable.

↑ Kanto earthquake of 1923
→ Occupying army at Yokohama

Financial markets in Japan and around the world subsequently witnessed an economic backlash which was most profoundly and consistently felt in the London insurance and underwriting markets. Relief efforts found worldwide contributors with exceptional beneficence offered by the United States, while the Japanese government offered support to both individuals and businesses by making recovery funds available through local financial institutions.[26] Although the reconstruction of Yokohama was tackled with a great deal of energy the clock had been put back many years. The Government set up the *Tokyo Rehabilitation Committee*, and its *Rehabilitation Plan* was enlarged to include Yokohama at the city's request. Under this new plan Yokohama was to be provided with an enlarged port, the city was to be expanded, and the streets would be given a new layout. Ultimately the section concerning the port was dropped, and the development of the city restricted to a minimum.

History repeated itself during the Second World War. As a result of American bombardments about 42% of the city was destroyed by fire. The Japanese defense system could do little against the American bombing. In Tokyo the entire Low City went up in flames. It was the dry season, and the strong winds fanned the fires caused by the incendiary bombs. The industry along the Sumida River was distributed amongst residential neighborhoods, so it was impossible to separate military from civilian targets. Moreover, everyone had remained at their station; no one had left the city. The Kannon Temple in Asakusa had survived the earthquake, but was now destroyed in the fires. A little later the Zōjōji and the two Tokugawa temples were also destroyed. There were something like four thousand American raids in that last year of the war. In 1923 just one ward had escaped the earthquake, but now in 1945 not a single ward of the 35 excaped war damage. After the war the most important areas remained in the hands of the occupying army. Barracks were quickly built in the center of the devastated area, which later became the base for the American troops stationed in Yokohama. 90% of the port facilities were requisitioned. This severely impeded distribution, and as a result trading and banking facilities left the city.

Yokohama paid the price for Japanese participation in the Second World War. The implementation of the *War Reconstruction City Planning* hardly got off the ground. In 1952 the occupation was partially rescinded, and work could begin on the reconstruction plan. By now the number of inhabitants had increased to a level above that before the war. The

Tokyo **Yokohama, urban planning during Meiji**

infrastructure was hopelessly outdated in comparison with that of other cities. In fact it was the Korean War of 1950 that gave a new impulse to the economy; the manufacturing industry picked up speed, and American help was no longer required. However, the Korean War increased the chance that the occupation army would remain, and trading withdrew from the city. Post-war development was largely focused on heavy industry and petrochemicals. By 1955 the requisition orders had been lifted, and the reconstruction plans were finally put into action. Fireproof buildings were constructed in the central areas that had previously been requisitioned. Yokohama was on the road to recovery. But at the same time the status of the Port of Yokohama suffered as a result of the outflow of business to Tokyo, the decrease in the number of ships calling on the port, the development of aviation, and the poor container facilities. Conversely, the promotion of heavy and chemical industries which was supporting the country's period of rapid economic growth had a very favorable influence on Yokohama. As a result Yokohama's urbanization and industrialization proceeded even more rapidly, and the nature of Yokohama Port changed into that of an industrial port.[27] Top priority was given to the development plans for the Coastal Industrial Belt. The development of the Honmoku Pier and the industrial sites continued, whilst the Tsurumi Coastal Industrial Belt was expanded following the reclamation of the Daikoku area.

Yokohama: Minato Mirai 21

Yokohama is located some 12 to 25 miles south-west of Tokyo. With the highly-developed transportation network it takes only about half an hour to reach Central Tokyo from Yokohama. As a result of its proximity to Tokyo Yokohama's population and industry began to integrate with those of Tokyo after the war. In the 1960s Japan attempted to double incomes by reviving the economy. Tokyo merely increased in size, but Yokohama, which until shortly before had primarily been a dormitory town, grew very rapidly. The number of inhabitants had already grown to about 2.7 million by 1978, which in Japan made the city the second only to Tokyo in size. The problem was that the infrastructure had hopelessly failed to keep pace with the growth in population. Moreover the oil crisis of 1973 hadn't done the economy any good (in Japan this was called the 'oil shock'). The population grew rapidly in response to the increase in career opportunities offered by Tokyo, and people spread out to neighboring cities such as Yokohama. In the period 1960–1972 Yokohama gained an additional 80,000 to 100,000 inhabitants each year. The nature of the people moving into Yokohama indicated that it was becoming a dormitory town for those employed or studying in Tokyo. Before the Second World War Yokohama had formed an autonomous Metropolitan Region, centered around the Keihin Industrial Belt together with the Port and its industry. During these years there was a strong organic relationship between Tokyo and Yokohama. War damage and requisitioning caused Yokohama to stagnate in the years following the war. As a result of the outflow of commerce and industry to Tokyo, Yokohama increasingly became part of the Tokyo Metropolitan Region.

Yokohama's central business district grew along a pier on which the trading companies were located, the Kannai district. The growth in international trade and the industrialization resulted in the expansion of Kannai. The waterfront was soon occupied by port facilities, ship's wharves, transshipment storage and a railroad station. A new center was formed around the station following the increase in population in the 1960s and '70s and a drastic worldwide restructuring of the economy. This was also the time in which Yokohama's first Master Plan was drawn up, the *Six Major Projects* of 1969.[28] The center is located at the estuary, close to Kannai. The Yokohama station area was separated from Kannai by the Mitsubishi ship wharf. In 1965 the problem of the separated central business districts was recognized, and it was decided to reinforce the center of the city by developing a new central business district, to be sited between the two existing centers. Takashima-chō station is located further up the line from Yokohama Station on the Tokyu-Tokoyo railroad. The next stop is Sakuragi-chō station, a railroad that had existed since 1879 when the first rail link was built between Shimbashi, south of Ginza, and Sakuragi-chō in Yokohama. The old Shimbashi station disappeared in 1923. Entrance to the area is via the Minato Mirai Boulevard. A 'people mover' transports you to the Nippon-Maru Park and the Landmark Tower. This moving walkway is part of the Queen Mall pedestrian network. Furthermore, as everywhere in Tokyo and Yokohama, there is a subterranean connection (underpass) under the Sakuragi-Higashi Totsuka railroad to the bordering areas. The underpass must be completed in the year 2000. 30 million people live within a radius of 30 to 40 miles from Tokyo. That constitutes about a third of the entire population of Japan, all living and working in an area of about 4000 square miles in the Tokyo Capital Region.[29]

Virtually all important decisions affecting Japan are made in the center of Tokyo. Not only does this concentration result in the enormous

↗ Kannai district
↓ Yokohama 1998

prices for the land, it also explains Yokohama's great degree of dependency on the Region. The railroad is primarily focused on Tokyo. Of the six railroads connected directly to Tokyo no less than five feed into Yokohama Station, which has facilitated the growth of the surrounding area. These lines further Yokohama's role as a dormitory town for Tokyo, so they in fact weaken

Yokohama's independence.[30] It is little different with the energy supplies. Electricity is supplied to the entire area by The Tokyo Electric Power Co., a public utility. Gas is supplied by another public utility, The Tokyo Gas Company. To promote the distribution of the economic functions of the Region and to reduce the level of congestion it was proposed (at the end of the 1970s) that the business activities should be distributed. The idea of multiple cores was introduced in the *Third Master Plan for the National Capital Region.* This referred to a multi-core structure by the development of several core cities around Tokyo. Yokohama was expected to play an important role as the biggest core city. The development of a new central business district in Yokohama was to result in a move from old industrial areas, and the transfer of port facilities. In 1970 the Kanazawa land reclamation project was proposed, which would provide land for the relocation of industry that was to move from the old areas. Modernization also meant the construction of long container piers, the Daikoku and Honmoku piers.[31] In 1981 agreement was reached about the relocation of the ship's wharf belonging to Mitsubishi Heavy Industries, which was to move to the Kanazawa Reclamation District. The decision to relocate the wharf created increased opportunities for the city's development. The project was called *Minato Mirai 21* (Port of the Future). The Rincho period also began in 1981 (*Rinji-Gyosei Chosa-Kai*, the Provisional Commission for Administrative Reform), which constituted an improvement in the administrative system.[32] Since then the third Master Plan has been launched, the *Yumehama 2010* plan. Yume is Japanese for 'dream' and 2010 is, of course, the year in which the plan should be completed. This plan takes account of the by now drastically weakened economy.[33] *Minato Mirai* encompasses about 460 acres, of which about 270 are existing land and 290 reclaimed land.[34] The project was initiated with the aim of bringing capital to Yokohama, away from Tokyo.

Tokyo **Yokohama: Minato Mirai 21**

As already mentioned, to a certain extent Yokohama is a dormitory town for Tokyo. The ratio of the night-time to day-time population was 100 to 89, the lowest among ten major Japanese cities. Every day about 400 thousand people travel between home and work or school. The solution to this problem is obviously to strengthen Yokohama's own economy. Minato Mirai is to provide work for about 190,000 people. The project is comprised of hotels, a convention center, commercial centers, and centers for culture and amusement. The investments involved amount to about 24 billion us $ (as a comparison Battery Park City in New York was a landfill of 92 acres with development costs amounting to 4 billion us $). The project has been established in the form of a public-private partnership. Although the development of the infrastructure is being carried out by public sectors including the City authorities, the major facilities such as the convention center and the district's heating and cooling facilities are being constructed by what are known as 3rd Sector Companies, from both the public and private sectors. Even the subway planned for the district is to be financed in this manner. The line will be incredibly expensive

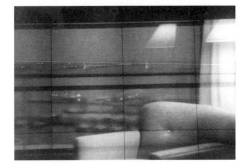

↑ Landmark Tower, Yokohama
↙ Takashima-cho station, Yokohama

because of the many tunnels under the bay. At present nothing more than an excavation site for the planned station is to be seen. These '3rd Sector' companies receive the necessary financial support from the authorities. The Japanese Development Bank grants them loans that are either inter-est-free or at a very low interest rate with a long-term spread. 75 billion yen has already been invested in the Convention Center, which is usually empty since the competition from Tokyo is very fierce. A large part of the MM21 project consists of parks as the waterfront is, of course, destined for parks and hotels. The stone docks and the brick warehouses have been restored, and now await a new purpose.

Tokyo **Yokohama: Minato Mirai 21**

The Tsukiji project

Tsukiji lies in the south-western part of Tokyo's Kyobashi, the former low city. At present it is the location of Japan's largest fish market. The market was originally located next to the Nihombashi Bridge, in the middle of the Low City. After the 1923 earthquake the fish market was moved to Tsukiji, first to a provisional site and then later to the definitive site once the present warehouses had been built. The market already seems small for Tokyo, and by Japanese standards the buildings have stood there for a long time. The fish market opens early, and most activity takes place before five in the morning. Almost all of Tokyo's (and Japan's) sushi and sashimi comes from this market. During the day there is much less activity, as the many sushi bars sell most of their produce in the morning. The fish market is not a tourist attraction as all sales are wholesale, to distributors and restaurants. Like the final location in the next chapter – Manhattan's Meat Market – this is a place where people are pleased to see the backs of their visitors.

The waterfront will undoubtedly be developed in the coming years. Like many other cities Tokyo will develop its Bay Area further, catching the wave of metropolitan development around the world, Tokyo will realize the potential to redevelop deserted city centers and obsolete industrial waterfront areas into sites of entertainment and recreation, hoping to capitalize on the discretionary spending income of the tourist and sightseeing market: a point that Boyer argues similarly.[35] Like many industrial markets they must turn their focus from the commodity of product based on utility and need to that of leisure time rooted in fantasy and desire. To avoid new a Ariake or Minato Mirai, we are submitting a different proposal for the development of the area. Although it is no longer present spatially, the area is rich in history. Nagai Kafū lived here; it was part of the water city of Tokyo. Tsukiji literally means 'built land' – and that is exactly what it is, reclaimed from Tokyo Bay after a major fire in 1657.[36] Today it is miles from Tokyo's port and the open sea, but in the days when the city breathed and sweated through its waterways, according to Paul Waley, Tsukiji was one of Tokyo's busiest and most exciting places. At the end of the 18th century this was where the feudal lords lived. The area even has a story associated with the Netherlands.[37] Historification inevitably ends in nostalgia. Minato Mirai's reproduction dock and the Nippon-maru, a clipper that once served as a training ship, are examples of this phenomenon. However, other approaches are also possible.

Tange Kenzo, Tsukiji Project

It would seem possible to develop part of the area on the principle of a *contemporary heterotopia* for Tokyo's day laborers. Day laborers, especially in construction, construction-related industries and longshoring, all major industries in Japan, are supposedly registered and entitled to unemployment compensation, according to Saskia Sassen. There are specific locations where jobs are listed and allocated by government employees who staff the various desks or counters, give workers their job slips, and write the information in the workers' carnets. These workers presumably can also write themselves into a waiting list for housing. The recent massive expansion of this category of workers has meant that a minority of them are actually covered by these regulations. Day labor has increasingly become a residual category, formed by those who were fired from other jobs, including white-collar workers, elderly men who no longer can work in the jobs they once held, and young men unable to get any other job. Sassen mentions four major hiring halls for day laborers in the country, two in the Tokyo-Yokohama area and one each in Nagoya and Osaka. The largest of these hiring halls is in the Taito ward in Tokyo. It has a reputation for being a rather dangerous place. The hiring halls are also frequently places for homeless men. Sassen's description of Kotobuki-chō in Yokohama is quite impressive and worth quoting at length.

On my first visit to one of these halls, Kotobuki-cho in Yokohama, we walked over at five in the morning. It was still dark. There was a gray concrete structure, the equivalent of four stories, with wide-open platforms at street level and one at the equivalent of two stories up, covered by a flat, slablike roof. It was a square structure with about 50 meters per side. Both on the street level and on the second-story platform on one of the enclosed sides were what looked like train station ticket counters, with long lines of men at each one. Through the ticket window I could see lists of jobs, with wages listed. At the other end of the platform were large groups of men, lying on the ground or just rising, clearly homeless, covered with tattered clothes, lying on dirty blankets, unshaven, unhealthy. An image of absolute misery. There were also young, neat men, among them many immigrants, and many older men standing in line. Amongst this vast and varied sea of men walked about twenty flashy, flamboyant men, arrogant and aggressive looking, with dark sunglasses notwithstanding the predawn darkness. They were the yakusa's. They acted in rather threatening ways toward me, encircling me. But I knew I was safe for a complicated set of reasons, not the least being that murder is still extremely rare even in the absolute bottom of the Japanese social structure. At about 8 a.m., the contractors have left with their hired laborers, and the large numbers that stay behind have nothing much to look forward to. They sit at the edges of the streets and talk, play various games. There is no place beneath this place. I visited some of the living quarters of those who had been left behind. You enter an old, minute version of a New York City tenement: a long very dark and narrow hallway, with an extremely low ceiling. There is an endless row of roughly made wooden doors. Behind each door is a cubicle the size of a narrow double bed and, at least in the ones I saw, a small window. Some of the quarters I visited were extremely neat, the occupant intent on salvaging as much as he could of his dignity.[38]

It is a place of no name, with no image to call it forth, she says. Our Tsukiji project is an architectural research into the possibilities of a new type of hiring hall with living accommodation for day laborers.

Tokyo:

Tsukiji project

hiring hall with living accomodation for day laborers, Tokyo

Architects **Diana Juranovic-Ishida, Toshikazu Ishida/KID** Conceptual Research & Development **Arie Graafland** Design team at Kyushu Institute of Design/Ishida Studio (cad preliminary studies, study models, site model, site research) **Toshikazu Ishida, Fumio Ohkubo, Kazutoshi Sakaguchi, Toyofumi Nakashima, Yasuhiro Yamada, Christian Ricart** 3D Graphics **Shuhei Nemuto** Model **Limited Editions, Rotterdam** Digital Assemblings **Arie Graafland, Hans Schouten and Bureau Piet Gerards** Model Photography **Photographic Department Faculty of Architecture, TU Delft, Hans Schouten**

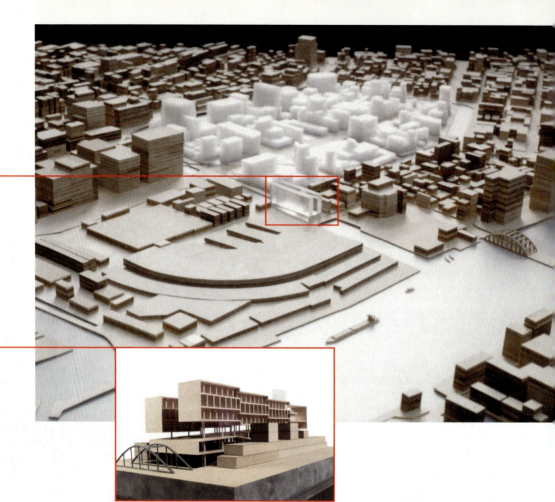

The space in which we live, which draws us out of ourselves, in which the erosion of our lives, our time and our history occurs, the space that claws and gnaws at us, is also, in itself, a heterogeneous space. In other words, we do not live in a kind of void, inside of which we could place individuals and things. We do not live inside a void that could be colored with diverse shades of light, we live inside a set of relations that delineates sites which are irreducible to one another and absolutely not superimposable on one another. (Michel Foucault)

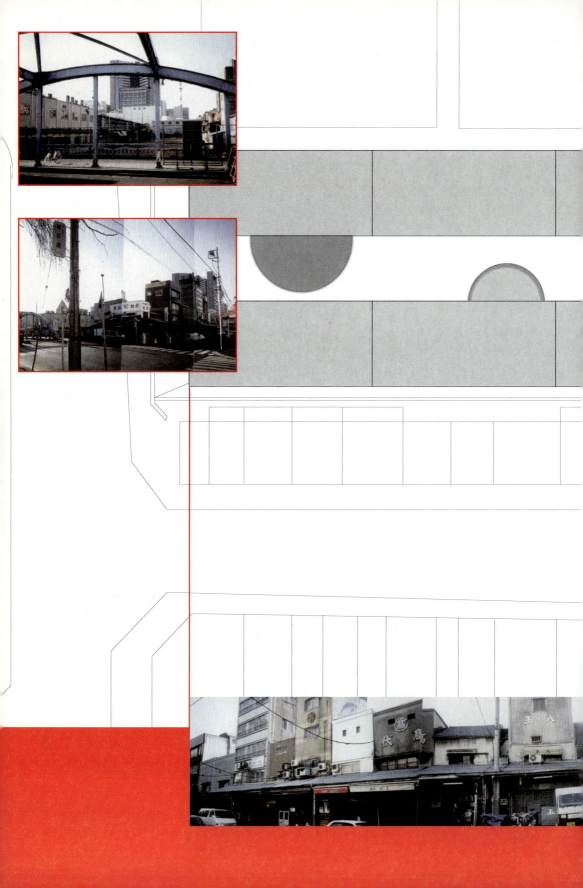

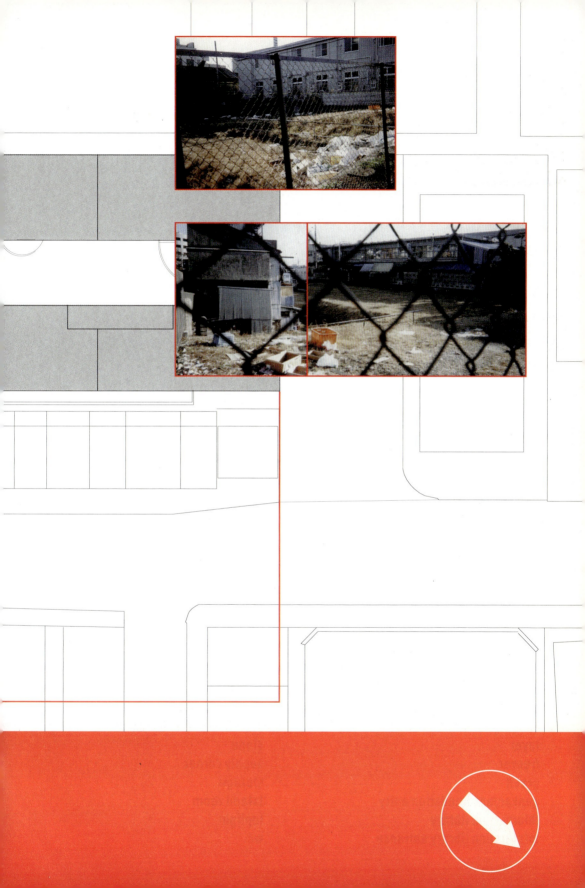

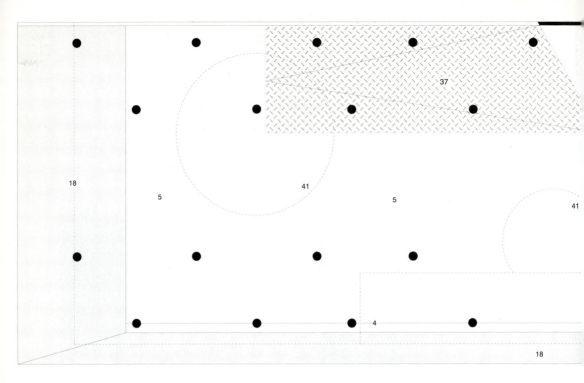

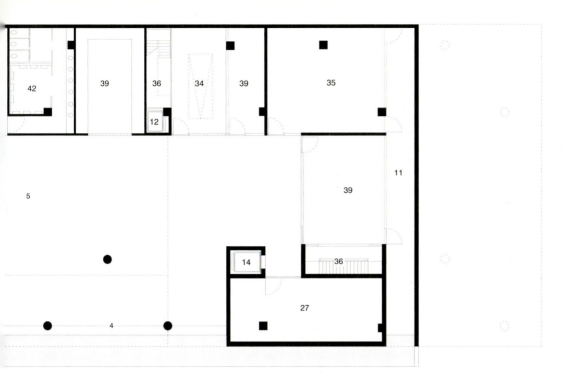

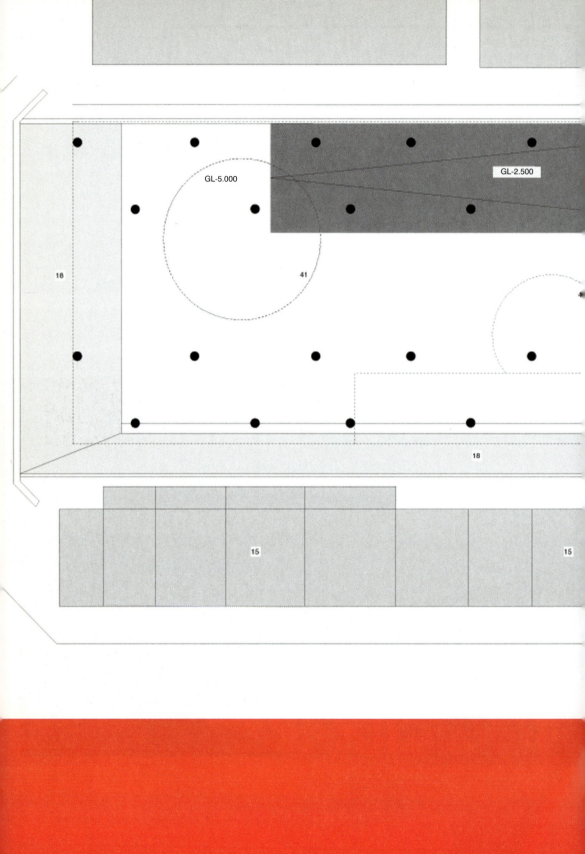

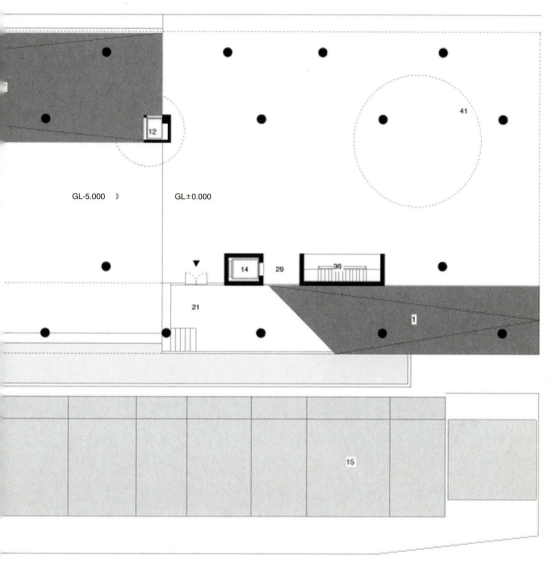

GL-5.000

GL±0.000

41

12

14   29   36

21   1

15

Plan 1F

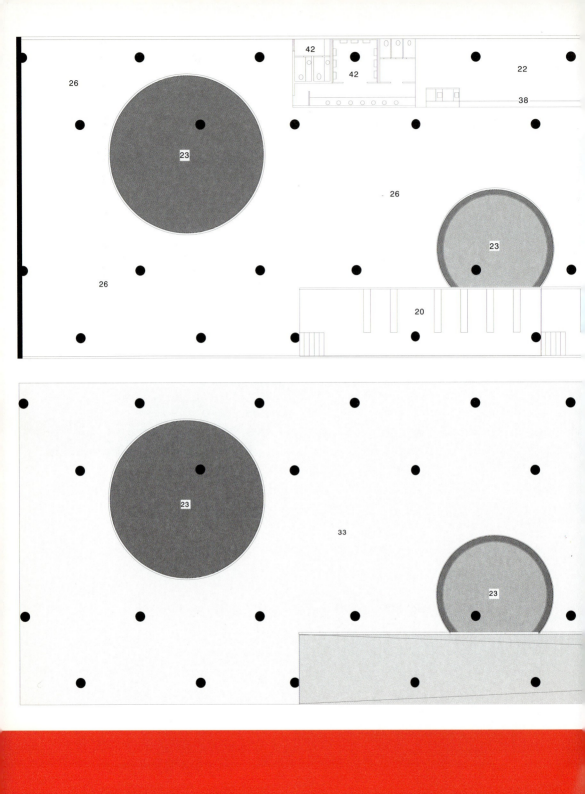

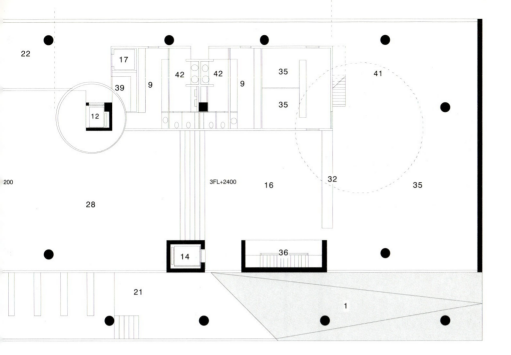

Plan 2F

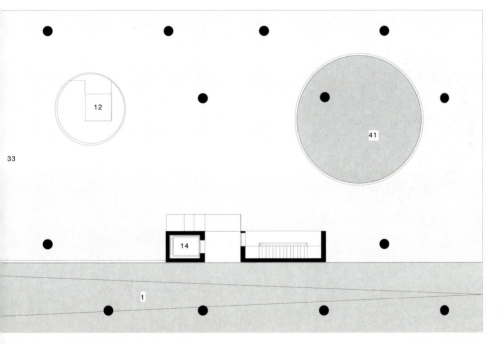

Plan 3F

Top plan numbers:

19	19	19	19
22	22	22	22

10

| 40 | 40 | 40 | 40 |

2

Middle plan:

2

| 40 | 40 | 40 | 40 |

| 22 | 22 | 22 | 22 |
| 19 | 19 | 19 | 19 |

10

Average dwelling space apartments 194 sq.ft. /18 m^2,

全国名産つけ物御問屋
株式会社 山本商店

鰹節・海産物
(株) 伊勢正

TEL 541-5551

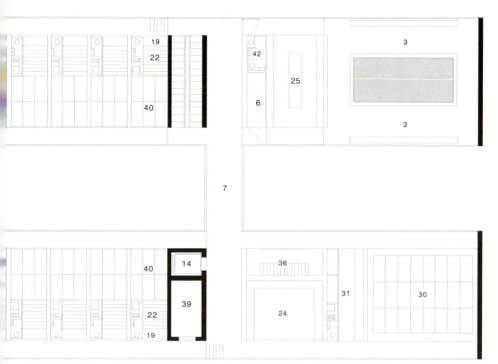

Plan 4F–6F

22 sq. ft. / 2 m² outside space

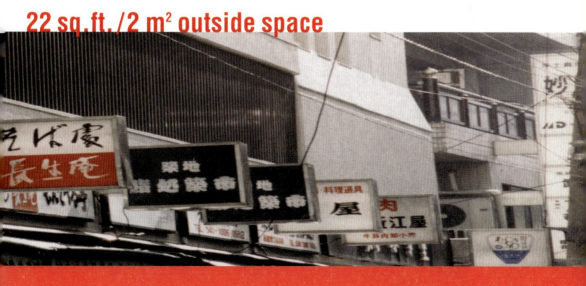

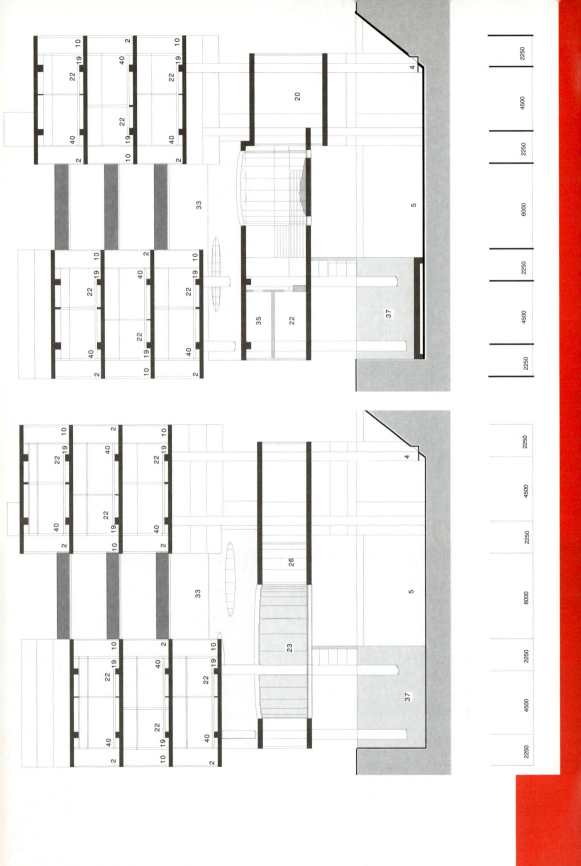

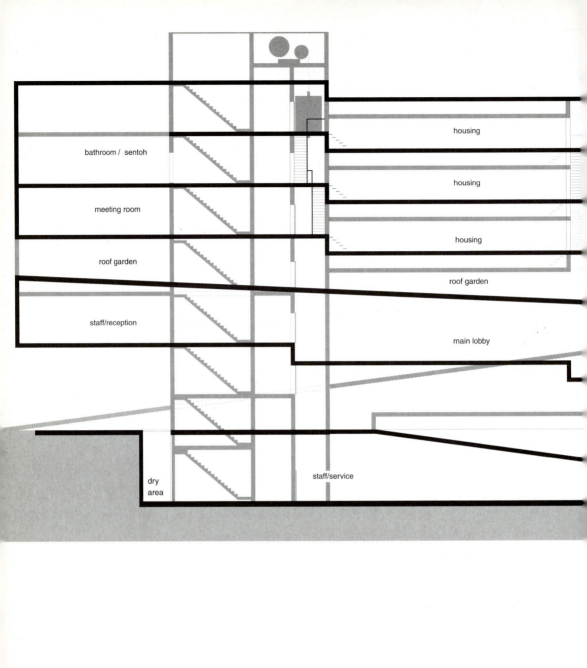

housing

bathroom / sentoh

housing

meeting room

housing

roof garden

roof garden

staff/reception

main lobby

dry
area

staff/service

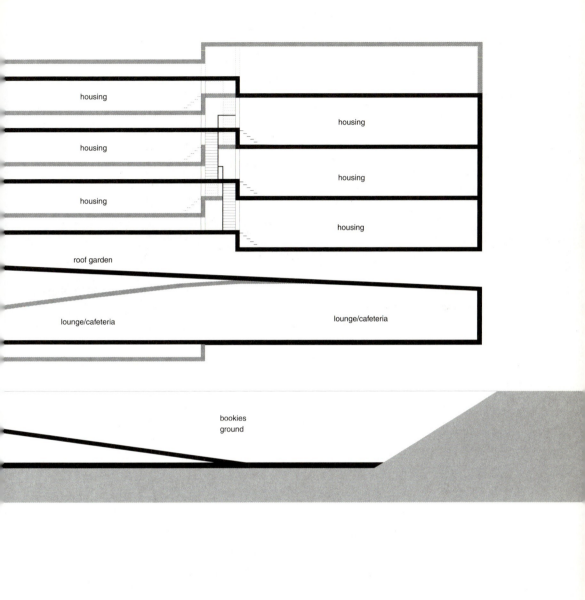

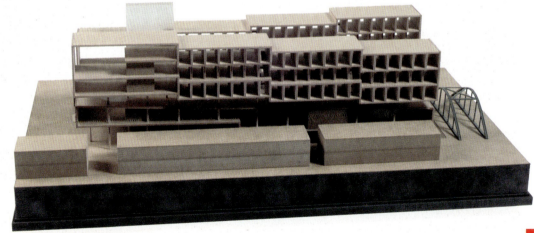

CITIES New York City

Lines of Flight in the City

He pushed up the window and leaned out. An L-train was rumbling past the end of the street. A whiff of coal smoke stung his nostrils. He hung out of the window a long while looking up and down the street. A world's second metropolis. In the brick houses and the dingy lamplight and the voices of a group of boys kidding and quarreling on the steps of a house opposite, in the regular firm tread of a policeman, he felt a marching like soldiers, like a side-wheeler going up the Hudson under the Palisades, like an election parade, through long streets towards something tall white full of colonnades and stately. Metropolis.

John Dos Passos, *Manhattan Transfer*

The homeless, shelters and the City

The eastern boundary of Manhattan is demarcated by the South Street Elevated Highway, which gives access to the Brooklyn Bridge. On one side lies the East River, on the other side the buildings of the financial heart of Manhattan, Wall Street. Countless photos of this part of Manhattan have been taken, but the view is still unbelievable: the towering buildings, and the river with its bridges to Brooklyn. Here the traffic is never still, but thunders ceaselessly to and from Manhattan Island.

If you cross South Street – for which you will need a total disregard for your safety – then on the opposite side of the street you arrive under the Elevated Highway. This area serves as a temporary shelter for continually changing numbers of homeless persons and for tramps. When you stand under the raised road, feeling a little lost, and listen to the noise of the city above you and look at the homeless around you, then you realize you are confronted with what is probably one of the most explicit images of modern life. Above you lies the world of Robert Moses' Elevated Expressways which were built at the time of the New Deal to open up the new enclaves of New York's middle class; but beneath the roar of the traffic you are confronted with the now stationary life of the outcast, whom Moses had wanted to eliminate, without exception, from the American Dream. The immigrant neighborhood of the Lower East Side had to be demolished for the Manhattan East River Drive (now Roosevelt Drive). This slum was partly replaced by the now cheerless modernism of Vladeck Houses. Vladeck Houses were erected by the City Housing Authority to offer accommodation to some 1770 low-income families. When building began in 1939 this plan was financially linked to the construction of the East River Drive. The more expensive homes in the original plan were ultimately never realized. In their place came the Vladeck Houses. They were considered to be a paradise by the new tenants who had all previously lived in extremely dilapidated housing.

There was a presage of the Elevated at the end of the previous century, when one for trains was constructed. The Lower East Side was a trading area. Here ship's supplies were sold, and as in Tokyo workers offered their services for casual labor. The 1895 photo of Coenties Slip gives an impression of the situation at the time; the elevated railroad runs over the heads of the workers, modernity has more than one face. Only above and below have remained unchanged. We should remember that the history of the homeless, the unemployed and tramps in New York City encompasses some 350 years, beginning with the foundation of the small Dutch trading post of Nieuw Amsterdam, where the financial heart of the United States is now located.

In the 1920s the Lower East Side became the subject of urban development. The ideas about the development of the area give some indication of the social relationships at the time of the New Deal. The Lower East Side, the 'mother of urban slums' (Joseph Platzker), was ready for demolition. Frederick Law Olmsted, Burnham and Lewis's approach had resulted in considerable improvement of the waterfronts of New York, and it could also be used for the Lower East Side. Moreover, the run-down housing could be tackled at the same time. The Expressway was an argument for the construction of more expensive housing.[1] The Lower East Side Chamber of Commerce approved the plans immediately; the project would constitute a financial injection in the laborers' districts. The Regional Plan Association (RPA) published their first ideas in 1929; the first report about the East Side waterfront appeared in 1930.

→   South Street Elevated, New York
→→ Coenties Slip, Manhattan 1895

The plan provided for the construction of monumental apartments, offices, railroads, garages and public buildings. Ann Buttenwieser points out that the tensions that were seen some ten years earlier between economic and more general interests, and between the wishes of traders and residents, resurfaced once again. Dumps and abattoirs were to disappear; and the power stations could be clad in an architectural mask, one of Venturi's first sheds. The ideology of the New York RPA is incomprehensible when viewed separately from the ideas of the financier, the Russell Sage Foundation. The designer of the Adams Plan and the Russell Sage Foundation were both examples of the philanthropic side in the American antagonism between property speculation and philanthropy.[2] The plan to revitalize the Lower East Side provided for the construction of homes for the middle class and for the lower-income groups, together with the necessary facilities and access with roads and walkways at two levels. It was supplemented by the construction of a series of separate commercial skyscrapers on both sides of the projected Chrystie-Forsyth Parkway. This boulevard was an important element in the total plan for this area, which lies between 14th Street and Manhattan Bridge, and from the East River to Third Avenue.

The chief criticism of the plan came from Lewis Mumford, who was of the opinion that although the plan included parks it was actually

New York City **The homeless, shelters and the City**

↑   E. Maxwell Fry, Lower East Side
renovation, Regional Plan of
New York and its environs,
Christy Forsyth Parkway, 1923

↗   Robert Moses (1888-1981)

nothing more than a continuation of the chaotic planning of urban developers. According to Mumford, Adams's plan was mainly based on a continuation of the existing rules for urban development, without changing the institutions who were to execute the plan. In his opinion the plan, which claimed to outline the development for the coming thirty-five years, actually reached no further than the day after tomorrow. In Mumford's view the execution of regional planning could no longer be left to the existing institutions, since they had allowed the city to become what it was. He believed that institutional change was a condition for regional planning. This requirement touched on a fundamental tenet of the New Deal, which held that government intervention was a stimulus for the construction industry.

So Adams's reply to Mumford was no surprise: Mumford's ideas could only be realized with the help of a 'despotic' – i.e. socialist – government.

Adams's plan didn't make it. It wouldn't have initiated the innovation of the urban economy. The situation changed in 1934, when the Public Works Authority (PWA), established under the New Deal, provided funds for homes for people with low incomes. The newly-elected Mayor of New York, La Guardia, made immediate use of the PWA schemes and started by tackling the first section of the East River Drive. As early as 1935 the Drive was already being described as a 'continuous lane for fast traffic'. From that time onwards the image of American modernity unfurled on and below the Elevated; the perspective of this image depends on the position of the observer: *on* or *under* the road.

For Giedion the position was on the road. At the end of his nearly nine-hundred-page book *Space, Time and Architecture* he concludes that as far as the USA is concerned we should view the new urban world in a different way; we will have to learn to live with a city 'dictated by the advent of the automobile'. Robert Moses' 'parkways' are the feature which make the American landscape so attractive. Their beauty can be enjoyed most from the air; the 'parkways', to be used solely by the automobile, meander gently through the unspoiled nature.[3] The Henry Hudson Parkway on the west of the island and the projected Chrystie-Forsyth Parkway are examples of these roads. However the Elevated never had that beauty: speed instead of pleasure has become the goal.

The regime of speed may rule on the road – but below the road it is a completely different story. This desolate area consists of parking lots, empty space, and a detention center located right on the water's edge. Here, people live in structures made of fabric, sticks and supermarket pushcarts. Although located right in the center of Manhattan the scene is reminiscent of the countryside; even though there is no question of natural surroundings, the waters of the East River and the open spaces create a more or less artificial nature.

There are some similarities with what Nels Anderson wrote about Chicago seventy years ago. 'The hobo has no social centers other than the "stem" and the "jungle"'.[4] The tramp was to be found either in the city or in the 'jungle', an improvised camp outside the city where the inhabitants lived in the same kind of structures as can now be seen in Manhattan. The railroads still played a part in the life of the tramp in the 1920s and '30s, when he traveled from city to city. The present-day hobo is much less mobile than his predecessor. The romance of city nomad life has gone for good, and the 'tramp' and 'hobo' increasingly belong to the past. In Manhattan the hobo has now come to a standstill, while the traffic on the Elevated has become many times more intense. His most important mode of transport is the supermarket pushcart, which has become a means of scraping together an income. He uses his cart to collect the empty beer cans everyone throws away; these cans are highly sought after, since the supermarket across the road refunds five cents deposit for every empty can. The tramp patiently awaits his turn with his trolley full of empty cans. No one is in a hurry, and no one seems to take any notice of the traffic. It is a striking image: a number of people sitting on rickety garden chairs, right next to the expressway, waiting until they can hand in their cans to the supermarket. Cans and empty bottles are the tramp's small change. They have their own exchange rate: one cigarette for three empty cans.

The homeless in the modern metropolis pose more than just a pointed question for our economy and society, since their existence also undermines the very basis of architecture: housing and urban structure. For them the concepts of 'home', 'at home', 'privacy' and 'public' have lost their meaning. A homeless person has no house, and he is usually unfamiliar with society. For him, going home doesn't exist. The street, sometimes a shelter, constitutes his 'privacy'. His life is 'public', even though it usually remains 'invisible' to those who do have a roof over their heads. Words such as economy, society, work, etc. have acquired a completely different meaning for the homeless. The economy consists of his empty cans, and society is comprised of his fellow homeless; a society without any form of cohesion. From our point of view the life of the homeless has become stationary. It consists of an established pattern of waiting and of struggling to survive from day to day. The homeless live in a different world, because the concept of time is something which belongs to our world. We live with a past, a present, and a future – but the homeless are aware only of the present. As is the case with all the economically deprived, life is overshadowed by the struggle for existence. A large part of the day is devoted to making plans to get hold of some food, and to finding a place to sleep.

Like every minority with a history they also have their own language. A place to sleep is called a 'flop': 'I got my flop for the night'. Everything can serve as a flop[5]: a 'flophouse' (cheap lodgings), a grid, the subway, a lost corner of the city, a shelter or a mission. But it can also be the temporary accommodation in a police station when the tramp has been arrested for public drunkenness – or a longer stay in prison, the 'bucket', when the tramp has received his sentence, where many have been imprisoned at one time or another ('doing time'). The present-day homeless often move from one official agency to another ('making the loop'). His circle of friends, if he has one, is called the 'bottle gang'. Since drinking in public is forbidden the best protection for the tramp is to keep on moving ('carrying the banner'), so he keeps out of sight of the police. In and around public buildings he is continually told to 'take a walk', when he then goes off to look for another place where he won't be able to stay either.

For the tramp the past is not something he remembers with much pleasure, and his future is uncertain. He is actually extremely vulnerable: the police can chase him off, one of his fellow homeless can rob him, and his income is at the mercy of the favors from others.[6] To survive he uses the world in a different way than we do: New York's subway is a place to sleep, the church means temporary accommodation and a little soup – for which he is prepared to suffer the sermon ('you have to take some ear beating') – and the parks are a place where he can spend the day. His currency is food stamps and empty cola cans.

The strategy of the homeless consists of temporarily obeying the rules of those who have authority over them at the time. This is reflected in the language, from which every nuance has disappeared. As just mentioned, any and every place he can sleep is called a 'flop'; the transfer from one agency to another is known as a 'loop', unavoidable once you've landed in it, but at the same rather reassuring, since in the system you'll see friends and acquaintances again. When you have been arrested by a 'bull' (policeman) you are put in the 'cement drunk tank', a concrete room in which you await your sentence together with some thirty others. 'Space' is experienced as a container, a 'tank'. When you have been sentenced you end up in the following container, the 'bucket' (prison). But first your clothes will be deloused in the 'delousing tank', a procedure everyone finds humiliating. You stand together 'bare-assed' in the 'tank'. There's another wait, 'killing time', while the clothes are deloused. Most clothing comes out of the drums in a worse condition than when it went in; the drums are often not cleaned between loads. So dead vermin join the next load.

They don't even bother to delouse the clothes in the shelters, where they consider that there are other dangers greater than vermin. Two burly members of staff who stood at the entrance of the 'big room' of Fort Armory at the time sent everybody through a metal detector and confiscated any weapons they found.

The outside world is often referred to in terms of a thing, a container, or a 'place', and they have few terms to describe it. They have a much greater vocabulary for their own world. 'Tramps' can be divided into 'mission stiffs', 'working stiffs', 'rubber tramps' (tramps who lift to move

around), or 'box car tramps' (nowadays rare). Their own world is differentiated, but outside everything consists of indifferent 'flops'.

'Space' is reduced to a container. For the homeless 'time' has a meaning
completely different from ours. For us time is a scarce commodity, both in
economical terms in relation to working hours, and in personal terms, as
valuable free time to be spent doing something useful or pleasant. But for
the homeless time refers to things that happen to him. Once you are in the
'bucket' there is 'soup time', 'pill time' and 'lockup time'. Time is something
you undergo ('doing time'). Back on the street things aren't much better.
There, too, you have to fill your time. So drink has always been a good
escape – nowadays joined by crack and heroin supplied by the 'pusher'.
These kill every sense of 'time'; so 'hard time' soon becomes 'easy time',
at least for as long as it lasts.

Apart from collecting and selling empty beer cans another way the
homeless or jobless can earn a little money is the sale of the *Street News*.
The *Street News* is for sale in the subway for one dollar. This is the best
point of sale because people can't walk on by, unlike on the street. The
vendor gets a reasonable margin. It won't make him rich, but selling
the paper is more pleasant than begging. The former editor-in-chief,
Hutchinson Persons, was the foremost driving force behind the paper.
The paper is based on the idea of helping yourself. Everyone, however
poor they may be, should try and lead their lives without having to depend
on others. Charity is acceptable only in emergency situations, and then
only temporarily. *Street News* wants the soup kitchens to ask for money for
their services. Persons disagreed with rent protection; he is of the opinion that it helps maintain inequality. In some cities rent protection is an
impediment for people who want to enter the housing market, while at
the same time it awards a bonus to the very group of people who have
profited from a low rent for many years. The lawyer of the homeless,
Peter H. Rossi, notes in his book that this regulation is not the only factor
limiting the amount of affordable accommodation for the poor, although
it undeniably forces up the prices of the houses that just meet the minimum requirements.[7] However, the idea that the market is capable of self-
regulation is wishful thinking – for the simple reason that those seeking
accommodation just don't have the money to pay the rent. Persons was
probably thinking of the old cheap hotels in the Skid Rows, where there
still was a real system of supply and demand. Many of these hotels (Single
Room Occupancy hotel, SRO) are gone, because the income of the home-

less is appreciably lower than it was thirty years ago. For the landlords the homeless are the least attractive group to whom they can rent their accommodation.

Persons's paper is a mixture of ideas about self-help, militancy, naiveté and optimism. His optimism refers to the pre-war situation in the United States. The homeless, often casual labor, were considerably more militant. The layout of the paper is unmistakably American. At the back of the paper you can find coupons which you can cut out and give to another homeless person: 'No excuses, you can get a job today'; indeed, as a vendor of the *Street News*. In pre-war Chicago there were a number of left-wing papers that were read widely amongst the hobos. To a certain extent *Weekly People*, *Truth*, *Industrial Solidarity*, *Worker*, *Hobo News* and *Voice of Labor* were forerunners of New York's *Street News*, although the latter has discarded their socialist ideals. These radical papers urged their readers to read now classic Marxist writers such as Lewis Morgan, Herman Cahn, Paul Lafargue and Archille Loria.

The sociologist Nels Anderson gives a description of a number of soap-box orators on a Sunday afternoon, chosen at random, in July 1922. One of the members of *Industrial Workers of the World* (iww) talks for twenty minutes about the need to organize. He argues that the reason the rich are so successful is that they have organized themselves properly. It isn't in the interests of the rich that casual laborers should organize themselves, because that could mean that they could also gain a measure of power. 'He didn't blame the rich man for organizing; he blamed the poor man for not organizing' (Nels Anderson, *The hobo*). The papers were a source of income for many speakers, in the same way that the *Street News* is now bought and resold.

Before the Second World War a large part of the population consisted of casual laborers who often did seasonal work and were continually on the road, underway from one boss to the next. They formed a sub-culture that was more positive and militant than the present sub-culture. At the beginning of this century a tramp was someone with money in his pockets, i.e. someone who could create his own world. This was how the millionaire James Eads Howe even went so far as to found the famous *Hobo College* in 1913 in Chicago, where Ben Reitman, Jim Tully and E. W. Burgess were appointed as members of the faculty. The curriculum included subjects such as philosophy and social studies.[8] Many traveling casual laborers were affiliated to the iww, 'conceived in the stem' in Chicago in July 1905, as Anderson put it. This union began as an alternative for the *American Federation of Labor*. It had its own newspapers, songs and skilled work, which had a beneficial effect on the self-image of its members. Some legendary stories about the 'wobblies' can still be heard.

The number of homeless remained fairly constant up to 1927. When the depression crippled the American economy in 1929 wages began to plummet, and the number of homeless increased enormously. Between October 1930 and September 1931 the city of Chicago provided one million nights' temporary accommodation. In the next twelve months (1931-1932) this number increased by more than three-quarters of a million. It increased by yet another million in the next year. In the period 1933-1934 there were 4,288,356 nights' temporary accommodation provided by Chicago alone. The total number of homeless in the United States was estimated to be one million. Nels Anderson made a statement to the Senate in which he estimated the number to be more than one and a half million, a figure many thought to be on the low side.

Anderson has described the difference, essential for this subculture, between a 'peddler' and a 'panhandler'. A peddler had a permit to sell pencils or shoelaces. He tried to survive by 'by touching hearts' – that was his work. But a beggar who was sound in body and mind, that was repugnant. That was 'panhandling'. The peddler usually had a fixed pitch, often in front of a church. But beggars could be found everywhere; and they were already 'outcasts'. The workplace of the peddlers has always been 'on the stem'.

The living conditions were – as they still are – bad. In 1922 an observer reported that in one Chicago SRO hotel he had found two toilets for one hundred and eighty men, and in another seven for three hundred and eighty people. Some toilets had no ventilation, and sometimes they were in a hall scarcely separated from the dormitories. There was hardly any hot water, and one washbasin had to be shared by forty to fifty men.[9]

In the New York City of the 1930s some fourteen organizations were already involved in the provision of temporary accommodation.[10] Only when the economy began to recover in 1936 did the number of night-time residences provided in New York drop dramatically to just 550 a day, compared with 19,000 in 1935.

The process of 'shelterization' had already started. The homeless now became dependent on the good-will of others, and their apathy increased.[11] In 1931 Anderson was already voicing severe criticism of social work, which he considered to be a result of the 'machine age'. According to him social workers never made any real contribution to a solution, if there was one. Social work, in his view, was too closely tied to the institutions. A lot has changed since his manual *The Milk and Honey Route* was published. The institutions are no longer focused on returning the homeless to the labor market. Their work has become more differentiated. The only feature that has become more significant is the *loop*. Anderson's criticism of this was not only very early; it was also very justifiable.

The homeless after
the Second World War

The relatively favorable pre-war subculture changed dramatically after the Second World War. Nowadays New York City does everything it can to cope with the problem of the homeless. It is spurred on to do so by the *Coalition for the Homeless* (CFTH), run by the jurist Robert Hayes. Hayes investigated the various shelters, interviewed the homeless, and represented their interests in a series of legal actions. For example, in the case of *Callahan versus Carey* (1981) he succeeded in enforcing the right to temporary accommodation in 'community based shelters', i.e. shelters to be found throughout the city. Until then everyone had been allocated a place in the Bowery shelter, which itself had only a limited number of beds. Most men are now referred to the cheaper hotels in the Bowery, such as The Union, The Kenton, The Palace, Sunshine, Delevan and Stevenson, using vouchers.[12] The homeless are distributed over the whole island, and are not concentrated only at Grand Central, Penn Station, Port Authority Bus Terminal or the Bowery. There are shelters for men, who form by far the largest group of the homeless (88%), for women, and for families – the fastest growing group. The buildings are the property of the city and are run by welfare work.

The *Partnership for the Homeless* was set up in 1981 in response to Koch's request for help, and is an umbrella organization for all religious institutions offering help to the homeless. They offered a total of 1577 extra beds. The new form of homelessness (the 'old' form too was always associated with economic recession) began in the 1970s and increased dramatically during the 1981-82 recession; but unlike the old form, the new form continued to grow during the economic recovery which continued into the 1990s. The differences in income had never been so great. In 1984 the poorest section of the population, about 40% of the total, received about 15% of the national income; while the richest section, also about 40%, received about 67%. This means that the middle groups were also worse off. In the past twenty years the very rich have seen their income rise by some 38%. Nowadays the number of the homeless is directly related to the changes in the economy. About 11.5 million workers lost their jobs when their factories closed during the de-industrialization at the beginning of the 1980s. The service economy that took industry's place meant that many blacks and Latinos were out of work for good. Poverty is still the most important reason why people become tramps. Many tramps come from families that had always balanced on the edge of the subsistence level. And then it doesn't take much to land on the street. The sociologist Rossi listed a number of characteristic differences between the group who ended up on the street in the 1950s and '60s and the group who became homeless in the '80s. One of the differences is that the problem is much more visible nowadays, as many people who used to live in the former SROs now live on the street. This group may have been poorly housed in the past, but at least they had a roof over their heads. The number of people who have had to go onto the streets has increased dramatically in the last few decades. And as mentioned earlier, the homeless are much poorer than they were in the 1950s.

Another difference is that in the past casual work was sometimes available — but now there is no work at all. The make-up of the group has also changed completely. Nowadays the homeless are much younger than they used to be, and the proportion of homeless women is greater than it has ever been.[13] In the 1970s half the one-parent families lived under the poverty line. In the period between 1970-1991 welfare payments under the AFDC program (*Aid to Families with Dependent Children*) were cut back drastically. On average the purchasing power of these welfare payments decreased by no less than 42%. During Ronald Reagan's presidency three major cutbacks in the payments were made, which amounted to a total of about 3.6 billion dollars. 11.4 million people still drew welfare payments in 1990; the total budget amounted to 18.5 billion dollars. As a result of these cutbacks the welfare payments fell below the official poverty line throughout the United States.

Since the 1960s the number of black one-parent families has more than tripled. In the 1980s more than half of all families were one-parent families (with a woman as the head of the family), of which more than 60% lived in poverty. The number of households that did not form a family quadrupled in the period between 1950 and 1980, while the total number of families increased by only 50%.[14] One-parent families appear to be particularly vulnerable. The proportion of homeless women with children is also increasing. As early as 1984 the New York social service reported that the overwhelming majority of families in the accommodation centers were comprised of women with children. The lack of suitable accommodation can result in these women losing their rights to an AFDC welfare payment, and they end up in a vicious circle. This may then be reason for these women to be dismissed from parental authority, and the *State Social Service Departments* can prevent the children returning to their mother while she has no suitable accommodation. About half of the families in temporary accommodation in 1984 had ended up on the streets because living in with their families had ultimately proven to be an impossible situation.

The street creates its own social world, in which food and drink are of paramount importance. It seems as though Dos Passos's New York is increasingly metamorphosing into Lou Reed's:

Outside it's a bright night, there's an opera at Lincoln Center
Movie stars arrive by limousine
The klieg lights shoot up over the skyline of Manhattan
but the lights are out on the mean streets
A small kid stands by the Lincoln Tunnel
He's selling plastic roses for a buck
The traffic's backed up to 39th Street
The TV whores are calling the cops out for a suck
And back at the Wilshire Pedro sits there dreaming
He's found a book on Magic in a garbage can
He looks at the pictures and stares at the cracked ceiling
'At the count of 3', he says,
'I hope I can disappear'
And fly, fly away

Lou Reed, *New York, Dirty Blvd*

Skid Row

Nowadays 'shelterization' means that an alcoholic or a psychiatric patient is transferred from one institution to another. Admittance to one institution often constitutes a bridge to another, since there is always a formal or an informal relationship between the various forms of treatment. Most of the homeless come into contact with this system, and they rapidly become familiar with its workings. In her book, Jacqueline Wiseman accurately describes this as the 'underground conveyor system'. After his treatment a homeless person will end up back on *Skid Row*, usually until his next admittance to an institution. In the language of the homeless this circle is called 'making the loop': 'I never worry when a friend of mine is missing (from Skid Row). I know he's out making the loop and will be back'.

Cohen and Sokolovsky name three main reasons for today's homelessness as poverty, drink and 'idiosyncratic factors', i.e. factors and experiences that can push people off the edge of a normal existence into a nomadic way of life, such as the death of the partner, a physical disability that makes work impossible, divorce, and other similar circumstances. George Orwell's 1930s observation in *Down and Out in Paris and London* continues to be valid: poverty still 'annihilates the future'.

Manhattan Transfer, our plan for the Washington Street shelter is primarily aimed at providing short-term accommodation. A return to regular society is considered to be important, but it does not have priority. The most important element in the program is the provision of accommodation (and food), or in specific terms the replacement of the large shelters. The creation of accommodation for the homeless, the most important objective of this architecture, is reduced to the simplest possible level. For this social group 'architecture' means nothing more than a roof over their heads. When all margins have been cut away, all that remains of the architecture of the shelter would, in the first instance, seem aptly describable as 'functional'. But only in the first instance, for although this functional architecture manifests itself without any form of aesthetic ideals it does in fact transform the program into an architectural form, just like any other kind of architecture. This form doesn't 'follow'; it has its own terms of reference, as this book will show.

'Gentrification' is used to describe the process in which the uneducated make way for more qualified residents in certain neighborhoods of the city. A revaluation of old and neglected residential areas occurs when the homes in these neighborhoods are occupied by new wealthy tenants and owners. As a result of this process most of New York's one-room apartments have been lost in the upgrading to expensive apartments. In social terms the result has been a dramatic increase in the number of homeless; other homes are too expensive, and there is little cheap accommodation available. Other important factors are the expiry of federal subsidies for existing homes, and the fact that federal funding for the lower-income groups has shrunk to 10% of the 1981 level. The housing program for the lower-income groups was cut back drastically during the Reagan years. The federal authorities devoted some 31 billion dollars to the program at the beginning of his presidency, but towards the end of his second term this amount had dwindled to 7 billion. In New York the number of people registered as seeking a home exceeds the total number of homes, whilst only half of the homes fall under the distribution scheme. Moreover the number of single-room-occupancy hotels or SROs in New York City has decreased greatly since the 1970s. About one-third of these SROs were located between West 59th and West 110th Streets.

One quarter of the SROs contained more than one hundred apartments, and about half contained between 10 and 99 apartments. The average building was larger in Manhattan's West Side than elsewhere on the island, and the lots contained a relatively greater number of SROs. The exterior of the buildings might look the same as a normal residential block, but the interior is very different. To discourage people from gath-

Manhattan Transfer Shelter, New York, Arie Graafland and Harry Kerssen, 1998

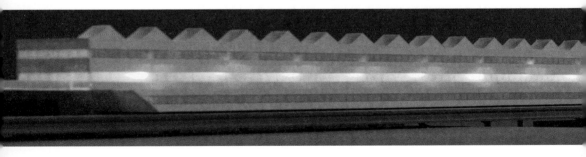

ering there the lobby is never furnished. The manager has a barred office, located so that he can watch what is going on. He has an ostentatious display of a number of weapons such as baseball bats, lead pipes and guns – just in case someone might get the wrong idea. Mirrors ensure that he can see into hidden corners, where attackers could lurk.[15]

The majority of these SROs have been converted into expensive apartments. 89% of the 113,000 single-room-occupancy hotels were lost in the years between 1970 and 1983. About 1,116,000 SRO units disappeared throughout the country in the period between 1970 and 1982, equivalent to half the total number of apartments. The cost of the remaining SROs is continually increasing. In 1994 all federal subsidies were stopped for the 900,000 privately-owned apartments. There is a very real risk that these apartments might come onto the open market. The authorities allotted 5.1 billion dollars for their ten-year plan, of which the majority came from their own funds since the federal authorities failed to provide the funds. The authorities' construction program was the largest in the whole of the United States. The tax paragraph J-51 was an important inducement to convert SRO units into luxury apartments. This law was originally intended to enable home-owners to carry out home improvements. Under paragraph J-51 the upgrading of 535,272 units was financed between 1978 and 1985, which involved a sum of 860 million dollars.

In 1982 about three-quarters of the housing subsidies went to the more prosperous neighborhoods of Manhattan. Cheap accommodation became more and more scarce. The New York *City Housing Authority* estimated that in the last ten years 17,000 New York families had moved in together because they couldn't find a home, which is equivalent to about one in ten families. The shortage of cheap housing enabled both landlords and people selling houses to increase the price. In the tax year preceding

New York City **Skid Row**

July 1983 the rents in the Consumer Price Index increased by 5.4%, while the other expenses increased by only 2.2%. As a result compulsory eviction became increasingly more common. There were five hundred thousand evictions in New York City, which has nearly 2 million rented homes. But paragraph J-51 also had another effect: the city lost about 280 million dollars in tax income. A considerable proportion of the housing from which the present homeless were driven was not rented out again but sold as apartments.[16] And New York is anything but an exception. The *Annual Housing Survey* (which is made by the *Census Bureau for the Department of Housing and Urban Development*) reveals that city after city lost housing with a rent equivalent to 40% or less of the minimum income. The number of cheaper rental homes in twelve large cities decreased by an average of 30% in the period between 1978 and 1983. In the same period the number of households living on or below the poverty line increased by 36%. As a consequence rental accommodation became unaffordable for an increasing number of the poor.

Housing is a human right,
Martha Rosler, Times Square

New York City spends more money on the homeless than any other city. The cost of temporary accommodation for the homeless has increased enormously in the last fifteen years: from 8 million dollars in 1978 to 58 million in 1984 and 173 million in 1990. Half of the 8.4 million people who earn less than 7000 dollars per year have to spend a disproportionately large amount of their income, about 60%, on the rent. A couple of years ago the city had 30,500 beds available for the homeless (the total number of homeless is estimated to be about 90,000).

New York does more for the homeless than any other city. But even that isn't enough as long as unemployment continues to grow, especially amongst the Afro-Americans and Latinos.

During the Reagan years jobs certainly were created, but most of these were in the low-paid and uncertain services sector. 44% of all new jobs created since 1980 provide an income fluctuating around the poverty line. The gap between the rich and the poor has never been so large: in 1983 0.5% of American households earned 45% of the national income, not counting personal property.[17]

The only way the family's income could increase was for the woman to get a paid job. But the 1980s was a golden time for the young and ambitious rich. Real estate agents, financiers and art dealers did good business. There were only a handful of artists in New York's art world of 1945, but now there are some 150,000 artists exhibiting their work in 680 galleries. Together they produced about 15 million works of art in the last ten years: the heyday of postmodernism.[18] The economy of New York City is based on fictive capital. The Yuppie culture has left its traces, ranging from gentrification of the neighborhoods to the streets dominated by Armani suits. The opposite of this culture is the culture of the homeless. Just before Christmas 1987 Congress announced that about 35 million dollars had been cut from the budget for the homeless.

The accent of New York's economy is still shifting. The tourist industry has now become the most important source of income; even more important than the financial markets. The various groups – people involved in the tourist industry, the financiers, the bankers, and the homeless – are not very compatible with each other. The city must continually serve different interests at the same time. This is a difficult task since, for example, too great an emphasis on the creation of permanent employment and affordable accommodation quickly becomes detrimental to the economic interests of the business world in the city.

This simultaneous care for these different conflicting interests is becoming increasingly difficult, if not impossible. Slowly but surely an 'urbane schizophrenia' (Manuel Castells) is developing.[19] The different worlds which together constitute a city like New York are developing in directions which increasingly exclude and ignore each other. The worlds of the ghetto, the more protected middle-class suburbs, high-tech, the services industry and the banks are becoming more and more isolated in New York. According to Castells we are witnessing the creation of mutually exclusive super-cities. These metropolises act like magnets, attracting people, capital, knowledge, information and energy – but the channels along which the city's activities are governed from a central point become increasingly isolated. This is no longer a question of the contrast between urban and regional structures, but of a process of interactive growth between elements that deny each other, whilst they are all part of the same system. There is the threat of a real urban schizophrenia, the parallel existence of conflicting social, cultural and economic systems which each have their own solutions to their problems within the same spatial context. In this situation it is still possible to talk of 'space' as defined by Giedion, but this space becomes increasingly fluid and mobile. This even seems to be true for the homeless, who are transformed into a mobile problem.

New York City **Skid Row**

A few years ago New York City suggested the possibility of accommodating the homeless in ships. Trailers, Liberty Ships taken out of the mothballs and even the old Staten Island ferries seemed to be suitable. Le Corbusier had a similar idea for the Seine. When the homeless became a problem for the neighborhood then it would only be necessary to move the ship accommodating them. This was a contemporary version of the fabled Ship of Fools from the Middle Ages that was forced to sail incessantly from harbor to harbor.

Deinstitutionalization; from State Hospitals to CMHC's

Although there are about 270 shelters in New York most people still come across a homeless person asleep on the street on their way to work, or in the area where they live. In the city's six 'outreach' projects the staff drives around the city in small buses, on the lookout for the mentally disturbed homeless. Homeless psychiatric patients are a separate problem. The increase in their numbers is blamed on the deinstitutionalization of the psychiatric clinics. In the period between 1969 and 1981 the number of patients in these institutions decreased by 66%, although the financial cut-back in this sector amounted to only 3%. The number of mentally ill tramps is unknown. However high percentages are given in a summary from the United States Conference of Mayors published in 1986. According to these figures the proportion of mentally ill tramps is 60% in Louisville, 45% in San Francisco and Salt Lake City, and 25% in New York City. Rossi cites similar figures in his study *The Condition of the Homeless in Chicago* (1985-1986). Almost one in four of the homeless in Chicago has been admitted to a psychiatric clinic at least once. The majority of them showed a repetitive pattern: 60% had been admitted once before, and 30% more than four times in total.[20] Other studies on the homeless show a similar picture. It is estimated that one third of the homeless are psychiatric patients. A comparison of 17 studies on the homeless made by Rossi indicated that 34% were mentally disturbed during a longer period of time. These studies are based on assessments varying from the empirical impression of an interviewer to a clinical diagnosis by an experienced psychiatrist.

There were a total of 116,136 patients in all the psychiatric clinics (State Hospitals) in the USA in 1984. This included all psychiatric cases caused by alcohol and drugs. Today there are probably twice as many patients on the streets as have been admitted to the clinics.[21] Fuller Torrey gives a poignant example of the situation in New York City. In the 1960s and '70s many of the clinics of the Manhattan State Hospital were closed, and the patients were discharged. The number of homeless grew rapidly in this period, so it was decided to reopen one of the clinics, but

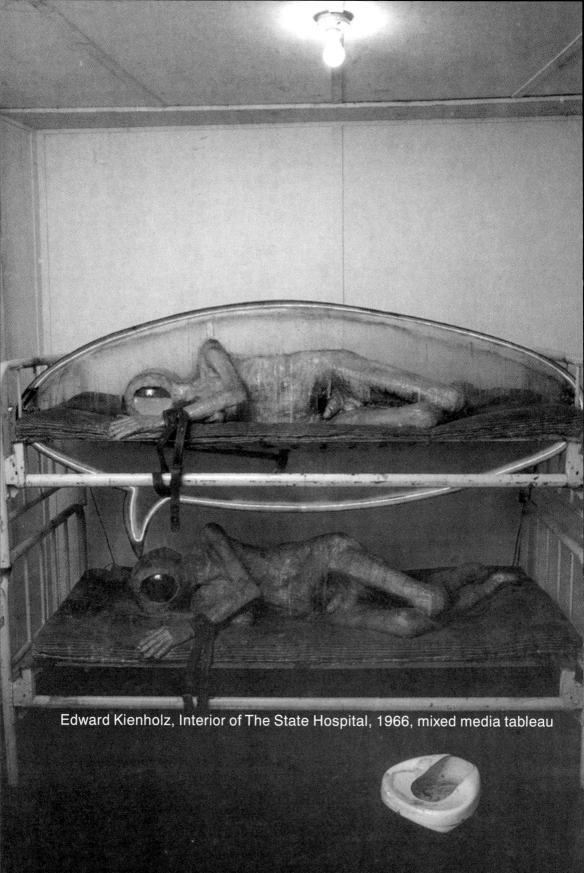

Edward Kienholz, Interior of The State Hospital, 1966, mixed media tableau

now as a shelter. Keener Building on Ward's Island is one such building, an abandoned psychiatric clinic that used to accommodate 180 patients. It was reopened in the summer of 1981, but in the following spring the building was already accommodating 625 homeless people. In 1982 two dormitories with a total of 850 beds were completed. These cost 7 million dollars, equivalent to 17,500 dollars a bed.

One of the homeless in the Keener Building was a former patient in the clinic. Now he had come back after a time in the Bowery: 'A long way round to go nowhere', as he put it. There were even beds in the offices and the lobby. Facilities such as rooms for the staff and the number of showers and toilets had originally been based on 180 patients. They hadn't been increased to take account of the increased numbers. As such the number of beds was already much smaller than the enormous number of homeless in New York. Only a couple of the TVs in the communal rooms actually worked. Hayes, the lawyer representing the homeless, brought a case against the city which resulted in them tripling the funds in order to take on more staff. But in spite of this the accommodation is still anything but an improvement for the ex-patients. A number of them once again live under the same roof they used to – but now without medication, and without nursing.

However the majority of the former patients from these clinics have not been able to find accommodation in one of the shelters. They can be found in the city's parks, where they talk to the invisible shadows around them. More than 58% of the total number of schizophrenic patients have no fixed abode, but the authorities (*National Institute of Mental Health*) don't seem concerned. The *Community Mental Health Centers* (CMHC's) program started in 1963 under President Kennedy has turned into a disaster. And history now appears to be repeating itself.

In the previous century psychiatric patients were accommodated in poor houses. These were abolished in response to the dissatisfaction at the time with the inhuman accommodation they provided, as well as the lack of any treatment. The first attempts to improve the lot of psychiatric patients were made in New York in 1860. These resulted in the *State Care Act* of 1890, which had an influence throughout the entire country. This Act ultimately resulted in the foundation of the State Hospitals, where the problem rapidly resurfaced. The first clinics were comparatively small, with about 300 patients, but ten years later they had already become so large that they housed 2000.[22] Even at the time urgent pleas were being made for smaller clinics with improved treatment facilities.

New York City **Deinstitutionalization; from State Hospitals to CMHC's**

The State Mental Hospitals – where the facilities for treatment were abominable – began to discharge patients in 1955. The pace of the discharges increased during the 1960s and '70s. The reduction in the number of beds can be explained in part by the high death rate amongst the patients at the beginning of the deinstitutionalization; according to Blau's estimates this amounted to between 20 and 40% of the total number of patients.[23] In the period 1955-1984 the number of beds in the state clinics fell by 80%, i.e. 433,407. There were still 552,150 beds in 1955.[24] In New York alone the number of beds fell from 71,066 to 23,000. This was the largest discharge of patients ever to take place.

During the first few years there were no real problems with accommodation, since the less severe cases could often be looked after at home. The real problems surfaced in about 1960. Patients without a home were discharged while there was insufficient accommodation available in the CMHC's. Many people ended up in lodgings and SROs. This is how the boardwalk hotels along the Long Beach coast came to be full of patients from the neighboring Creedmore and Pilgrim State Hospitals. Estimates indicated that a quarter of the SRO inhabitants in New York were severely mentally disturbed. Ellen Bassuk, who made a study in a shelter chosen at random in Boston, arrived at a considerably higher number. According to her figures 90% suffered from a psychic disorder. However she also included all persons with an alcohol problem in this group.[25] Her investigation was carried out in cooperation with her colleagues (psychiatrists and social workers), and examined 78 visitors to the shelter. It revealed that 40% suffered from some form of psychosis. Most were schizophrenics. About 29% were chronic alcoholics, and 21% had a personality disorder. The majority of this group were not members of any kind of network such as families or a circle of friends. And this isolation only increased once patients had been admitted for treatment. About 74% initially indicated that they had no family ties or friends. After hospitalization the figure increased to 90%.

Bassuk is of the opinion that the lack of a social network is one of the reasons people become homeless. According to her deinstitutionalization is another reason. The number of homeless began to grow around 1970. At the same time the distribution of the homeless through New York City also began to change. Men who had until then hung around in the Bowery now began to gather in Grand Central Station. Homeless people who had customarily stayed mid-town now began to spread over the whole island.[26] Many of them had psychological problems. Since then their number has continued to increase. Later studies, such as Bassuk's, confirm this trend. Her investigations revealed that between one-fifth and one-third of the homeless needed psychiatric treatment. At the time of her study (1983) the average age of the tramps was already decreasing (34 years). It is certain that a number of people became psychotic as a result of the changes to the welfare system.[27]

In between times the CMHC's had discovered a new group of patients; not the severely mentally ill patients from the State Hospitals, but those who have been named the 'worried well' by Fuller Torrey. The CMHC's no longer talk of patients, but of clients. Their main therapeutic activities are now counseling and psychotherapy, which account for about 80% of all forms of treatment. About 10 million (!) counseling and therapy sessions were held in the 600 CMHC's in 1978.

During this period the psychotic patients on the Long Beach board-walk had to make do without any medication or therapy. The City Council failed in their attempts to have these patients re-admitted for treatment because the *Civil Liberties Union* successfully challenged this action as being unconstitutional. In New York Koch contested the lawyers of the *Union*, but in vain, since every individual – however psychotic they might be – has the right to refuse treatment.

Apart from their mental problems many tramps are also in very poor physical shape. A study by the *Office of Mental Health* (1982) showed that 27% of the men who visit the shelters suffer from some kind of chronic disease requiring long-term treatment. 24% of the men had a physical disability that would have caused problems if they had had a job. This poor physical condition is largely due to the termination of financial support for people with a physical disability. An amendment to the *Social Security Act* adopted by Congress in 1956 granted persons of 50 years and older who suffered from a chronic ailment the right to financial support. This right was further extended in 1960, and again in 1965, to cover persons of all ages, subject to the condition that the person concerned had been unable to work in regular employment for a period of at least one year. This caused an astronomical increase in the costs of the benefits, from 533 million dollars in 1960 to 3 billion dollars in 1970 and 15.3 billion dollars in 1980. For this reason a 1980 Act was approved by Congress which required that all cases should be re-examined, effective from 1982. President Reagan advanced this date by ten months. In a period of seven months the benefits of 106,000 people were discontinued. As early as April 1982 400,000 cases had been re-examined, and the benefits of another 190,948 people were withdrawn. In 1983 yet another 408,000 lost their rights to AFDC. In addition 2 billion dollars were cut from the 12 billion-dollar budget for 'food stamps'. The cut-backs in the AFDC hit women with children particularly hard, and caused an increase in the number that had no permanent accommodation. Most of the literature on the homeless deals with men; not only because there are fewer homeless women (about 4000 in New York City in 1979), but also because women are less 'visible'. Their favorite places are station 'rest rooms' – in this instance the American euphemism for toilets is a very apt description. Most homeless women live in their own world and only a very few talk to others. Little is known about them, but studies that have been made reveal that in relative terms twice as many homeless women have a history of psychiatric problems than do men.[28] Most prefer to be left alone, surrounded by their possessions propped into plastic shopping bags.[29]

Problems and solutions

Dinkins, then Borough President of Manhattan, was of the opinion that Koch's plan for family support took insufficient account of the income groups. The plan had nothing to offer to families with an income of less than 16,000 dollars per year unless the family had no roof over their heads. Like many others Dinkins also stressed the importance of social counseling – which was an absolute necessity, as the Reagan government had drastically cut back all social welfare. The *Family Support Act* replaced the AFDC in 1988, with the intention of helping needy families to find work by active mediation and by training programs. About 20% of the people who had received AFDC, including women with children younger than three years, could count on this support. The goal was to have about 40% of the people drawing benefits at work for sixteen hours a week by 1992, and the ultimate objective was to get about 70% back to work in 1997.

The Federal 'food stamps' program was also cut back. The budget was reduced by 6.8 billion dollars between 1982 and 1986. One million people lost their rights to the benefit and the number of stamps was reduced for the other 20 million. The city is trying as best it can to compensate for this reduction, but its means are limited. The police have been instructed to bring the homeless to shelters in emergency situations, for example during near-freezing weather. The police 'fact sheet' lists exactly how often help is offered, and how often it is accepted. During the winter months of 1990 14,000 people were approached, and half were brought to a shelter. During that winter a total of about 21,000 people were provided with accommodation.

At present there are nine centers which are open day and night, where the homeless can go to receive accommodation, food, a shower, and social care. East Third Street Men's Shelter in the Bowery is the central reception point for many of the homeless. A couple of hundred people can be accommodated in the 'Big Room' at one time. Until recently (1993) Fort Washington Armory on 168th Street could accommodate 1200 men in beds arranged in rows on a concrete floor the size of a football field. John Coleman went on the streets for a few days to witness what life is like for the homeless, and he gave the following excellent description of life in the Men's Shelter on East Third Street.

At 3.30 PM, with more cold ahead, I sought out the Men's Shelter at 8 East 3rd Street.

This is the principal entry point for men seeking the city's help. It provides meals for 1300 or so people every day and beds for some few of those. I had been told that while there was no likelihood of getting a bed in this building I'd be given a meal here and a bed in some other shelter. I've seen plenty of drawings of London's workhouses and asylums, in the times of Charles Dickens. Now I've seen the real thing, in the last years of the 20th century in the world's greatest city. The lobby and the adjacent 'sitting room' were jammed with men standing, sitting, or stretched out in various positions on the floor. It was as lost a collection of souls as I could have imagined. Old and young, scarred and smooth, stinking and clean, crippled and hale, drunk and sober, ranting and still, parts of another world and parts of this one. The city promises to take in anyone who asks. Those rejected everywhere else find their way to East 3rd Street. The air was heavy with the odors of Thunderbird wine, urine, sweat, and above all, nicotine and marijuana. Three or

Fort Washington Armory, The big room, 1992

four Human Resources Administration police officers seemed to be keeping the vio-
lence down to tolerable levels, but barely so. After a long delay, I got a meal ticket for
dinner and was told to come back later for a lodging ticket. [30]

And the accounts in the papers don't mince words either. For example, the following excerpt could be found in the *New York Times* of January 1 2
1992:

After the lights go down at night at the Fort Washington Armory in upper
Manhattan, paranoid schizophrenics lie nervously next to ex-convicts they right-
fully fear. Noises arise in the darkness: the moans of men having sex with men, the
cries of the helpless being robbed, the hacking coughs of the sick, the pounding of
feet running through a maze of 700 cots packed into one vast room.

Violence was a frequent and regular feature of life in the Fort, with
an eruption every four to six hours. For safety reasons a number of temporary residents slept on their side; in their words, on their backs they
were 'a flat target'.

The situation changed drastically in 1993. The 'running track' has
now been restored to its former glory in the hall where the homeless
used to sleep. The capacity of the Fort has been reduced to about seventy
beds, divided between four dormitories. Violence is much less commonplace, as there is now a 'guard' in front of the door to every dormitory.
During the day the residents have to leave, and go onto the street. Everywhere the Fort reeks of Lysol. The Fort's new limited capacity is obviously more manageable, but no-one knows where or how its lost capacity
has been compensated.

Koch had already made an announcement in 1989 that he planned to
close the large and dangerous shelters and replace them with a smaller
and more humane form of accommodation. Large shelters are not very
suitable. They are often the last refuge for the homeless, but even so
many don't like to use them. Proof of this is to be found in Chicago: the
shelters were not filled to capacity during the winter of 1986, having an
occupancy of only 80%. The occupancy rises with an increasing feeling of
safety in the shelter. In order to further safety, some shelters simply
refuse to admit tramps who are under the influence of alcohol or drugs.
But a really good solution would be to compartmentalize the shelters to
create more privacy.

The sites for the new shelters need to be carefully chosen, in view of
the many protests from the various neighborhoods. When plans were
announced for the conversion of a school building in Harlem on 156th

Street the residents of the Polo Grounds on the opposite side of the street rose in a massive protest. *Don't Bring the Bowery Uptown* could be read on one of the placards. Usually, the HRA (Human Resources Administration) no longer even asks for the opinion of residents in the neighborhood, as they assume that no-one wants the homeless around them ('not in my backyard'). Dinkins adopted a very cautious approach to the designation of sites for shelters. In 1991 he had Andrew Cuomo, son of the Governor of New York, make recommendations on 24 to 35 possible locations of smaller units where improved services could be provided.[31]

The five-year plan to dismantle the city's barracks-style shelters in favor of shelters with a maximum capacity of 150 has sparked a fury of criticism since it was released two months ago. While most praise the intent of the plan, neighborhood residents have opposed virtually all of the 35 potential sites, and the plan has come under fire from politicians ranging from community board members to the two leaders of the City Council, Speaker Peter Valone and President Andrew Stein.

New York Newsday, 9 December 1991

Our *Manhattan Transfer Shelter System* (MTSS) won't solve the problem of the homeless. But it will help people survive, as it will provide them with accommodation and food for a few nights. One of the forms of help offered by the *Manhattan Transfer Shelter System* is a detoxification department for alcohol and drugs. The State Mental Hospitals recommend a ninety-day period of treatment. But Wiseman's survey indicates that the *Pacific City Hospital* allows only one to five days for detoxification.[32] The *Manhattan Transfer Shelter* detox has a comparable duration; only a short-term treatment is offered. Emergency shelter, where possible as an ambulant patient, is combined with a treatment of a maximum of five days.

A comparison with the *St. Francis Residences* of the Franciscan monks is illustrative. The monks' project consists of two (smaller) buildings, one of which is at 124 East 24th Street and the other at 155 West 22nd Street. The operating costs are relatively low; and as the homeless are treated with respect life in the *Residences* is completely different from the large HRA shelters. However the *Residences* provide long-term accommodation and in that respect, are somewhat similar to the HVO shelter *De Veste* in Amsterdam, which combines overnight accommodation with a boarding house. *Manhattan Transfer* is designed for *overnight accommodation*, but aims at a a population comparable to that of the Residences.

To determine the distribution of the shelters on the island we used our inventory of possible sleeping-places in combination with the inventory of the *Department of City Planning*, who developed a computer program containing a precise list of the location of the 66,206 beds in shelters, foster group homes and other forms of accommodation, and their distribution.

This computer inventory was compared with an inventory of possible building sites of more than 35,000 square feet. The computer generated a list of 490 sites, some of which were in twenty neighborhoods that already had more than enough shelters. 252 sites were rejected as unusable, and the remaining 238 were visited. At the end of the analysis 24 sites remained. A criticism often heard of this method is that the distribution cannot be left to the computer. The *New York Times* wrote in December 1991 that 'Artificial intelligence is no substitute for common sense'. That may be so, but a computer model is of great importance since it can form the basis for a discussion. We compared the count of the sites with the abstract grid of the distribution of the sleeping-places in the *Manhattan Transfer*; the 'urbane schizophrenia' becomes clear only when it is visualized in a map.

Fair share, said Frederick A.O. Schwarz, chairman of the Charter Revision Commission, forces politicians and the public, including the affluent communities, to think about the fundamental social pathologies causing the problems and not, like Pontius Pilate, to wash their hands of these problems by hiding them.

New York Times, December 1991

Private initiatives and government intervention

Private institutions such as the American Red Cross provide accommodation for an additional 1200 people. The American Red Cross ended up providing accommodation for the homeless in a roundabout manner. Obviously their primary duty is to provide temporary accommodation for people who have become homeless as a result of a disaster, such as fire. This became a major task with the large number of fires in the 1970s. An increasing number of families became homeless, and in conjunction with New York's *Human Resources Department* this help was institutionalized to combat the growing dependence of the city on the welfare hotels at a time when Federal funds were beginning to dry up. One of the stopgap solutions was to use old warehouses, particularly in the Bronx. However it was not possible to guarantee either sufficient privacy or enough sanitary facilities. And these shelters were too expensive. The vacant hospital and school buildings that were offered for use as shelters were unsuitable for the accommodation of a large number of people, and there were usually insufficient funds to carry out the major modifications the buildings needed.

The *Department of Health and Human Services* granted compensation for about half of the costs of the temporary accommodation. In 1987 the department wanted to reduce this compensation to an amount equal to half of the city's costs. The costs for the city are considerable; on average 20,000 dollars a year is needed to house a family in a welfare hotel. There were about 3000 families in the scheme in 1986, for which the *Human Resources Administration* paid a total of about 72,000,000 dollars.

In a number of cases the hotels were no longer welfare hotels, but ordinary commercial hotels which – without their knowledge – were providing accommodation to homeless people who had been assigned to them by the city. It transpired that the *Human Resources Administration* had a list of 45 commercial hotels, mainly in the vicinity of the La Guardia and Kennedy Airports. About 750 families had been given accommodation in this way in 1991, each for about 2300 dollars a month. When this leaked out there was a great deal of indignation. Hotel owners told journalists that they were of course prepared to accommodate the homeless, as long as they knew that they had been sent by the city.

However, Dinkins had previously approached the hotel industry with a request for accommodation, but he had never received an answer. For this reason the HRA gave the homeless cash (100 dollar a night), with the instructions to say nothing about their situation. The press quickly came with stories about homeless people watching pay-per-view films all evening and telephoning long-distance, and all at the taxpayers' expense (*New York Times*, 25 August 1991).

A redistribution of the financial resources could solve part of the problem of the homeless, but a Proposed Act with this in mind stranded in Congress in June 1987. A number of campaigns from within Congress succeeded in delaying the implementation of the Act covering the costs of temporary accommodation until 1991. The withdrawal of most of the Federal support forced the city to close the already unpopular welfare hotels. In the first instance this was to be completed in 1992, but the deadline was advanced to July 1990. Although this deadline wasn't met, they certainly made progress. On the day of the deadline only 147 families still lived in these hotels, compared to 3600 three years earlier.[33]

In 1984 the Red Cross took the initiative to rent a vacant building of the Travel Inn close to Times Square to provide accommodation for mothers with children. The building opened its doors in 1985, and the Red Cross brought in all the staff needed to run the project. Each room has a couple of beds, a refrigerator, cupboards, a table, chairs, and its own bathroom. Part of the garage is used as parking space, another part is used as storage space, and yet another serves as a communal area.

There is an enormous number of homeless single mothers with young children. Joan Forrester Sprague's book about them makes an inventory of a large number of initiatives to provide accommodation for homeless mothers. There is a very good reason for her description of these institutions as 'lifeboats for women and children'.[34] Many of these women have suffered from beatings and violence in the past. Only women are admitted to the accommodation, so they are protected from their former partner.

One of the most important current programs that have been set up by private initiatives is HELP, which is run by Andrew Cuomo. HELP is the acronym for *Homeless Emergency Leverage Program*. It is a private initiative, in part financed by the authorities. In the last few years the program has grown from a few hostels on the East Side into eight centers with a total of one thousand units. Cuomo's plan is popular, since his centers cost only about two-thirds of what the former New York welfare hotels cost. Cuomo built an AIDS hospital in the Bronx where nursing costs 200 dollars a day, which is low in comparison with the 700 dollars a day it costs in the city. Apart from being cheaper than the authorities Cuomo is also faster. Theoretically speaking, about eight years is needed to get through New York's procedure for social housing. In most cases this can be reduced to four years, by beginning several procedures in parallel rather than consecutively. An efficient manager like Cuomo, who has a legal background, can obviously gain some extra savings in this time. Cuomo is a fervent supporter of private initiative. In his opinion the authorities can't get on top of the problem because of all the procedures involved, and the legislation. The private nature of HELP also allows him to set more stringent requirements on the people he accommodates. The female residents – women with children make the most use of the provisions HELP offers – must report to the social worker. They must follow a detoxification program or a training, if necessary. In addition they must keep their children at school. If they don't, they're out. A minority, about one-tenth of the total, stay for a longer period of time. Most stay between two to eight months until a permanent address has been found for them.

The name of the program would appear to be rather unfortunately chosen. *Help* strongly suggests permanent support, which is precisely the opposite of what is intended. Roger Hart, who is a professor at the City University of New York and is acting as an advisor to a project in Brooklyn, was informed that 'condominium' would be a much better name.

The hopeless conditions in the welfare hotels was the reason why Ed Koch took the initiative in 1986 to start a program for temporary accommodation for the homeless in the city, to be sited at seven locations. The construction program was completed under Mayor David Dinkins. The city provided the funds and invited Skidmore, Owings and Merrill (SOM), one of the largest architectural practices in the USA, to submit a design. The commission was accepted and they drew up a design, at cost price. The SOM design was awarded a prize in 1988. The buildings designed by SOM provide accommodation for about 100 families. The reception is on the ground floor, with an office for the intake. A communal room is located on the first floor. There are two types of residential units: smaller

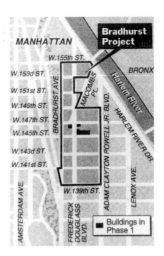

↑   Skidmore, Owings & Merrill,
    Transitional Housing for the homeless, 1991

→   Bradhurst project, Manhattan, New York

families have a room with two or three beds and a built-in kitchen and
bathroom, while larger families have a separate room for the kitchen and
dining room. The accommodation for single persons is in 'houses' con-
sisting of eight separate rooms arranged around a communal kitchen and
living room. The exterior is vaguely reminiscent of the Amsterdam
School, although the design is much more formal.

Another project is located in Crotona Park West, the Bronx. This
involves an extensive renovation project of twenty buildings, which are
intended for permanent residence. Each group of three buildings has a
laundry, a communal room and a management center. Every three groups
have a joint children's day care center; a new center has recently been
promised. A problem with this project is that the complex is relatively
isolated from the city's facilities. A lot of criticism could be made about
this project in urban development terms – but here too it should be realized that anything is better than the street.

The largest project is the *Bradhurst* project in Harlem. It is located in
one of the most neglected and poorest neighborhoods of the city, a desolate area stretching over 40 blocks. The project covers the area between
139th Street and 155th Street and between Adam Clayton Powell Boulevard and Bradhurst, Edgecombe and St. Nicholas Avenues. The area has
been completely neglected since the 1970s: most families are long gone,
and the crime rate is the highest in the city. It is an urban 'wasteland' and
in need of investors. The project involves the alteration of eighteen buildings to make some 320 apartments for homeless people and families with

a low income. In total 2200 new residential units will be created, and within the next ten years 300,000 square feet will be made available for commercial purposes. A number of services will also be included in the project, which will provide opportunities for job-training and cultural activities. The estimated cost of the housing program alone amounts to no less than 160 million dollars.

The *Harlem Urban Development Corporation* and the *New York Urban Coalition* disagreed as to how this area should be redeveloped. *Harlem* doesn't want outsiders involved in the development – but unfortunately the *Urban Coalition*, a private multi-cultural concern established in the aftermath of the riots of the 1960s, has its offices downtown in Soho, on Hudson Street. So it is not considered to be a 'black' organization. The solution seemed to be to split the efforts. The Urban Coalition will initially participate in 26% of the homes, and the Harlem Development Corporation will provide the remaining 74%. When more homes are built later in the project the roles will be reversed.

Prototype on Washington Street, the first location of the Manhattan Transfer Shelter System (MTSS)

The first prototype of the *Transfer Plan*, with detox, is projected in the west of the island on the site of the *14th Street Wholesale Meat Market*. The grid of Manhattan has a kink south of 14th Street. The kink begins at the Avenue of the Americas (6th Avenue) and continues to the Hudson River. The site is demarcated by West 14th Street to the north, Greenwich Street to the east, and West Street on the Hudson side. The prototype will be built on Washington Street, on the still stable remains of the disused Amtrak railroad that comes to a dead end on Gansevoort Street. In the 1960s the entire Market covered 14 blocks, or an area of 35 acres. The most important part of the Market was located on the 7 blocks between West 14th Street and Gansevoort Street to the north and south, and between Hudson Street and West Street to the east and west. Most buildings have three to five stories, although one or two are higher. All the buildings are badly neglected, and most are in a hopeless condition. Too little account was taken of the Market in the urban planning, so the trucks arriving to load or unload meat often get stuck in the narrow streets. Robert Holland and Donald Bowers's 1962 report on the Market for the Mayor already included a long list of faults. The buildings were actually already out of date; not that it would be possible to adapt them for use with modern transshipment methods. And the days of the Meat Market must surely be numbered now the Amtrak railroad is no longer in use, and a number of refrigerated warehouses have been closed.

The 14th Street market is not a pleasant place to work. Manual labor still is used instead of modern handling equipment; it must be used, because few of the facilities were planned for modern mechanical handling methods. Adequate and clean welfare facilities are not available for most employees in the market. Many of the welfare facilities are dark, dirty and poorly equipped. Few meet modern standards, nor is that possible for most of them because of their constructions, size and location within the facilities. Many facilities have crowded work areas, lighting is bad in some, many are dirty,

Meat market, land use

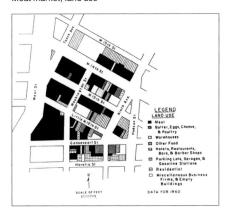

few have proper facilities for cleaning, and many have equipment that is impossible to clean even if proper cleaning facilities and equipment were available. ... The environment, in and around the market, is far from pleasant and attractive. It is depressing not only to the employees but to visitors and others who frequent the market. Many of the buildings are old, weather-worn, and in poor repair. The entire area is poorly drained, and a sloppy condition prevails in rainy or snowy weather. In the winter, trash, garbage, and other refuse is often burned in the streets, not only to get rid of it but to provide heat for employees working outside.[35]

The two consultants give detailed proposals for new refrigerated stores and improved delivery and shipment. However the underlying problem remains unsolved, as the implementation of these proposals would have needed an area of at least 80 acres. The 35 acres of the 14th Street Market are nowhere near enough. The report does however see possibilities for the site between Hunts Point and Jersey Meadows; but since the continuation of meat transshipments in the present circumstances is no longer feasible the *14th Street Wholesale Market* will be given a new function: the *Manhattan Transfer Shelter System.*

The building works like a SONnaia SONata. Those of us who are used to thinking in terms such as housing, home and comfort would experience the shelter as Ginzburg's mechanized hell. But for the homeless person it is a refuge where he is glad to stay, it gives him the chance to stay off the street for a while.

Milyutin provided a housing cell, but the shelter has only a sleeping cell. All other functions are collective – as with the Constructivists – although in the shelter this has been chosen for other reasons. The dom-kommunas were intended for the workers' elite, and drunkards, vulgarity and ignorance were shut out; in the shelters the reverse is the case, they are shut in. The building is elevated, not in some kind of modernistic reference, but to provide protection from the 'demand' for a place to sleep.

The access to the elevated Amtrak construction was a problem. From the very beginning it was certain that we would use a linear structure for this part of the building, which is in fact a critical paraphrasing of the OSA ideology. We accentuated the entrance in a 'dramatic' fashion with reference to Melnikov's Svoboda Club. This was a worker's club Melnikov built in 1928, together with another club. These clubs were greatly different from his usual style, because they were so linear. The

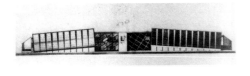

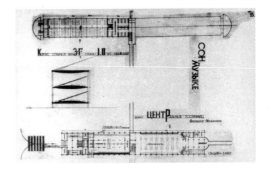

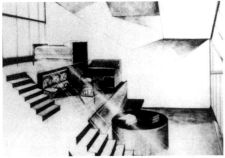

Konstantin Melnikov, SONnaia SONata, 1929

Frunze Club on the river and the Svoboda on the Vyatskaya Ulitsa seem to have come directly from an 18th century drawing book.

It seems as though the linearity is being tested by the disharmony. In the Frunze Club the longitudinal symmetry is disrupted by the monumental elevated facade, which serves for propaganda purposes. In the Svoboda Club this is achieved with the stairs, which are at the extreme ends of the facade. This places a strong emphasis on the entrance, which then becomes the focus of attention since it is placed centrally and is completely symmetrical. Starr calls it a 'restless element', whilst the entire structure exhibits a harnessed symmetry. With the Manhattan Shelter, the entrance is closer to the end of Washington Street, close to the junction with Gansevoort Street, and set asymmetrically to the length of the building. The entrance consists of a staircase combined with an elevator. This can be accessed easily by people who often have their possessions

New York City **Prototype on Washington Street, the first location of the Manhattan Transfer Shelter System (MTSS)**

with them. And anyone who might have a push-cart, or someone with a prosthesis or in a wheel-chair is able to reach the entrance with ease.

The stairs can be seen as a homage to Melnikov, the famous loner in Russian mass society. In this respect the user of the shelter is similar to his. The reference relates to the first design of the Svoboda Club. This had no stairs, but was instead provided with a ramp which served as a metaphor for a waterfall from the reservoir of the club. This design was rejected by the trade unions because it

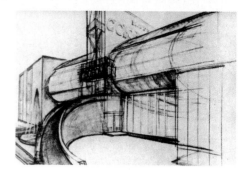

Konstantin Melnikov, Svoboda Club, 1927

was too daring. Sick and tired of their criticism Melnikov returned to work, and made a proposal for stairs instead of the ramp. For the *Washington Street Shelter* we chose a pragmatic solution, with a respectful nod to Melnikov. In many respects it is thoroughly 'banal' architecture. Its day-to-day use may evoke on occasion an emotion that I have previously described as sublime, and this may yet transform the building into architecture.

Prototype Manhattan Transfer Shelter System (MTSS)

New York

Washington Street Manhattan, New York

Architects **Arie Graafland, Harry Kerssen** Model **Limited Editions, Rotterdam** Digital Assemblings **Arie Graafland, Hans Schouten and Bureau Piet Gerards** Model Photography **Photographic Department Faculty of Architecture, TU Delft, Hans Schouten**

The appropriation of a growing area of the city for high-priced rehabilitation and redevelopment has also contributed to a sharp increase in homelessness, especially in New York, but also in London and, on a much smaller scale, in Tokyo. All three cities have long had a significant concentration of poor people. But the extent of the segmentation and spatial unevenness has reached dimensions not typical of earlier decades. (Saskia Sassen)

The prototype will be built on Washington Street, on the still stable remains of the abandoned Amtrak railroad that comes to a dead-end on Gansevoort Street. In the nineteen-sixties the entire Market covered 14 blocks, or an area of 35 acres. The most important part of the Market was located on the 7 blocks between West 14th Street and Gansevoort Street to the North and South, and between Hudson Street and West Street to the East and West. Most buildings have three to five stories, although one or two are higher. All the buildings are badly neglected, and most are in a hopeless condition. Too little account was taken of the Market in the urban planning, so the trucks arriving to load or unload meat often get stuck in the narrow streets.

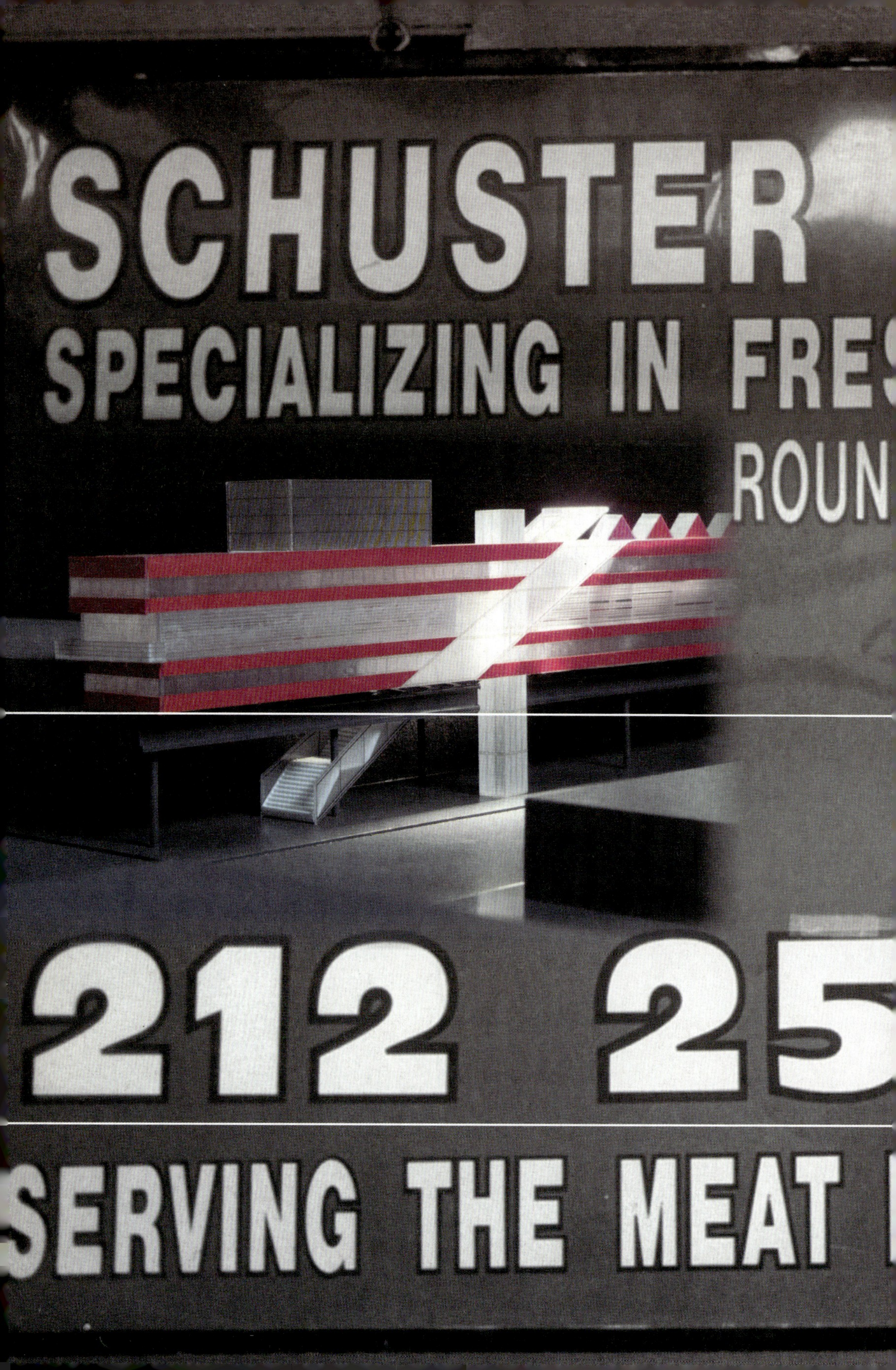
SCHUSTER
SPECIALIZING IN FRES
ROUN
212 25
SERVING THE MEAT

EAT CORP.
LY CUT LEAN MEATS
★ FLANK STEAK
★ SHINS
★ FLANKS
5-1
DUSTRY SINCE 1941

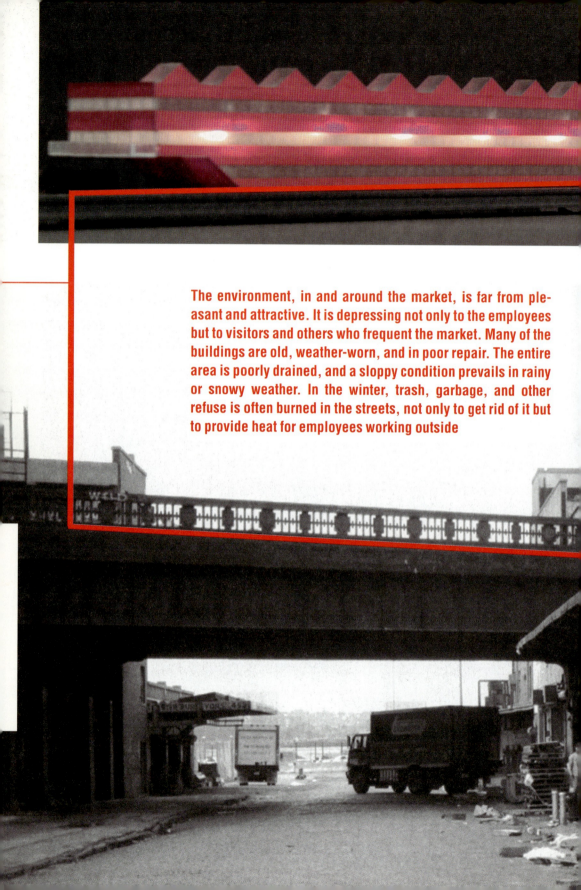

The environment, in and around the market, is far from pleasant and attractive. It is depressing not only to the employees but to visitors and others who frequent the market. Many of the buildings are old, weather-worn, and in poor repair. The entire area is poorly drained, and a sloppy condition prevails in rainy or snowy weather. In the winter, trash, garbage, and other refuse is often burned in the streets, not only to get rid of it but to provide heat for employees working outside

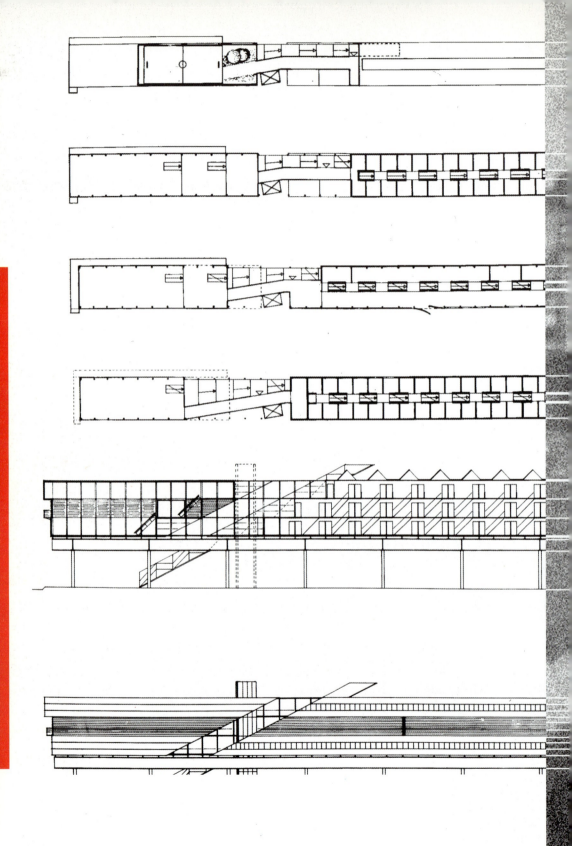

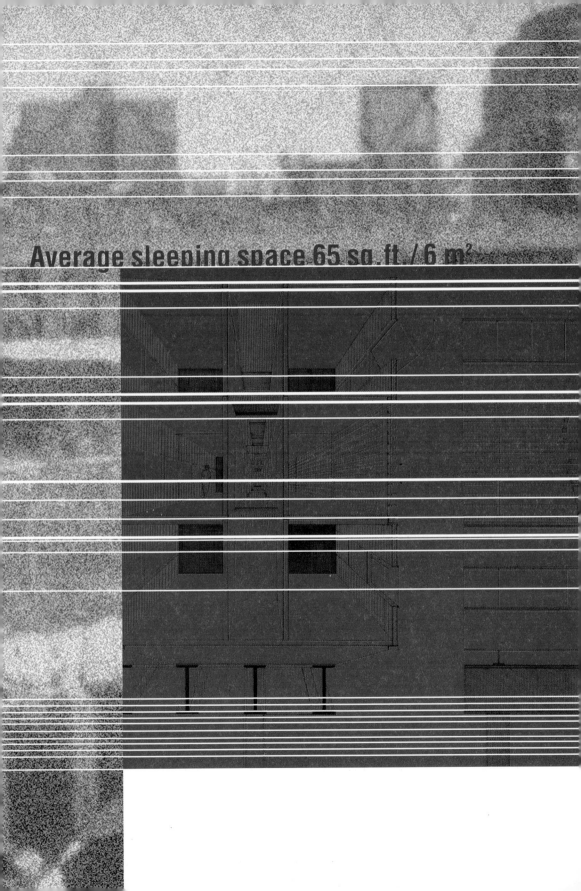

Average sleeping space 65 sq. ft. / 6 m²

Notes

1 Architecture: Introduction

1 Mark Wigley in Philip Johnson and Mark Wigley, *Deconstructivist Architecture*, New York, 1988, p.11. Catalogue for the exhibition of the same name in the Museum of Modern Art.

2 Walter Benjamin, *Das Passagen-Werk*, in *Gesammelte Schriften*, Volumes v-1 and v-2 (Ed. Rolf Tiedemann), Frankfurt a/M, Suhrkamp Verlag, 1983, p.12.

3 Walter Benjamin, 'Konvolut M (Der Flaneur)', [m3a, 4], in *Das Passagen-Werk*, p.533.

4 Susan Buck-Morss, *The dialectics of seeing. Walter Benjamin and the Arcades Project*, Cambridge, MIT, 1989, pp.39-40.

5 In *The dialectics of seeing* Buck-Morss has reconstructed Benjamin's *Passagen-Werk* on the basis of the cities involved.

6 Walter Benjamin, 'Erfahrung und Armut', in *Gesammelte Schriften*, Volume ii-1 (Ed. Rolf Tiedemann and Hermann Schweppenhäuser), Frankfurt a/M, Suhrkamp Verlag, 1977, pp.213-219.

7 In his opening article 'Die Neue Einfachheit. Mutmassungen über die Jahrtausendwende' in the *German Year Book* Vittorio Magnana Lampugnani makes a plea for a 'neue Einfachheit'. He also makes a distinction between movements such as Deconstructivism, Postmodernism and the very nostalgic 'Modernism' in contemporary architectural culture. This last form is above all a repetition of the work of Le Corbusier, Gropius and Mies, or in other words the architecture of Richard Meier and Norman Foster. Lampugnani makes a plea for another approach, that of neutrality. In his view monotony is often more honest than compulsive variation. Like Modernism, values such as simplicity, clarity and unity would once again adopt a central role. Architectural chaos was to be contained. Although I am broadly in agreement with his criticism, it does unmistakably imply a return to Modernism. However such a return is impossible. Experiment and complexity should be retained.

Fritz Neumeyer's plea for a 'Mut zum Normalen, zum Konventionellen' is of the same order, and consequently is not an answer for *contemporary* architecture. Fritz Neumeyer, *Hinterhergeschaut. Die Architektur der Stadt und der Architekturpreis des BDA*, Berlin, 1992.

8 Jacques Derrida, 'A letter to Peter Eisenman', and Peter Eisenman, 'Post/El Cards; a reply to Jacques Derrida', in *An exchange between Jacques Derrida and Peter Eisenman*, Assemblage 12. Derrida's letter was written in October 1989, in reference to the conference *Postmodernism and Beyond. Architecture as the critical art of contemporary culture* at the University of California, Irvine.

9 K. Michael Hays, *Modernism and the posthumanist subject. The architecture of Hannes Meyer and Ludwig Hilberseimer*, Cambridge, MIT, 1922, p.286.

10 Benjamin, *Das Passagen-Werk*, p.574.

11 Manfredo Tafuri, 'L'architecture dans le boudoir', in *The Sphere and the Labyrinth. Avant-Gardes and Architecture from Piranesi to the 1970's*, Cambridge, MIT, 1987, p.283. Original title *La sfera e il labirinto; avanguardie e architettura da Piranesi agli anni '70*, Turin, 1980.

12 Claes Caldenby, 'Bold if rare beginnings', in Irina Chepkunova, Claes Caldenby and Otakar Máčel, *Soviet Architecture 1917-1987*, Amsterdam, 1989, p.9.

13 Samuel IJsseling, Mimesis. *Over schijn en zijn*, Baarn, Ambo, 1990, p.11.

14 In this respect Janet Abrams's work is of interest; see, for example, her *Site Work, Architecture in Photography Since Early Modernism*, London, 1991.

15 Aaron Betsky, *Violated Perfection. Architecture and the Fragmentation of the Modern*, New York, 1990, p.188.

16 *Indesem* 1993, Congress of the Department of Architecture of the TU-Delft, papers and design workshops, *Dark is the night*, December 1993.

17 Lebbeus Woods, *Onefivefour*, New York, 1989.

18 R. Sierksma, *Massa en minoriteit. Een essay over een (post)modern tijdsgewricht*, Delft, 1991. Sierksma discusses this kind of consciousness in the context of the relationship between Modernism and Postmodernism. The latter is characterized by a lack of self-reflection, combined with an increasingly rapid flow of meaningless information units. This results in isolation and pseudo-social relationships, p.55 ff.

19 Liane Lefaivre, 'Dirty realism' in der Architektur', in *Architese* no. 1, 1990, 'Neue Ansichten'.

20 Fredric Jameson, 'Spatial equivalents in the world system', in *Postmodernism or the Cultural Logic of late Capitalism*, Durham, 1992, p.101 ff.

2 Constructivism

1 Johan Meyer, 'De zinnen te buiten', in *Oase* 39, spring 1994, pp.35-57.

2 Otakar Máčel, 'Tradition, innovation and politics', in *Soviet Architecture 1917-1987*, Amsterdam, 1989, p.15. I call this 'socio-realism', not socialist realism. The latter assumes that socialist ideals can be communicated by the use of art. I suspect that this is impossible. This is, in brief, Adorno's criticism of Lukács. Art as a positive ideology is doomed to failure. Socialist realism was always a straitjacket, Russian agit-prop remained an emblem on the exterior of the building. In neither Melnikov's nor Leonidov's architecture did they have anything to do with the actual building. (The same can also be said, mutatis mutandis, of Terragni; the other side of the story.)
In 1934 socialist realism was simply short-circuited with politics. With the help of the trade unions (established in 1932, and financed by the state) it was possible to proclaim it the 'method' for the benefit of the proletariat. Máčel lists five characteristics of socio-realism, all of which represent a positive ideology of a classless society: faithful representation, the unstoppable progress of socialism, solidarity between all workers, revolutionary romanticism, and socialist realism as a phase in the development of the history of art. All five characteristics are the subject of Adorno's aesthetic and philosophical criticism.

3 After Roger Scruton, *The Aesthetics of Architecture*, Princeton, Princeton University Press, 1979, p.168.

4 Peter Eisenman, 'En terror firma, in de sporen van groteksten', in Arie Graafland (Ed.), *Peter Eisenman. Recent Projects / Recente projecten*, Nijmegen SUN, 1989, p.21 ff.

5 After Anthony Vidler, *The Architectural Uncanny. Essays in the Modern Unhomely*, Cambridge, MIT, 1992, p.17 ff.; for Walpole see R. Sierksma, 'Anekdotische architectuur, Horace Walpole's *Strawberry Hill*', in *Oase* 39, spring 1994, pp.11-34.

6 See chapter 1, note 8.

7 Klaus Jürgen Bauer, *Minima Aesthetica*, Banalität als strategische Subversion der Architektur, Weimar, 1996.

8 The situation is no different in the Netherlands: according to his colleagues Koolhaas is one of the 'five worst' architects; see *De buitenkant van Nederland,* interview, 1997.

9 S. Frederick Starr, *Konstantin Melnikov, Solo Architect in a Mass Society*, Princeton, Princeton University Press, p.25. See also A.M. Voigt, *Russische und Französische Revolutionsarchitektur 1917/1789*, Cologne, 1974.

10 For this theme see Leszek Kolakowski, *Der Mensch ohne Alternative* (1956) and *Traktat über die Sterblichkeit der Vernunft* (1967); for the Netherlands Ger Harmsen, *Marx contra de marxistische ideologen* (1968).

11 Christoph Mohr and Michael Müller, *Funktionalität und Moderne. Das Neue Frankfurt und seine Bauten 1925-1933*, Frankfurt a/M, 1984.

12 Moisei Ginzburg, *Style and Epoch*, Opposition Books, Cambridge, MIT, 1982, pp.80-81. Originally *Stil' i epocha* (1924).

13 ibid., p.102.

14 For the relationships between Berlin and the USSR see Manfredo Tafuri's extremely informative article, 'USSR-Berlin, 1922: From Populism to "Constructivist International"', in *The Sphere and the Labyrinth*, p.119 ff.

15 Christina Lodder, *Russian Constructivism*, New Haven/London, Yale University Press, 1983, p.113.

16 Starr, *Melnikov*, p.67.

17 N.A. Milyutin, *Sotsgorod, The Problem of Building Socialist Cities*, Cambridge, MIT, 1974. Originally *Socgorod* (1930).

18 Anatole Kopp, *Town and Revolution*, London, 1970, p.115. Originally *Ville et révolution. Architecture et urbanisme Soviétique des années vingt*, Paris, 1967.

19 Cited by Kopp, *Town and Revolution*, p.81.

20 Anatole Kopp, *Constructivist architecture in the USSR*, London, 1985, p.70. For a comprehensive description see S.O. Khan-Magomedov, *Moisei Ginzburg* (1972); the Italian translation by Claudio Masetti (Milan, 1975) has a preface by Vieri Quilici. See this edition, pp.122-162.

21 Andrei Gozak and Andrei Leonidov, *Ivan Leonidov. The complete works*, Ed. Catherine Cooke, London, 1988, p.10.

22 Elke Pistorius, *Der Architektenstreit nach der Revolution. Zeitgenössische Texte Russland 1925-1932*, Basle/Berlin/Boston, Birkhäuser, 1992, p.9 ff.

3 The sublime

1 Scruton, *The Aesthetics of Architecture*, (chapter 2, note 3).

2 Edmund Burke, *A Philosophical Inquiry into the Origin of Our Ideas of the Sublime and Beautiful*, with an introduction by J.T. Boulton, London, 1958.

3 ibid., volume one, section II, 'Pain and pleasure', p.33.

4 Immanuel Kant, *Kritik der Urteilskraft*, Zweites Buch, 'Analytik des Erhabenen', 23, p.105. For the references to *Kritik der Urteilskraft* I have made use of volume x of Wilhelm Weischedel's edition of Kant's writings: Immanuel Kant, *Werkausgabe*, 12 volumes, Frankfurt a/M, Suhrkamp Verlag, 1968. See also Jean François Lyotard, *Lessons on the Analytic of the Sublime. Kant's Critique of Judgment*, Stanford, Stanford University Press,

1994, p.68. Originally *Leçons sur l'analytique du sublime*, Paris, Galilée, 1991.

5 Immanuel Kant, *Beobachtungen über das Gefühl des Schönen und Erhabenen*, Königsberg, 1764. John Goldtwait's English translation was based on volume 2 of Kant's *Gesammelte Schriften*, in the edition of the Königlich Preussische Akademie der Wissenschaften. It was published in a book entitled *Essays and Treatises in Moral, Political andVarious Philosophical Subjects*, London, 1798.

6 Paul Crowther, *The Kantian Sublime. From Morality to Art*, NewYork, 1989, p.9.

7 Scruton, *The Aesthetics of Architecture*, p.173.

8 Gilles Deleuze, *Kant's Critical Philosophy.The Doctrine of the Faculties*, London, 1984, p.51. Original title *La Philosophie Critique de Kant*, Paris, 1983. See Kant, *Kritik der Urteilskraft*, 'Vom mathematisch-Erhabenen', pp.25-27, in particular p.27.

9 Wolfgang Welsch, *Aesthetisches Denken. Adorno's Aesthetik: Eine implizite Aesthetik des Erhabenen*, Stuttgart, 1990, p.117 ff.

10 Rem Koolhaas, 'Bigness.The problem of Large', in *Wiederhall* 17, devoted to 'Art architecture aesthetics now', Amsterdam, 1994.

11 Kant, *Kritik der Urteilskraft*, 'Analytik des Erhabenen', 23, Ed.Weischedel, p.166.

12 Jean-François Lyotard, 'Complexity and the sublime', in ICA Documents 4, *Postmodernism*, London, 1986, p.14. See also idem, *Lessons on the Analytic of the Sublime*, p.69 ff.

13 P.H.J.M. Heydendael and M.H.R. Nuy, *Achtergronden van thuisloosheid*, Groningen, 1992, p.141.

14 Joel Blau, *The homeless of New York. A case study in social welfare policy*, unpublished dissertation, Columbia University, 1987, p.22.

15 AfterWalter Benjamin, *Ursprung des Deutschen Trauerspiels* (1926); in *Gesammelte Schriften*, volume 1-1, p.213.

16 Lyotard gives an explanation of this problem in *Le différend*, Paris, Minuit, 1983; English translation *The Differend. Phrases in Dispute*, Manchester, Manchester University Press, 1988. A lucid discussion with a critical commentary is to be found in Wolfgang Welsch, *Unsere postmoderne Moderne*, Weinheim, 1988.

17 'Deklaration der Vereinigung proletarischer Architekten (VOPRA)', in Pistorius (Ed.), *Der Architektenstreit nach der Revolution*, p.85.

18 A. Mordwinow, 'Die "Leonidowerei" und ihr Schaden', in *Iskusstvo v massy*, 1930, pp.12-15; translation in Pistorius (Ed.), *Der Architektenstreit*, p.120.

19 Thomas Weiskel, *The romantic sublime. Studies in the Structure and Psychology of Transcendence*, Baltimore, Johns Hopkins University Press, 1976, p.85 ff.

20 'Man sieht hieraus auch, dass die wahre Erhabenheit nur im Gemüte des Urteilenden, nicht in dem Naturobjekte, dessen Beurteilung diese Stimmung desselben veranlasst, müsse gesucht werden'. *Kritik der Urteilskraft*, 'Vom Mathematisch-Erhabenen', Ed.Weischedel, p.179.

21 Terry Eagleton, *The Ideology of the Aesthetic*, Cambridge, 1990, p.73.

22 This refers to two articles: 'The Sublime and the Avant-Garde' and Newman: 'The Instant'. Both articles were included in Andrew Benjamin (Ed.), *The Lyotard Reader*, Oxford, 1989. The first originally appeared in *Art Forum* 22, no. 8, April 1984. The philosophical background of this concept is to be found in *Lessons on the Analytic of the Sublime*, in the paragraph 'Negative Presentation': '"Negative presentation" is the sign of the presence of the absolute, and it is or can only make a sign of being absent from the forms of the presentable. Thus the absolute remains unpresentable...' (p.150 ff.) and further on 'the imagination suggests the presence of what it cannot present' (p.152).

23 Adorno was never really en vogue. His thoughts were too complex, often too cryptic, but he had in fact already committed many of the ideas for Foucault's genealogy and Lyotard's differential concepts to paper. It is possible that he didn't play a major role in the Marxism 'debate'. He is undoubtedly no postmodernist or post-Marxist, but it is certain that many of his ideas can be of assistance to us in gaining an understanding of today's world. His criticism of metaphysics, of the usual relationship between the general and the specific, system and detail, his artistic *material concept* (a reference to the Russians), his rejection of socialist realism, and not least his manner of writing, characterized by the figure of the ellipse, are also to be found in differential thought. Lyotard's articles about the sublime could also have been written by Adorno.

24 Anthony Vidler, *The Architectural Uncanny*, chapter 2, note 5.

25 Paul Crowther cites, for example: Jacques Derrida, *The Truth in Painting*, (translated by G. Bennington, Chicago, 1987), Paul de Man, 'Phenomenality and Materiality in Kant' in G. Schapiro and A. Sica, (Eds.), *Hermeneutics: Questions and Prospects*, Amherst, 1984 and Neil Hertz, 'The Notion of Blockage in the Literature of the Sublime' in G. Hartmann, (Ed.), *Psychoanalysis and the Questions of the Text*, Baltimore, 1978. After Paul Crowther, *The Kantian Sublime. From Morality to Art*, Oxford, 1989. Not unjustly he notes in the 'Introduction' that 'in all these cases, in other words, Kant's theory is out to use on the basis of, or in the service of, some much broader set of theoretical interests. There is little or no attempt to consider it in the context of possible tensions and distortions forced upon it by the broader philosophical position embodied in Kant's ethics and aesthetics. Until this issue is clarified, I would suggest that our understanding of both Kant and the status of sublimity as an aesthetic concept remain substantially incomplete'.

26 Crowther, *The Kantian Sublime*, p.164.

27 For Marshall Berman, see p.96 and 111 of this book.

28 Elaine Scarry, *The Body in Pain. The making and unmaking of the world*, NewYork/Oxford, 1985, p.161 ff.

29 ibid., p.170.

30 ibid., p.249.

31 Anthony Vidler, 'The building in pain, the body and architecture in post-modern culture', in *AA-Files* 19.

32 This was also the intention of my book *Esthetisch vertoog en ontwerp*, Nijmegen, SUN, 1986. It aimed to render these terms suitable for use in architecture via the *material concept* (see Chapter V. 'Aesthetic material').

33 Gilles Deleuze and Félix Guattari, 'November 28, 1947: How do you make yourself a body without organs?' in *A Thousand Plateaus. Capitalism & Schizophrenia*, Minneapolis, 1987, p.149 ff. Originally 'Comment se faire un Corps sans Organes?', in Gilles Deleuze and Félix Guattari, *Capitalisme et Schizophrénie. Mille Plateaux*, Paris 1980, p.185.

34 In his *Coldness and Cruelty* Deleuze refers to Theodore Reik's description of this. Reik draws attention to (1) the special significance of the fantasy: the scene, the rituals, (2) the suspense factor: the waiting, the delay, (3) the persuasive factor and (4) the provocative fear. Deleuze adds (5) the contract to these. After Gilles Deleuze, *Masochism Coldness and Cruelty*, New York, 1991, p.74. Originally *Le Froid et le Cruel*, Paris, 1967.

35 Gilles Deleuze and Félix Guattari, *Anti-Oedipus*, Minnesota, 1983, p.8, originally published as *L'Anti-Oedipe*, Paris, 1972.

36 Gilles Deleuze and Félix Guattari, *Anti-Oedipus*, p.8.

37 Arie Graafland, 'Peter Eisenman, architectuur in absentia', in Graafland (Ed.), *Peter Eisenman. Recent Projects / Recente projecten*, Nijmegen, SUN, 1989, p.116.

4 Amsterdam: Rhizome city

1 Gilles Deleuze and Félix Guattari, *A Thousand Plateaus. Capitalism and Schizophrenia*, translation and preface by Brian Massumi, Minneapolis, University of Minnesota Press, 1987, p.21. Original title: *Mille Plateaux,* part II of *Capitalisme et Schizophrénie*, Paris, Minuit, 1980, p.16.

2 Denis Hollier, *Against Architecture. The writings of Georges Bataille*, translated by Betsy Wing, Cambridge, MIT, 1989. Original title *La Prise de la Concorde*, Paris, Gallimard), 1974. The title refers to the famed Parisian square, the Place de la Concorde. I wouldn't be surprised if Tschumi's *Parc de la Villette* had been inspired by this book.

3 Richard Sennett, *The Conscience of the Eye. The design and social life of cities*, New York, 1990, p.190 ff.

4 The manager of the branch of a multinational located in the South-East lobe of Amsterdam resides in a splendid canalside house on the Binnenkant. In the hours of darkness he is a visitor to the Warmoesstraat; he goes from the Cockring to the all-night restaurant in the basement of the Film Museum, and then returns to the rhizome. He is also a valued member of the board of the Schorer Foundation; any free evenings he might have he spends at the Squash City on Bickerseiland. He flies weekly between Frankfurt, London and New York, in the pursuit of the international flow of capital. He studied at the Harvard Business School, and is based in the rhizome of Amsterdam at his own request.

5 Jan de Heer, 'AUP + AUP(ette)', in *Raderwerk*, 10 jaar Projektraad Bouwkunde, Delft, DUP, 1981, p.160.

6 ibid.

7 Sennett, *The Conscience of the Eye*, pp.54, 55.

8. Alan Colquhoun, *Modernity at the Classical Tradition. Architectural Essays 1980-1987*, Cambridge, MIT, 1991, p.28.

9 Arie Graafland, 'Rem Koolhaas en de Moderniteit', in *Hoe modern is de Nederlandse architectuur?* Rotterdam,

010 Publishers, 1990, p.79.

10 Deleuze and Guattari, *A Thousand plateaus*, p.22; *Mille plateaux*, p.33.

11 The two works that Deleuze and Guattari wrote together in the 1970s; *L'Anti-Oedipe* and *Mille plateaux* constitute the project *Capitalisme et Schizophrénie* (see note 1).

12 *El Croquis*, special issue: *Encontrando Libertades: Conversaciones con Rem Koolhaas / Finding freedoms: conversations with Rem Koolhaas*, March 1992, no. 53, Koolhaas in discussion with Alejandro Zaera Polo, pp.6-32.

13 A. Zaera Polo in ibid., p.35 ff.

14 Jacques Derrida, 'Point de Folie – Maintenant l'Architecture', in Bernard Tschumi, *La case vide. La Villette*, Architectural Association, folio VIII.

15 The history is described in Mary McLeod, 'Le Corbusier and Algiers', in *Oppositions*, no. 19/20, 1980. This number, edited by Kenneth Frampton, is devoted to the subject: Le Corbusier 1933-1960.

16 For the Sea Terminal in Zeebrugge see my paper 'Architectuuronderwijs en het einde van de Glazen Doos', presented to the European Association for Architectural Education on 24 April 1992 at Eindhoven, and published in R. Sierksma (Ed.), *VF-progress report II*, Delft 1992.

17 Rem Koolhaas, in *Hoe modern is de Nederlandse architectuur?* (this chapter, note 9).

18 Janny Rodermond and Harm Tilman, 'Een scenario voor de IJ-oever. Strategie en ontwerp', in *de Architect*, November 1992.

19 ibid.

20 Rem Koolhaas, *Delirious New York*, New York / London, 1978, p.23; republished in Rotterdam, 010 Publishers, 1994, p.30.

21 Fredric Jameson in discussion with Michael Speaks, 'An architectural Conversation, Envelopes and enclaves:

the space of post-civil society', in *Assemblage*, 1994, no. 17, p.33.

22 H. Brugmans, *Geschiedenis van Amsterdam*, part v, Utrecht/Antwerp, 1973, p.136 ff.

23 Rem Koolhaas, 'Precarious Entity', in Cynthia Davidson (Ed.), *Any-one*, New York, Rizzoli, 1991, p.146 ff. Koolhaas's paper discusses his design for the Bibliothèque de France from 1989. Although it doesn't contain an explanation of the concept of the 'critical mass', it does discuss aspects he took into consideration in his design of a specific commission, a library. Two passages are devoted to this concept in the AWF scenario. Critical mass 1 refers to the concentration on the Oostelijk Eiland around Amsterdam's railway station, the cs, and critical mass 2 refers to a new kind of work place on the Oostelijk Eiland. According to the scenario the linearity of the design, in which a large volume of buildings is spread along a 3-mile stretch of the riverbank, ensures that the mass never becomes 'critical'. For more details see the *Ruimtelijk Scenario IJ-oevers Amsterdam*, 1 September 1992. The client was the Amsterdam Waterfront Financieringsmaatschappij, and the project was supervised by the Office for Metropolitan Architecture.

The concept of critical mass actually comes from the real-estate world. Garreau's study indicates that about five million square feet of office space are needed for the creation of an 'edge city'. With five million square feet the rest will follow of its own accord. This easily amounts to as many as 20,000 office staff. Joel Garreau, *Edge City. Life on the new frontier*, New York, 1991, pp.30-31.

5 Tokyo: The Sugoroku Board

1 Jinnai Hidenobu, 'Journey into a mysterious city', in *Ethnic Tokyo*, Process 72.

1 Edward Seidensticker, *Low City, High City*, Tokyo from Edo to the Earthquake: how the shogun's ancient capital became a great modern city, 1867-1923, Harvard University Press, 1991.

3 Jinnai Hidenobu, *Tokyo, a spatial anthropology*, University of California Press, 1995, p.67.

4 Jinnai Hidenobu, op. cit., p.92.

5 Jinnai Hidenobu, op. cit., p.93.

6 Edward W. Soja, *Thirdspace, journeys to Los Angeles and other real-and-imagined places*, Blackwell, 1996. p.283.

7 I have adopted the Japanese custom for Japanese names, according to which the surname is written first.

8 Edward Seidensticker, *Low City, High City*, p.186.

9 Arata Isozaki, 'Wayo Style, The Japanization Mechanism', in *Visions of Japan*, 1992.

10 Michael Foucault, 'Of Other spaces', in Politics, *Documenta X*, the book, p.262, *Diacretics*, 16-1, spring 1986.

11 Daniel Defert, 'Foucault, Space, and the Architects', in Politics, *Documenta X*, the book, pp.274-283.

12. Edward Seidensticker, *Tokyo Rising, the City since the Great Earthquake*, Harvard University Press, 1991, p.52.

13 Botond Bognar, 'Archeology of a fragmented landscape: the new avant-garde of urban architecture in Japan', in *New Japanese Architecture*, New York, Rizzoli, 1990, p.16.

14 M. Christine Boyer, 'Cities for Sale: Merchandizing History at South Street Seaport', in Michael Sorkin (Ed.), *Variations on a Theme Park*, New York, 1992, p.184.

15 Edward W. Soja, *Thirdspace*, pp.163, 311. Soja uses this term in connection with his analysis of Henri Lefebvre's work. 'Thirding' as an *active* term presumes that there are three forms of spatial thinking: the *perceived* space of materialized Spatial Practice; the *conceived* space he (Lefebvre) defined as Representations of Space; and the *lived* Spaces of Representation. Soja defines *Thirdspace* as 'another way of understanding and acting to change the spatiality of human life, a distinct model of critical spatial awareness that is appropriate to the new scope and significance being brought about in the rebalanced trialectics of spatiality-historicality-sociality'. It is not merely an analytical term, but also a design tool to be used for another approach towards space.

16 Edward Seidensticker, *Tokyo Rising, The City since the Great Earthquake*, Harvard University Press, 1991, p.40.

17 Manfredo Tafuri, Francesco Dal Co, *Modern Architecture*, Chapter v, 'The International Concept of Utopia', p.385.

18 In 1940 the then Minister of Foreign Affairs, Yosuke Matsuoka, referred to a Greater East Asia Co-Prosperity Sphere, a community that was 'to include southern regions such as the Dutch East Indies and French Indochina'. But much of the New Order was not applicable to the Co-Prosperity Sphere's 'southern regions', whose relationship to Japan was historically quite different from those between Japan and its closer neighbors, China and Manchuria. South-East Asia was geopolitically and economically a very different region from North-East Asia. In 1942 the Intelligence Section of the Ministry of the Navy drew up the document 'On the Greater East Asia Co-Prosperity Sphere' (*Daito-A kyoeiken-ron*). This document made a distinction between five categories, in which Japan was the 'leading country' and China, Manchukuo and Thailand were independent countries classified in the second category. These latter countries were subject to the 'mediating leadership' (*shido bakai*) of Japan. For more details see J. Victor Koschmann, 'Asia's Ambivalent Legacy', in Peter J. Katzenstein and Takashi Shiriaishi, *Network Power, Japan and Asia*, Cornell

University Press, 1997, p.102.

19 Michel Random, *Japan, strategy of the unseen*, A guide for Westerners to the Mind of Modern Japan, 1997.

20 For details refer to Hajime Yatsuka, 'An architecture floating in a sea of signs', in *The New Japanese Architecture*, p.38.

21 David B. Stuart, *The Making of a Modern Japanese Architecture, 1868 to the Present*, Kodansha International, Tokyo and New York, p.182.

22 Kisho Kurokawa, *Intercultural Architecture, The Philosophy of Symbiosis*, The American Institute of Architects Press, 1991, p.202.

23 *Japan Almanac*, Ashai Shimbun Publishing Company, 1997.

24 Saskia Sassen, *The Global City, New York / London / Tokyo*, p.276. Princeton University Press, 1992. See also her *Globalization and its discontents*, The New Press, New York, 1998, p.59ff.

25 Sidney Giffard, *Japan among the powers, 1890-1990*, Yale University Press, 1994, p.27.

26 Sidney Giffard, op. cit., p.67.

27 See *Yokohama, Portrait of a city from its port opening to the 21st century*, 1982.

28 For details see an overview of the spatial planning of Yokohama; *Urban Design Yokohama, Concepts and Development*, Yokohama Urban Design Forum (YUDF), 1992.

29 See *Yokohama, Facts & Figures*, Business Development Division, Economic Affairs Bureau, City of Yokohama, 1995.

30 See *Transportation in Yokohama*, Bureau of Urban Planning and Road & Highway, City of Yokohama, 1991.

31 See *Guide to the Port of Yokohama*, Port of Yokohama Promotion Association, 1993, and *Ports and Harbours in Japan*, International Affairs Office, Tokyo, 1996.

32 F. Medda and P. Nijkamp, *Waterfront Revitalization and Yokohama's Minato Mirai 21*, Tinbergen Instituut Amsterdam, p.14.

33 *Yumehama 2010 Plan*, design for a New Yokohama Renaissance, City of Yokohama, (Planning Bureau, City of Yokohama), 1995. The Yumehama plan is much more than a spatial plan: in fact it is a comprehensive development program containing long-range objectives, and is to some extent comparable to the integral structural planning as practiced in the Netherlands.

34 *Minato Mirai 21, Our Community and its Members*, Yokohama MM21, Corporation Sakuragi-chō Naka-ku, Yokohama and Yokohama MM21, Overview of Minato Mirai 21, Planning and Individual Operations, 1997.

35 M. Christine Boyer, op. cit., p.189.

36 Paul Waley, *Tokyo: City of Stories*, Tokyo / New York, 1991, p.104.

37 One of the residences in Tuskiji was the Okudaira, where in the years 1771-1774 the first medical manual was translated from the Dutch. The *Ontleedkundige Tafelen* was an anatomical manual written by Johann Adam Kulmus, from Dantzich. The book had been translated from the original German into Latin, French and Dutch. The Dutch version had been acquired by Ryotaku Maeno, a physician in the Okudaire fief, who lived in Nagasaki. Ryotaku deciphered the Dutch text as best he could. The Japanese version, *Kaitai shinsho*, was published in 1774. Ryotaku was one of the first to break through into the Dutch culture; as a consequence he was given the name of 'our Dutch freak'.

38 Saskia Sassen, *The Global City, New York / London / Tokyo*, p.297.

6 New York City: Lines of flight in the city

1 Ann L. Buttenwieser, *Manhattan Water-Bound, Planning and Developing Manhattan's Waterfront from the Seventeenth Century to the Present*, New York, New York University Press, 1987, p.171.

2 Manfredo Tafuri, 'The disenchanted Mountain: 'The Skyscraper and the City', in *The American City. From the Civil War to the New Deal*, Cambridge MIT, 1979, p.436 ff. Originally *La città americana dalla guerra civile al New Deal*, Rome, 1973.

3 Siegfried Giedion, *Space, time and architecture. The growth of a new tradition*, Cambridge, Harvard University Press, 1967, p.825.

4 Nels Anderson, *The hobo, the sociology of the homeless men*, Chicago, University of Chicago Press, 1923, p.11. Nels Anderson was the first and also the most important sociologist to study the homeless. He wrote several books and a great many reports. He knew the world from the inside. Under the pseudonym Dean Stiff he also wrote a handbook for the homeless, *The Milk and Honey Route. A Handbook for Hobos*, New York, 1931.

5 James P. Spradley arrives at a taxonomy of some one hundred places to sleep. From a sociological point of view his book is a very interesting urban ethnography of the *bum*, the *tramp* and the *hobo*. But the problem is that this group increasingly belongs to the past; much has changed in the last twenty years. After James P. Spradley, *You Owe Yourself a Drunk. An Ethnography of Urban Nomads*, Boston, 1970; see in particular p.227, where Spradley explains his motives.

6 For an extremely informative explanation of the background and theories about 'skid row' alcoholics see Jacqueline P. Wiseman's, *Stations of the lost. The treatment of Skid Row Alcoholics*, Chicago, University of Chicago Press, 1979, pp.5-14. Edmund G. Love's, *Subways are for sleeping*, London, 1958, contains an interesting collection of his experiences when he tem-

porarily landed outside our regulated society. The book reveals how inventive people become when they are faced with the need to survive in a large city.

7 Peter H. Rossi, *Down and Out in America. The Origin of Homelessness*, Chicago, University of Chicago Press, 1989, p.185.

8 Samuel E. Wallace, *Skid Row as a way of life*, Bedminster Press, 1965, p.20.

9 Ibid., p.22.

10 George S. Sobel, *Report to Committee*, summer 1922, cited by Anderson, *The Hobo* (this chapter, note 4), p.132.

11 Carl Cohen and Jay Sokolovsky, *Old Men of the Bowery. Strategies for Survival among the Homeless*, New York/London, 1989, p.54.

12 For a summary of these activities see Thomas J. Main, 'The Homeless of New York', in Jon Erickson and Charles Wilhelm (Eds.), *Housing the Homeless*, Center for Urban Policy Research, State University of New Jersey, 1986, p.82 ff.

13 Peter H. Rossi, *Down and Out in America* (this chapter, note 7), p.44.

14 Jill Hamers (Ed.), *The making of America's homeless. From Skid Row to new poor, 1945-1984*, Housing and Development Policy Unit and Institute for Social Welfare Research, December 1984.

15 For a description of the SROS see Harvey A. Siegal, 'A descriptive portrait of the s.r.o. world', in Erickson and Wilhelm (Eds.), *Housing the Homeless* (this chapter, note 12), p.223 ff.

16 Joel Blau, *The Visible Poor. Homelessness in the United States*, Oxford, Oxford University Press, 1992, p.137.

17 Peter Marcuse, 'Neutralizing Homelessness', in *Socialist Review*, Vol. 18, no. 1 Jan/March 1988, pp.69-97.

18 David Harvey, *The Condition of Post-modernity. An Enquiry into the Origins of Cultural Change*, Cambridge, MIT, 1989, p.311.

19 Manuel Castells, 'High technology, economic restructuring, and the urban-regional process in the United States', in *High Technology, Space and Society*, Urban Affairs Annual Reviews 28, 1985.

20 Rossi, *Down and Out in America*, p.146.

21 E. Fuller Torrey, *Nowhere to go. The Tragic Odyssey of the Homeless Mentally Ill*. New York, Harper and Row, 1988, pp.8-9; see also Ellen Baxter and Kim Hopper, 'The new mendicancy; Homeless in New York City', in *American Orthopsychiatric Association*, 52 (3) July 1982.

22 Michael B. Katz, *In the Shadow of the Poor House. A social history of Welfare in America*, New York, Basic Books, 1986, p.102.

23 Blau, *The Homeless of New York* (chapter 3 note 14), p.183.

24 Fuller Torrey, *Nowhere to go*, p.139.

25 Ellen L. Bassuk, 'The Homelessness Problem', in *Scientific American*, vol. 251, no. 1, July 1984, p.30.

26 Blau, *The Homeless of New York*, p.117.

27 Ellen L. Bassuk, Leonore Ruben and Alison Lauriat, 'Is Homelessness a Mental Problem?', in *The American Journal of Psychiatry*, Official journal of the American Psychiatric Association, vol. 141, no. 12, December 1989.

28 Pamela Fischer and William Breakey, 'Homelessness and mental health: an overview', in *International Journal of Mental Health*, vol. 14, no. 4, 1986, p.19; see also S. Crystal and M. Goldstein, *Correlates of shelter utilization: One day study*, New York, Human Resources Administration, 1984, and from the same authors *The Homeless in New York City Shelters*, New York, 1984.

29 For a documentation of this group see Ann Marie Rousseau, *Shopping bag ladies. Homeless women speak about their lives*, New York, Pilgrim Press, 1981.

30 John R. Coleman, 'Diary of a Homeless Man', in Erickson and Wilhelm (Eds.), *Housing the Homeless* (this chapter note 12), pp.44-45.

31 'Dinkins to Defer Plans to Scatter Homeless Shelters Across the City', in *New York Times*, 10 December 1991.

32 Wiseman, *Stations of the Lost* (this chapter note 6), pp.51-52.

33 Joel Blau, *The Visible Poor* (this chapter note 16), pp. 161.

34 Joan Forrester Spraque, *More than Housing. Lifeboats for woman and children*, 1991.

35 Robert L. Holland and Donald A. Bowers, *The 14th Street Wholesale Market for Meat and Poultry in New York City*, Report to the Commissioner of Markets of New York City, the Mayor's Market Advisory Committee, the Marketsmen's Association of Lower Manhattan, and Members of the Industry, New York 1962.

Index

Colophon

This book would not have been possible without the generous support of the Netherlands Architecture Fund, Rotterdam, and the Faculty of Architecture at Delft University of Technology.

The Critical Landscape
Stylos Series on architecture and urbanism, Faculty of Architecture, Delft University of Technology
Series editor Arie Graafland, Delft University of Technology
Editorial board K. Michael Hayes, Harvard School of Design, USA; Michael Müller, Art History, Bremen University, BRD; Michael Speaks, Southern California Institute of Architecture, USA

Advisory board Henco Bekkering, Jan Brouwer, Jasper de Haan, Deborah Hauptmann, Jeroen Mensink, Kyong Park, Yorgos Simeoforides, Carel Weeber
In 1996 the first volume in the series was published under the title *The Critical Landscape* (ISBN 90 6450 290 0).
In 2000 a third volume is to be published, *Cities in Transition*.

The Socius of Architecture
Guest editor Deborah Hauptmann
Translation by Alan Mynott
Text editing John Kirkpatrick
Book design by Piet Gerards, Heerlen/Amsterdam
Printed by Snoeck-Ducaju, Ghent

© 2000 The author and 010 Publishers, Rotterdam (www.010publishers.nl)
For the works of visual artists affiliated with a Cisac-organisation the copyrights have been settled with Beeldrecht, Amsterdam
ISBN 90 6450 389 3